Analyzing Food Security Using Household Survey Data

STREAMLINED ANALYSIS WITH ADePT SOFTWARE

Analyzing Food Security Using Household Survey Data

Ana Moltedo
Nathalie Troubat
Michael Lokshin
Zurab Sajaia

THE WORLD BANK
Washington, D.C.

Contents

Contents

Figures

Screenshots

Tables

Contents

Contents

Preface

This book and the development of the ADePT-Food Security Module (ADePT-FSM) were made possible by the financial support from the European Union under the "Improved Global Governance for Hunger Reduction" program. Both outputs are from part 2.1 of the program, managed by the Statistics Division of FAO, and are aimed at improving methodologies, tools, and guidance materials for generating food security and hunger-related statistics.

ADePT-FSM is the adapted version of the Food Security Statistics Module (FSSM), which began development a decade ago by Jorge Mernies and Ricardo Sibrián, former director and senior statistician, respectively, of the Food Security Statistics Unit of the FAO Statistics Division. Their work and determination were essential in creating ADePT-FSM and this book. Without their involvement and guidance, it is certain that these products would not exist, and for this we offer our deepest gratitude.

FSSM was designed to derive a comprehensive set of indicators on various aspects of food security at national and subnational levels, which greatly contributed to its attractiveness. It has been used in many countries by national statistical offices or institutions involved in food security analysis. However, since it was not simple to use, in December 2011, the FAO Statistics Division became involved in a joint collaboration with the World Bank to adapt FSSM into ADePT-FSM. This collaboration aimed to provide stand-alone software with a user-friendly interface to derive food security statistics from survey data. The authors wish to thank all the users of FSSM, as it was through their interest in the tool and their shared experiences that enabled FSSM to improve over time and to evolve into ADePT-FSM.

This book is a compilation of 20 years of experience in processing food consumption data from national household surveys, and it has greatly benefited from the expertise of many actors in the field of food security from nutritionists to analysts. To list all of them would be an impossible endeavor, but the authors wish to acknowledge at least a few and apologize for all those who are not listed here although they contributed directly or indirectly to the manual.

The authors are grateful to Pietro Gennari, director of the FAO Statistics Division, for his support and confidence in the project; to Ruth Charrondiere, nutrition officer at FAO, for her invaluable advice on building nutrient conversion tables; to Carlo Cafiero, senior statistician at FAO, for the tremendous work he did in revising the methodology and for sharing his knowledge; to Piero Conforti, senior statistician and leader of the Food Security Analysis team, who recently joined as a new member and facilitated the publication of the manual; to Sergiy Radyakin and Stanislav Kolenikov, who were involved in the development of the software; to Michele Rocca for providing technical support; and to Ellen Wielezynski, who edited the entire manual. All members of the FAO Food Security Statistics team have contributed either by writing part of this manual or by providing essential comments. Also, very special thanks goes to Seevalingum Ramasawmy, statistician at FAO, who has been deeply involved since the beginning in developing the FSSM and whose vision and commitment planted the seed for the collaboration with the World Bank.

Finally, the authors express their gratitude to the European Union for the financial support needed for this book, the development of the software, and the funding of many capacity development activities on deriving food security indicators using food consumption data from national household surveys.

Abbreviations

ADER	average dietary energy requirement
BMI	body mass index
BMR	basal metabolic rate
CPI	consumer price index
CV	coefficient of variation
DEC	dietary energy consumption
DER	dietary energy requirement
DES	dietary energy supply
DHS	demographic and health survey
EAR	estimated average requirement
EP	edible portion
FAO	Food and Agriculture Organization
FBDG	food-based dietary guidelines
FBS	food balance sheet
FCDB	food composition database
FCT	food composition table
FPI	food price index
FSSM	Food Security Statistics Module
ILO	International Labour Organization
INFOODS	International Network of Food Data Systems
KCAL	kilocalorie

Lcu	local currency
MDER	minimum dietary energy requirement
MDGs	Millennium Development Goals
NAS	National Academy of Sciences
NDS	nutritional dietary survey
NHS	national household survey
PAL	physical activity level
PoU	prevalence of undernourishment
RAE	retinol activity equivalent
RI	recommended intake
RNI	recommended nutrient intake
SOFI	*The State of Food Insecurity in the World*
U5MR	under-five mortality rate
USDA	U.S. Department of Agriculture
WHO	World Health Organization

Food Security

Ana Moltedo, Carlo Cafiero, Nathan Wanner

Introduction

In 2012, thanks to the collaboration of the World Bank Computational Tools Team,[1] and under the umbrella of the European Union program "Improved Global Governance for Hunger Reduction," the Food and Agriculture Organization (FAO) methodology was integrated into a user-friendly software named ADePT-Food Security Module (ADePT-FSM).

This book aims to provide the essential guidelines of the use of ADePT-FSM and of its background methodology. It is organized into five chapters:

- Chapter 1 introduces the background concepts of food security and food consumption data.
- Chapter 2 describes the methodology used to derive different food security indicators.
- Chapter 3 discusses the analysis of the derived food security statistics.
- Chapter 4 provides guidelines on how to prepare the input datasets.
- Chapter 5 explains how to install and use ADePT-FSM.

Background

Food and nutrition security has emerged as a primary development goal at the top of the global agenda.

During the 1996 World Food Summit hosted by FAO, the participating heads of state and government[2] committed to reduce the *number* of undernourished people to half their present level by 2015. Four years later the United Nations General Assembly adopted the UN Millennium Declaration in which it was resolved to halve, by the year 2015, the *proportion* of people who suffer from hunger.

In order to achieve these goals, the development of both a statistical methodology and software for obtaining reliable estimates of undernourishment was an essential step.

Other initiatives like the Poverty Reduction Strategy Papers[3] and the Rural Development Strategies also increased the need for reliable food security statistics at national and subnational levels. Food security statistics play a fundamental role in assessing the magnitude of food deprivation, estimating the level of food and nutrient consumption, forecasting the long-term food consumption demand, and evaluating the impact of food security programs over time.

Food Security

When international attention became increasingly focused on the problem of hunger following World War II, the term *food security* typically referred to the "incidence of famine" and the resulting deaths from starvation. The immediate cause of starvation was identified as a lack of sufficient food; hence "ensuring food security" was identified with providing an *adequate supply* of food to those in need.

The limitations of such an interpretation became immediately evident: a disconnection emerged between the success in increasing food supplies through improved agricultural production and the persistence of hunger and malnutrition around the world. A scenario could result in which there is adequate food supply for the population at the aggregate level, but with some households receiving an inadequate supply while others have more than is needed. These high levels of disparity revealed the limits of a concept based only on the availability of food. Since then, attention has shifted toward food *access* as a key dimension of food security: ensuring enough food is not a sufficient condition for food security unless equal access to food by individual households is guaranteed.

Over time, newfound impetus has been placed on some nonfood factors important for food security, such as access to clean water, sanitation, and health care. These factors are all involved in how effectively food is utilized to reach a state of nutritional wellbeing. The definition of *food security* has therefore further broadened to include a new dimension of nutritional concerns, *utilization*, which captures the elements important for the best use of food by the body to improve nutritional status.

The three dimensions of food security (availability, access, and utilization) are crucial at any point in time, though it is important to ensure that food security conditions are *continuously* met. The fourth and final dimension of food security is therefore *stability*. To be food secure, a population, household, or individual must have access to adequate food *at all times*, and should not risk losing access to food as a consequence of sudden economic, climatic, or political shocks. The stability dimension also aims to monitor the robustness of the food security situation to cyclical, predictable variations connected with annual weather patterns.

The definition of *food security* adopted by the 1996 World Food Summit[4] includes all four described dimensions: "Food security exists when all people, at all times, have physical, social and economic access to sufficient, safe and nutritious food that meets their dietary needs and food preferences for an active and healthy life."

Starting from the mid-1990s the nutritional aspects of food security gained increasingly more importance: the terms *food security and nutrition* and *food and nutrition security* have been increasingly used by the international community. The former term has been used to distinguish between actions needed at the global, national, and local levels from actions needed at the household and individual levels. *Food and nutrition security*, instead, highlights nutrition considerations throughout the food chain (CFS 2012).

In 2012, the Committee on Food Security recommended using the following definition of *food and nutrition security*: "Food and nutrition security exists when all people at all times have physical, social and economic access to food, which is safe and consumed in sufficient quantity and quality to meet their dietary needs and food preferences, and is supported by an environment of adequate sanitation, health services and care, allowing for a healthy and active life."

With the broadening of the definition of *food security* over time, it became clear that no single indicator would likely suffice in providing a comprehensive picture of the food security and nutrition situation.[5] Rather, a carefully chosen suite of indicators[6] is likely necessary to describe food insecurity in all its dimensions in order to reliably inform the international community and decision makers on how to design appropriate responses.

Analyzing food consumption data collected in national household surveys (NHS) is one way of looking at food security. ADePT-FSM allows us to derive indicators at national and subnational levels that encompass some of the dimensions of food security.

Sources of Food Consumption Data

Food consumption can be captured at the national, household, or individual level. Food balance sheets estimate food consumption through a national account of food available for consumption in a given country. The difference between national household surveys and nutritional dietary surveys (NDS) is that the former capture food consumption at the household level and the latter at the individual level. National household surveys are multipurpose surveys not specifically designed for food security purposes but allow analysts to assess the distribution of food consumption in the observed population. NDS are specifically focused on food intake yet have some major limitations, mainly related with operational costs.

Food Balance Sheets (FBS)

Food balance sheets provide a national account of the food available for consumption in a given country, both in terms of calories[7] and nutrients over a reference period of one year, drawing on information on production, trade, and stocks. They are useful in monitoring many aspects of the food economy in a country, including efficiency of production, quality of the available food supply, and effectiveness of food policies in increasing food supply. The FAO Statistics Division has been producing FBS for about 180 countries since 1980 to monitor food availability across countries and over time. The derived dietary energy supply (DES) is a fundamental parameter for the estimation of the FAO prevalence of undernourishment (PoU) indicator in a country, the other two being the variability and asymmetry of the distribution of food consumption.[8] Historically, the dietary energy supply did not take into account food waste and losses at the retail level. However, share of food losses at the regional level and for broad food categories have recently been estimated by FAO (FAO 2011). In applying these shares to the DES of the country, it is now possible to account for food losses in the whole food chain, except for the food lost within households in the form of leftovers or spoilage due to improper food storage.

Although FBS are an important tool for characterizing the overall availability of food, their limitations in terms of potentialities should also be stated. First and most important, FBS data are not meant to be used to study the dietary diversity of a population because they do not provide information on how food is distributed within the population. Indeed, while national household surveys are able to capture information at the household level, the food balance sheets provide information only at the aggregate national level. Another consequence of this is that the estimates derived from FBS do not allow for statistics at the subnational level, or for assessments of seasonal variations.

Secondly, FBS measure food availability from a supply, rather than demand, perspective because the data refer to food availability at the level of commodities, without providing any piece of information on how these commodities are accessed. Another important drawback of FBS is that they do not capture food produced by private households for their own consumption. Finally, the reliability of data on stock fluctuations is often questionable, leading to some uncertainty in the estimates.

National Household Surveys

The general term *national household survey* encompasses different types of surveys, such as household income and expenditure surveys, household expenditure surveys, household budget surveys, and Living Standard Measurement Studies. They are designed for a number of different purposes, including updating the weighting basis of the consumer price index, studying household living conditions, and studying poverty and income distribution.

Although these surveys are not specifically designed for food security analysis, they collect data on food consumption as an integral part of their broader inquiry on household consumption expenditures. Usually, food consumption data are collected as food consumed or acquired by households from different sources, in terms of both quantities and monetary values. In addition, NHS provide data on household income and expenditure and other socioeconomic and demographic characteristics useful for classification purposes. National household surveys usually cover the entirety of a country's territory, with samples distributed throughout the year, thus taking into account the issue of seasonality. Moreover, they allow for the analysis of variations over time when the survey is repeated in different years or is conducted on a continuous basis.

Since launching surveys of this magnitude to specifically capture food security data is very costly, the ADePT-FSM attempts to efficiently utilize the information contained in these multipurpose surveys to obtain reliable food security statistics.

Despite the described positive attributes, national household surveys are rarely designed to capture the level of the households' *habitual* food consumption for a number of reasons. The first (and most important) issue is that NHS may collect information on food *acquisition* rather than *consumption*. In this case, it can be very difficult, if not impossible, to distinguish the food acquired for actual household consumption over the data collection period from the food acquired for storage purposes.

This issue could not affect food security statistics of poor populations (those most vulnerable to food insecurity) because they often cannot afford food storage.

An additional drawback is that NHS generally collect food data with short reference periods (one week to one month), leading to increased variability in the estimate of habitual consumption because of the inherently greater variability within a short reference period. This inherent variability is due to unusual events that may occur (such as a wedding), which call for increased food acquisition compared to what would normally be consumed. In addition, with short recall reference periods "telescoping errors" can occur whenever the respondents mistakenly recall events taking place more recently than they actually did. Contrarily, collecting data on longer reference periods has its own drawbacks because "recall loss" errors can take place when the respondent is unable to remember events that took place long before. Considering these two types of errors, food diaries are sometimes considered the gold standard for the collection of food consumption data since they minimize errors due to recall; nonetheless, they are more burdensome to the respondent and may therefore not be completely and accurately filled out due to respondent fatigue, causing a different type of survey error.

Another potential drawback of NHS is that the information on the *size* of the household may differ from the number of people who actually consumed the food (*partakers*) over the reference period; this may be due to the absence of some household members during the reference period, or to the consumption of food by guests or workers. Although this problem can be addressed in surveys that collect information on the number of food partakers, this piece of information is very often lacking. In addition, food consumed outside may not be well captured by the survey questionnaire due to the use of generic categories (e.g., meal consumed in restaurant), or to the inability of the questionnaire design to capture some aspects of the food consumed *away* (such as school lunches for children).

Even when information on household food consumption is accurately captured, data on intrahousehold food distribution are very seldom available, and hence there is no choice but to assume that each person within the household has equal access to food.

Furthermore, although food waste is generally considered to be more of a problem for households with higher incomes, low-income households can also have food waste when food spoils due to inadequate food storage technology.

Lastly, NHS do not always consider food acquired for purposes other than consumption (such as food given to other households or to charity, or used for resale).

To further illustrate the difficulty in characterizing habitual food consumption from NHS, consider that even if the overall average calorie consumption in the sample may still be a good estimate of the mean, since "households in a large population group are equally likely to be drawing down on food stocks as they are to be accumulating them" (Smith, Alderman, and Aduayom 2006), the values calculated for each *individual household* would likely be biased whenever household-level storage of food is relevant. This shall have consequences on the estimated distribution of food consumption across households, as the variability *within* households will be confounded with the variability *between households*.

Secondly, and perhaps more worrying, if the individual household status of being undernourished is going to be used to conduct disaggregated analysis by population subgroups (the possibility of which constitutes one of the most attractive aspects of household survey data), the risk exists that the analysis would yield inconsistent results if the difference between acquisition and consumption happens to be correlated with the grouping variable.[9]

It is hoped that in the near future more nationally representative household surveys explicitly collecting average quantities of food consumed over the year will be available to improve the precision of the estimates at the population level. This could also allow the analysis of households' food consumption in relation to other socioeconomic characteristics. A minimal set of requirements for such a survey should include features that would allow the following:

- A complete assessment of the type of food consumed by all household members, including food consumed away from home
- Differentiation of actual food consumption of household from that of food acquisition over the surveyed period, recognizing that the latter may include food acquired for other uses (partakers, storage, food given to guests, etc.) or for other periods of time
- Control for possible seasonal variation in food consumption (ideally by conducting repeated observation on the same household in different points in time)

One must remember, however, that even with all of the potential drawbacks, national household surveys are virtually the only source of available data to assess the distribution of food consumption, and can provide invaluable information for food security analysts and policy makers.

Nutritional Dietary Surveys

Nutritional dietary surveys focus on food consumption data, conducted in a few countries with small sample sizes on an ad hoc basis. They measure *individual* food intake by collecting both qualitative descriptions and quantities consumed of each food item during the last 1 to 15 days[10] by individuals.

Nutritional surveys have a number of limitations for estimating food security statistics. Firstly, the survey period[11] is normally shorter than three months, and hence it does not account for seasonal variations in individual food intake. Although seasonal intake is generally less variable in developed countries where some food products are globally imported and where there is a greater capacity for food storage, there can be huge variability in populations that eat locally produced food or that lack the resources necessary for proper storage.

A second problem with NDS is that they usually do not collect information on food intake occurred away from home. In countries where lunches at school or work, street food, meals at restaurants, etc., form a large part of the diet, these surveys can substantially underestimate the total dietary energy intake. Another potential problem is that nutritional dietary surveys do not collect information on household or individual food and nonfood expenditure, nor on their income.

Perhaps the biggest drawback of NDS, however, is that they are very complex, labor intensive, and expensive to implement. They require highly trained enumerators and costly measuring equipment to collect food intake data. Monetary costs and difficulty of implementation for these surveys can be a major drawback, and for this reason these surveys are usually more useful for studies of limited coverage, targeting selected socioeconomic or other specific population groups such as children and pregnant women.

Summary

The ideal source of information to assess food security in a country is represented by nutritional dietary surveys. However, as these surveys are costly and difficult to implement, national household surveys are often used as a readily available source of data on the distribution of food consumption. This piece of information is augmented with the parameter obtained from food balance sheets, the dietary energy requirement, to obtain the FAO estimate of the prevalence of undernourishment. The main differences between nutritional dietary surveys, national household surveys, and food balance sheets are shown in table 1.1 below.

Table 1.1: Comparison of Nutritional Dietary Surveys, National Household Surveys, and Food Balance Sheets

Nutritional dietary surveys	National household surveys	Food balance sheets
Estimate food consumption from food intake	Estimate food consumption from the demand perspective	Estimate food consumption from the supply perspective
Cover individuals	Cover private households	Cover private households and public establishments (hotels, residences, hospitals, military barracks, and prisons)
Estimates are at the individual level	Estimates are at national and subnational levels	Estimates are at national level
Do not capture seasonal variation in food consumption	Capture seasonal variation in food consumption	Do not capture seasonal variation in food consumption
Conducted for specific purposes	Conducted yearly in some countries and infrequently in others	Compiled each year
Not conducted in many countries	Since the 1990s, increasing numbers of countries are conducting them	Cover almost all countries

ADePT-Food Security Module

Over the past years, increasing attention has been paid to national household surveys by the international community in order to collect reliable and timely information on food consumption for the purpose of food security assessment. National household surveys are in fact the only available source of information to assess the distribution of food consumption within a country.

ADePT-FSM aims to derive consistent and readily available food security statistics from food consumption data collected in NHS. The software also provides a transparent platform in which the user can reproduce the FAO official estimates of the percentage of undernourished people within a country.

Countries conduct their NHS according to international recommendations and guidelines[11] and collect three levels of information related to (1) the household, (2) the household members, and (3) the household income and expenditures in goods and services, including food. In order to execute ADePT-FSM, the preparation of three datasets[12] from the original microdata is therefore required. ADePT-FSM also requires a fourth dataset including exogenous data on the nutrient content (proteins, carbohydrates, etc.) of the food commodities listed in the survey. Such data are found in food composition tables available for many countries all over the world.

Lastly, ADePT-FSM does not limit its outcome to statistics belonging to the "access" dimension of food security, namely caloric intake and macronutrients consumption. A balanced intake of macronutrients,[13] in fact, is not in itself a sufficient condition for conducting a healthy life, as human beings also need to consume adequate amounts of minerals and vitamins (micronutrients) and indispensable amino acids. ADePT-FSM therefore allows for the analysis of some micronutrients[14] and indispensable amino acids[15] available for consumption.[16]

The statistics produced are presented in standard Excel tables ready to be included in national food insecurity assessment reports.

Notes

1. This team belongs to the Development Research Group.
2. When *government* is used, it also refers to the European community within its areas of competence.

3. Prepared by countries every three years, the Poverty Reduction Strategy Papers describe a country's macroeconomic, structural and social policies, and programs over a three-year or longer horizon.

4. This definition was reaffirmed officially in the Declaration of the World Summit on Food Security, 2009 (CFS 2012).

5. For an example see De Haen (2002).

6. Several key indicators are published by the FAO Statistics Division on its website: http://www.fao.org/economic/ess/ess-home/en/.

7. This is the dietary energy supply.

8. These are both derived from national household survey data.

9. For example, consider the case in which most households build up food stocks in the period after the harvest. If this is not taken into account when defining the sampling plan, and that specific area of the country is surveyed in that period, the result will be biased in the data correlated with the location of the household.

10. Depending on the method used by the interviewer (often a nutritionist) to record food intake: (1) 24-hour weighted method; (2) 24-hour recall method; or (3) food frequency method. While for the former two methods the *reference period* (period of time over which the individual data are collected) is one day, for the food frequency method it is either 7 or 15 days.

11. The recommendations and guidelines include the UN National Household Survey Capability Programme (1989) and the UN manual *Designing Household Survey Samples: Practical Guidelines* (2005).

12. These datasets are prepared either in STATA® or SPSS® format.

13. Diet could be defined as balanced when all the following conditions are met (WHO/FAO 2003):
    - Proportion of dietary energy provided by protein is in the range of 10–15 percent
    - Proportion of dietary energy provided by fats is in the range of 15–30 percent
    - Proportion of total dietary energy provided by carbohydrates is in the range of 55–75 percent

14. These include vitamin A, ascorbic acid, thiamine, riboflavin, vitamin B6, cobalamin, and the minerals calcium and iron.

15. These include isoleucine, leucine, lysine, threonine, tryptophan, valine, histidine, methionine, cystine, phenylalanine, and tyrosine.

16. The analysis of micronutrients is made in terms of availability, rather than consumption, because different food processing methods have different impacts on the nutrient profile. For example high temperature processing can affect the vitamin content (e.g., vitamin C) and discarding of water used in cooking will lead to the loss of water soluble food components (e.g., B vitamins, vitamin C, and certain bioactive components) as seen in FAO/INFOODS (2012).

References

CFS (Committee on World Food Security). 2012. "Coming to Terms with Terminology." Final report 2012/39, Rome, October 15–20. http://www.fao.org/fileadmin/user_upload/bodies/CFS_sessions/39th_Session/39emerg/MF027_CFS_39_FINAL_REPORT_compiled_E.pdf.

De Haen, H. 2002. "Lessons Learned." Paper presented at the Food and Agriculture Organization conference "Measurement and Assessment of Food Deprivation and Undernutrition," Rome, June 26–28.

FAO (Food and Agriculture Organization). 2011. "Global Food Losses and Food Waste." Study conducted for the Messe Düsseldorf and FAO International Congress "SAVE FOOD" initiative at Interpack2011, Düsseldorf, May 12–18.

FAO, and INFOODS (International Network of Food Data Systems). 2012. *Guidelines for Food Matching: Version 1.2.* Rome: FAO. http://www.fao.org/infoods/infoods/standards-guidelines/en/.

Smith, L. C., H. Alderman, and D. Aduayom. 2006. *Food Insecurity in Sub-Saharan Africa: New Estimates from Household Expenditure Surveys.* Research Report 146. Washington, DC: International Food Policy Research Institute.

UN Department of Technical Cooperation for Development, and Statistical Office. 1989. *Household Income and Expenditure Surveys: A Technical Study.* New York: United Nations. http://unstats.un.org/unsd/publication/unint/DP_UN_INT_88_X01_6E.pdf.

UN DESA (United Nations Department of Economic and Social Affairs). 2005. *Designing Household Survey Samples: Practical Guidelines.* New York: United Nations. http://unstats.un.org/unsd/demographic/sources/surveys/Handbook23June05.pdf.

WHO (World Health Organization), and FAO. 2003. *Diet, Nutrition and the Prevention of Chronic Diseases*. Report of a Joint WHO/FAO Expert Consultation, Geneva, January 28–February 1, WHO Technical Report Series 961, Geneva: WHO.

Bibliography

Cafiero, C. 2011. "Measuring Food Insecurity: Meaningful Concepts and Indicators for Evidence-Based Policy Making." Paper presented at the Food and Agriculture Organization conference "Round Table on Monitoring Food Security," Rome, September 12–13.

———. 2013. "What Do We Really Know About Food Security?" Working Paper 18861, National Bureau of Economic Research, Cambridge, MA. http://www.nber.org/papers/w18861.

FAO (Food and Agriculture Organization). 2006. "Food Security." Policy Brief 2, Agriculture Development Economics Division, FAO, Rome.

Chapter 2

Theoretical Concepts

Carlo Cafiero, Ana Moltedo, Seevalingum Ramasawmy,
Nathalie Troubat, Nathan Wanner

Introduction

This chapter presents various food security indicators that can be derived from food data collected in national household surveys (NHS). It also introduces procedures to estimate the indicators as well as to standardize food consumption and expenditures data into dietary or monetary values.[1] Some of these procedures are done manually during the preparation of the datasets before executing ADePT-FSM, and others are automatically implemented in the software.

Food security indicators range from the prevalence of undernourishment to average consumption of various nutrients by source of food acquisition. These indicators are produced for different analytical groups based on the household and household's head characteristics collected in the NHS.

Section 1 of this chapter presents the food data collected in NHS, the procedures of standardization are further explained in section 2, and finally, indicators on food security and their related methodologies are introduced in the last section. Some practical examples related to the procedures of aggregation and standardization are provided in the annexes.

Food Data Collected in Household Surveys

Food data collected in household surveys are not standardized and strongly depend on survey design.[2] The way surveys are processed depends therefore on the unique characteristics of the food data collected. Specifically, this includes the sources of food acquisition, units of measurement of quantities collected, and whether food data were collected in quantity and/or monetary values.

Sources of Food Consumption

Household food consumption ideally refers to the habitual consumption of food commodities, including nonalcoholic and alcoholic beverages.[3] However, only a few surveys (such as yearly panel surveys) collecting information on food partakers are designed to capture household habitual food consumption. Usually the collection of food data in NHS refers to food acquired or consumed in or outside the sampled household during a given reference period.

Most food items acquired by the households are intended to be consumed by household members. Exceptions exist when acquired food is given to employees, guests, relatives, or pets. It may also be used to feed livestock, for small food businesses, or for resale. Therefore, to estimate the habitual household food consumption, the food not consumed by household members should be excluded in the food security analysis through proper identification at the collection stage. Ideally, any food losses and waste produced by the household should also be collected.

Households acquire food from various sources. Food can be purchased in markets, shops, food courts, restaurants, work canteens, from hawkers, etc. Food can also come from own production (farming, fishing, gathering, or hunting), or it can be withdrawn from private or business-owned stocks or received as payment or free from friends, relatives, and charity institutions.

During the data collection reference period, households may consume food items withdrawn from their own stocks, make bulk purchases, or accumulate stocks from their own production. For these reasons, especially for acquisition surveys, information on levels of initial and ending stocks should be properly reported during the food data collection period to avoid under- or overestimation of the habitual food consumption at the household level.

Summarizing, households usually consume food that is acquired from the following main sources:

- *Purchased food.* Food bought to be consumed inside the household, or food bought and consumed away from home, such as in restaurants, food courts, canteens, or from street vendors.

- *Nonpurchased food.* From own production (backyard gardens or farms), received free as gifts, donations, or transfers (including long-term food loan), received as payment in kind (including prepared food at workplaces), received as institutional food aid, or other (fishing, hunting, gathering, etc.).
- *Food stocks.* Composed of purchased or nonpurchased food items acquired prior to the starting date or during the reference period of food data collection.

Purchased Food

Purchased food items involve a payment by either cash or credit. Food purchases may be on a daily, weekly, or monthly basis depending on the type of food and payment of wages. Food can be purchased for consumption either within or outside the household. As the type of information (food quantities or monetary values) and the approach used to estimate dietary energy are different depending on whether the food is consumed inside or outside the home, it is important that the NHS captures food purchased for consumption at home and away from home separately.

In-House Consumption Perishable food commodities such as bread, milk, fresh fruits, and vegetables are usually purchased at shorter intervals (daily or weekly), while nonperishable commodities such as rice, flour, and sugar are usually acquired for consumption over a longer period of time (weekly or monthly). The payment of wages may be daily, weekly, fortnightly, monthly, or sometimes in relation to crop harvests (households usually purchase bulk quantities of specific food items in relation to the harvest cycles).

Consumed Away from Home Food purchases include food consumed away from home, such as drinks and ready-prepared meals from vendors, restaurants, food courts, school, work canteens, etc.

Nonpurchased Food

Own Consumption Households acquire some food commodities such as cereals, roots, tubers, vegetables, fruits, milk, and meat from their own production (from backyard gardens or farms). Some households consume all their food production, while others consume only part of it, selling the rest for income. This type of food acquisition is commonly referred to as *own production* or *own consumption* or *self-production* and does not involve any monetary transactions. However, it is important to have proper estimates of the food quantity and monetary values acquired from this source. Own production may constitute an important source of food for particular household groups involved in agricultural livelihoods, especially in rural areas.

In Kind Households may also acquire and consume food items obtained free of charge, such as gifts, donations, or transfers from relatives and friends. In some countries, fishing, hunting and/or gathering provide a substantial amount of food to certain groups of the population. Various international or national institutions give some basic and essential food items to individuals or households as food aid on a regular or ad-hoc basis. Household members may also receive food from employers as part of payment (income in kind), especially those working in food activities such as vegetable cultivating, farming, or livestock food processing, or those working as food vendors. Food acquired from these sources may constitute an important part of the total household food consumption.

Stocks

Food stocks are usually comprised of nonperishable food such as cereals and preserved food. However, in some developed countries, it is also common that people stock perishable food by freezing it. Stocks are mainly accumulated by people in rural areas from own production during the harvest period or by urban rich households that can acquire bulk quantities at lower prices.

Food Consumption Data Collected in Quantities and/or Monetary Values

National household surveys collect data on food acquisition or consumption from purchases in monetary and quantitative terms. The data are collected at the food commodity level. Food purchased for consumption inside of the home refers to food items available in the market and usually expressed in well-specified standard units of weight or volume. Therefore, it is expected that the data collected in the survey have details related to quantity, unit of measurement, and cost (in monetary value). However, the information collected may vary depending on the source of food acquisition.

In some surveys, food purchased is collected only in monetary value. When quantities are not available, they need to be estimated using market retail prices. These prices correspond to local or regional markets or local food shops, or are derived from surveyed households for the reference period. It is recommended that those estimates are worked out at the data collection stage by the field interviewer in collaboration with the respondent.

Food acquired for household members' consumption from sources such as own production, gifts, and aid does not involve monetary value transactions. In this case the monetary values could be estimated using market retail prices or from surveyed households in the region. In most recent surveys, households are asked to report the monetary value of food from these sources as if the item were bought at the market.

Finally, household members may purchase and consume food and drinks outside the home. The type of food can vary from a well-defined "takeaway" commodity such as beer, carbonated beverage, hamburgers, corn on the cob, roasted chicken, and fried rice to a more general, "ordered" description such as dinner, meal, or breakfast. While the takeaway food is purchased in standard local units such as a portion or plate, the ordered meal is consumed in bars, restaurants, or work canteens, and it mixes food items according to a recipe that may differ among the food outlets. For takeaway food, it is possible to have information on food quantities in standard units along with monetary values; however, for ordered food, usually only monetary values are available. For these reasons, nutrients and calories of these two food groups are estimated following different procedures.

Table 2.1 summarizes the most common availability of data by source of food acquisition and the limitations that may appear when processing the data.

Unit of Measurement

On the one hand, the unit of measurement of quantities acquired can be standard, such as gram, kilogram, liter, or milliliter, or a local unit, such as bag, basket, cup, or heap. On the other hand, all factors to convert quantities into nutrient values are expressed in terms of nutrient content per 100 grams of the food product. To ensure a proper conversion of food quantities into nutrient values, it is important to have factors to convert local units into standard ones. For instance, if a household declared the acquisition of a heap of parsley, the interviewer has to inquire how many standard

Table 2.1: Most Common Availability of Data by Source of Food Acquisition and Possible Limitations in Processing Data

Food source		Quantity details	Value details	Limitations
Purchased for inside household food consumption.		yes	yes	Availability of grams or milliliters conversion factors related to the local quantity units of measurement.
Food purchased and consumed away from home.	(1) Prepared standard takeaway meals acquired outside home.	yes (Standard portions collected from food providers)	yes	Availability of grams or milliliters conversion factors related to the standard portions. The calorie and nutrient densities of the food products should be available in food composition tables.
	(2) Prepared meals acquired and eaten away from home (Ordered meals consumed in bars, restaurants, hotels, schools, workplaces, etc.).	no	yes	Frequently only food monetary values are available.
Food from own production Food received free Food received as payment Food from stock Food obtained from institutional aid		yes	yes/no	Retail prices have to be estimated at the local market or obtained from surveyed households in the region.

units (for instance grams) of parsley are usually in a heap in this specific region. In some countries, the unit of the National Statistical Office that is in charge of collecting prices also records gram weight equivalences of the local units of measurement.

Standardization Procedures

Indicators are expressed in terms of quantities, dietary energy, and monetary values per person per day. This means that all data collected in the survey and needed for the food security analysis should be standardized before being aggregated over time and space. Procedures of standardization start with the conversion of food monetary values or quantities collected in the NHS into dietary energy. These procedures are complex and strongly rely on the quality of the food data collected, the food composition data, and the quality of the food matching.[4]

Estimation of Dietary Energy

The human body requires energy for different purposes, including metabolic process, muscular activity, growth, and synthesis of new tissues. Humans can access the required energy through the intake of energy-yielding macronutrients from foods that are protein, fats, carbohydrates (including fibers), and alcohol. Each contributes to the total calories but in a different proportion. Food energy is usually calculated on the macronutrients' content of the food product to which energy conversion factors are applied. In this way grams of nutrients are transformed into energy. There are two units for energy: calories (expressed in kcal) en joules (expressed in kJ). See table 2.2.

Joules is the recommended unit for energy due to historical reasons. However, the authors prefer to use calories as the unit of measurement for energy. Polyols and organic acids usually play a minor role and will therefore be omitted here.

The total amount of calories using the Atwater formula is calculated in ADePT-FSM as follows:

$$Calories(Kcal) = Protein(g) * 4 + Fats(g) * 9 + Av.\ Carbohydrates(g) * 4$$
$$+ Fiber(g) * 2 + Alcohol(g) * 7$$

Note: In the above equation: *Available carbohydrates = total carbohydrates − fibers*.

Macro- and micronutrient consumption are estimated by multiplying food quantities (collected in the survey or calculated based on prices) by nutrient values from national or regional food composition tables (FCT) or databases (FCDB). These nutrient values are usually expressed as grams (g), milligrams (mg), or micrograms (µg) of nutrients per 100 grams edible portion (EP) on a fresh basis.

The food reported in the survey must be matched to food in FCT/FCDB. This can be done only if the consumed foods are expressed in grams EP.[5]

Table 2.2: Atwater System

	kJ/g	Kcal/g
Protein	17	4
Fat	37	9
Available/total carbohydrate	17	4
Available carbohydrate in monosaccharide equivalents	16	3.75
(Dietary) fiber[a]	8	2
Alcohol (i.e., ethanol)	29	7
Organic acids[b]	13	3
Polyols[b]	10	24

Source: FAO 2002.
a. In case only a total carbohydrate value is available, no energy is attributed to the fiber value.
b. There are also specific conversion factors for individual polyols and organic acids.

When food quantities are given in milliliter or liter, they need to be converted in grams EP using density values.[6]

Unfortunately, the process to convert food quantities into nutrient content is not straightforward, mainly due to some limitations in the available data:

- Food quantities expressed in local units of measurement without a conversion factor into standard units
- Nonedible portions (e.g., bones, seeds, peels, etc.) are included in the reported food quantities but their proportion is not known to convert to EP
- Undefined food items such as dinner, lunch, meal, etc.
- No national or regional FCT/FCDB available
- The impossibility of getting nutrient values for local food items or food with a broad definition such as other cereals, other meat, etc.

Because of these limitations, the way to estimate the calories and nutrients consumed should be split into two procedures:

- *Procedure 1.* Used when food quantities can be expressed in grams EP and nutrient values of quantities are available for the food item
- *Procedure 2.* Used when food quantities do not exist or they cannot be converted to grams EP, but food expenditures are available

As households consume/acquire food for inside and outside household consumption, the estimated energy consumed/acquired is calculated using a combination of the two procedures. Table 2.3 shows the various cases where procedure 1 or 2 should be applied.

The steps to follow in both procedures are described below. A numeric example built on 19 households belonging to Region = 1, Area = Urban, and Income quintile = 2 is presented in annexes 2B and 2C.

Procedure 1: Estimation of Nutrients and Calories from Food Quantities

As was mentioned before, this procedure applies *only* when food quantities can be expressed in standard units (grams EP) and nutrient values are available.

Table 2.3: Data Availability

Food quantity	Conversion factors to convert local unit of measurement into standard unit (grams or milliliters)	Food monetary value	Calories and nutrients conversion factors from FCT	Procedure to follow in the estimation of calorie and nutrients consumption
YES	YES	YES	YES	PROCEDURE 1
YES	YES	YES	NO	PROCEDURE 2
YES	NO	YES	YES	PROCEDURE 1: If the quantities can be expressed in a standard unit using the food commodity price and the monetary value. PROCEDURE 2: If it is not possible to apply the PROCEDURE 1
YES	NO	YES	NO	PROCEDURE 2
NO	YES/NO	YES	YES	PROCEDURE 1: If the quantities can be expressed in a standard unit using the food commodity price and the monetary value. PROCEDURE 2: If it is not possible to apply the PROCEDURE 1
NO	NO	YES	NO	PROCEDURE 2

Six main steps are involved: the first two should be done manually, while the remaining are implemented in ADePT-FSM:

1. Standardization of the food quantities into grams or milliliters equivalent
2. Conversion of milliliters into grams
3. Adjustment of food quantities for nonedible portions
4. Estimation of grams of nutrients per household
5. Estimation of calories provided by each nutrient
6. Estimation of total calories per household

Step 1: Standardization of the Food Quantities into Grams or Milliliters Equivalent   Food composition tables always refer to nutrient values per 100 grams edible food product. Therefore, the first important step is to ensure that all food quantities are converted into grams. When food quantities are expressed in a unit of measurement such as kilogram, gram, milliliter, liter, a can of 200 grams, or a bottle of 750 milliliters, conversion into gram or milliliter is straightforward. In these cases food quantities can be converted into grams or milliliter just multiplying the amount of quantity per 1,000, 1, 1, 1,000, 200, and 750, respectively. However, food quantities may be expressed in local units such as bag, basket, cup, glass, heap, plate, tin, unit, etc. These local units are commonly used in many countries, and their gram equivalent differs by food product and country (in some cases, also by region within a country). If the local unit of measurement cannot be converted into standard units the analysis cannot be conducted; it is therefore important to estimate *the gram equivalent for the local units* by food item at the community level, based on a sample of food items. It is always recommended that households report the quantities of food consumed/acquired in a standard unit of measurement. When not possible the enumerator should convert local units into standard ones in the field at the time of data collection.

If after the data collection cases remain where food quantities are missing or cannot be expressed in grams, an indirect method can be applied. It has to be kept in mind however that this estimation is lowering the quality of the estimated energy and other nutrients, which should be taken into account in the interpretation of the results. This method estimates food quantities using food unit values ($/gram) at the most representative level. As unit values change across time, the monetary values should be adjusted before computing the unit values. These are the steps:

1. Estimate deflators as the food price index of the month in which the household was interviewed divided by the average of the food price index over the survey period.
2. Deflate all food expenditures using the correspondent deflator.
3. Convert all food quantities into the same standard unit.
4. For each household compute the unit value per food item using the quantities in standard units and the associated deflated expenditures.
5. Compute the median unit values grouping households by region, area, and income quintile.[7]
6. Estimate the food quantities using the correspondent expenditure and the median unit value associated with the households.

Step 2: Conversion of Milliliters into Grams Nutrient values in FCT are usually expressed per 100 grams EP, so the food quantities expressed in milliliters should be converted into grams. To do so, it is necessary to have information on the food product's density coefficient (food product mass per unit of volume). Water at 4 degrees Celsius has a density of 1, whereas for the rest of the food items, the value can be less than 1 (e.g., oils) or more than 1 (e.g., milk). Using density values,[8] quantities in grams are estimated as below:

$$Food\ Quantity_{jh}(g) = Food\ Quantity_{jh}(ml) * density_j \left(\frac{g}{ml} \right)$$

where j stands for food product for which a valid density coefficient exists and h stands for household.

An example on how to transform food quantities expressed in units of volume into standard units is presented in annex 2A.

Step 3: Adjustment of Food Quantities for Nonedible Portions   While food quantities acquired include nonedible portions such as peels, bones, seeds, etc., nutrient values in the FCT are usually expressed per 100 grams EP. For this reason, there is the need to transform "as purchased" quantities into edible ones.[9] This transformation is done for each food commodity by applying the appropriate refuse factor.[10] Some food commodities, such as rice, milk, or sugar, are 100 percent edible, but this is not the case for other food items such as bananas, meat with bones, peaches, and walnuts in a shell. Therefore, the refuse factor depends on the food product, and when it is expressed as a percentage varies from 0 (all edible) to 76 (walnuts in a shell) or to even more for some food items. In many FCT/FCDB, the refuse factor is not reported, but instead the edible coefficient (ranging between 0 and 1), which is defined as the edible portion of the food, i.e., the portion of the food without refuse. For example, an edible coefficient of 0.70 means that 70 percent of the food is edible while 30 percent is inedible.

Summarizing the food quantities obtained in grams after applying steps 1 and 2 are adjusted for nonedible portions with the formula:

$$Edible\ Food\ Quantity_{jh} = Food\ Quantity_{jh} * \left(1 - \frac{Refuse_j}{100} \right)$$

Or

$$Edible\ Food\ Quantity_{jh} = Food\ Quantity_{jh} * (Edible\ Coefficient_j)$$

where *Food Quantity*$_{jh}$ refers to the grams of food product j consumed/ acquired by household h; including the refuse (nonedible portion); *Edible*

Food Quantity$_{jh}$ refers to the edible grams (excluding bones, peels, seeds, etc.) of the food product j consumed/acquired by household h; *Refuse$_j$* refers to the percentage of nonedible grams in the food product j; and *Edible Coefficient$_j$* refers to the proportion of the food item being eligible.

Step 4: Estimation of Grams of Nutrients per Household   The estimation of the nutrient content by food product is done by applying the nutrient values of the macronutrients (fat, protein, carbohydrates, fiber, and alcohol) as published in FCT/FCDB to the edible quantities expressed in grams. The total grams of nutrient, at household level, is the sum of the nutrients provided by each food item:

$$Q_{ih} = \sum_{j=1}^{g} ((Edible\ Food\ Quantity_{jh} * Nutrient\ Value_{ij})/100)$$

where i represents the nutrient (fat, available carbohydrate, protein, alcohol, or fiber) in household h; j represents the food items for which there are valid nutrient values, and the food quantities are expressed in edible grams following steps 1, 2, and 3; and g is the total number of food items for which valid nutrient factors exist. The value of g is lower (or equal) to the total number of food items consumed/acquired by household h. Q_{ih} refers to the total grams of nutrient i in household h, and Nutrient Value$_{ij}$ is the total grams of nutrient i per 100 grams edible portion of the food product j.

Step 5: Estimation of Calories Provided by Each Nutrient   The macronutrient consumption contributes to the estimated energy available for the human body. The amount of calories provided by protein, fats, available carbohydrates, fiber, and alcohol can be estimated using the Atwater system coefficients (see table 2.2 above):

$$N_{ih} = A_i * Q_{ih}$$

where N_i stands for dietary energy (kcal) provided by nutrient i in household h; A_i represents the Atwater coefficient (kcal/gram) associated with the nutrient i; and Q_{ih} refers to the total grams of nutrient i consumed in household h.

Step 6: Estimation of Total Calories per Household   The total estimated energy from these g food items consumed/acquired per household is finally derived summing from all foods the calories provided by protein, fats, available carbohydrates, fiber, and alcohol.

$$DEC_h = \sum_i N_{ih}$$

where DEC_h represents estimated energy (kcal) acquired/consumed by household h from the g food items for which a valid nutrient factor exists; and N_{ih} represents the dietary energy (kcal) provided by nutrient i in household h from the g food items for which a valid nutrient factor exists.

A numerical example following steps 3 to 6 of procedure 1 is presented in annex 2B.

Procedure 2: Estimation of Nutrients and Calories from Food Expenditure

Procedure 2 applies when (1) food quantities are not available, (2) the unit of measurement cannot be expressed in standard units, or (3) nutrient values for the food product are not available. For instance, this procedure is usually applied to food consumed away from home, prepared food, or food not well defined. Since procedure 2 generates estimations of lower quality, it is best to explore other possibilities to obtain the necessary data. For example, if nutrient values are not found in the national or regional FCT/FCDB, other FCT/FCDB should be consulted, or they should be calculated using recipes, etc.

Procedure 2 involves monetary values and follows four main steps, implemented in ADePT-FSM, to estimate the following:

- Proportion of calories provided by protein and fats
- Total missing calories
- Corresponding calories from protein, fats, carbohydrates (including fiber), and alcohol
- Missing grams of protein, fats, carbohydrates (including fiber), and alcohol

The steps are described below, and annex 2C provides a numerical example based on 20 households.

Step 1: Estimation of the Proportion of Calories Provided by Protein and Fats When procedure 1 was applied in a household to one or more food items, the proportion of calories provided by these products from protein and fats are estimated with the formulas:

$$SPORT_h = \frac{\sum_{j=1}^{g} PROT_{jh}}{\sum_{j=1}^{g} DEC_{jh}} \quad \text{and} \quad SFAT_h = \frac{\sum_{j=1}^{g} FAT_{jh}}{\sum_{j=1}^{g} DEC_{jh}}$$

where for household h, $SPORT_h$ and $SFAT_h$ stand, respectively, for the proportion of dietary energy (kcal) derived from the content of protein and fat in the g food items to which procedure 1 was applied; for household h, $PROT_{jh}$ and FAT_{jh} calories stand for the dietary energy (kcal) derived from the content of protein and fat in the food item j; and for household h, DEC_{jh} stands for total dietary energy (kcal) provided by the food item j.

Step 2: Estimation of Total Missing Calories   Missing calories are those corresponding to food items for which it is not possible to apply procedure 1. The estimation of these calories is done using the median household calorie unit value ($/kcal) at region/area/income quintile level. This median calorie unit value is calculated with data corresponding to the food items for which procedure 1 was applied, and is equal to the ratio between the expenditures (adjusted for temporal price fluctuations) and the corresponding dietary energy values.

$$UVal_h = \frac{\sum_{j=1}^{g} FDEXP_{jh}}{DEC_h}$$

where $UVal_h$ represents the calorie unit value of household h in local currency per kcal; $FDEXP_{jh}$ represents the total food expenditures occurred by household h to acquire the g food items to which procedure 1 was applied; and DEC_h represents the total dietary energy of household h brought by the n food items.

The final calorie unit value corresponds to the median household calorie unit value at region/area/income quintile level. This median calorie unit value is applied at the household level to the food expenditure of all the k food items for which corresponding calories were not estimated using procedure 1.

$$DEC_{kh} = \frac{FDEXP_{kh}}{UVal}$$

where k represents all the food products acquired by household h and for which no quantity or nutrient value exists (e.g., food consumed away from home); the sum of g and k corresponds to the total number of food items consumed/acquired by the household h; DEC_{kh} represents the dietary energy of household h from the k food items; $FDEXP_{kh}$ represents the expenditures occurred by household h to acquire the k food items; and $UVal$ represents the median calorie unit value.

Step 3: Estimation of the Corresponding Calories from Protein, Fats, Carbohydrates (Including Fiber), and Alcohol The amount of calories provided by protein and fats are calculated applying the proportion of calories provided by them (computed in procedure 2, step 1) to the estimated missing calories (computed in procedure 2, step 2). Using the same notations as introduced in step 1 and step 2 of procedure 2, it becomes:

$$PROT_{kh} = DEC_{kh} * SPORT_h \quad \text{and} \quad FAT_{kh} = DEC_{kh} * SFAT_h$$

The calories provided by total carbohydrates (including fiber) and alcohol are calculated as the difference between the total estimated missing calories (computed in procedure 2, step 2) and the sum of calories provided by protein and fats (computed in procedure 2, step 3):

$$CAR_{kh} = DEC_{kh} - (PROT_{kh} + FAT_{kh})$$

where $PROT_{kh}$, FAT_{kh} and CAR_{kh} represent, respectively, the calories from protein, fats, carbohydrates (including fiber), and alcohol provided by the k food items acquired by household h.

Step 4: Estimation of the Missing Grams of Protein, Fats, Carbohydrates (Including Fiber), and Alcohol To obtain the missing grams of protein, fats, and carbohydrates the respective Atwater coefficients are applied to the estimated missing calories provided by each of these nutrients (computed in procedure 2, step 3).

Quality Consideration

The quality of the calculated energy content of food products will heavily influence the quality of the energy consumed/acquired and therefore the food security statistics. Therefore, when interpreting the results several issues need to be taken into consideration:

- Food consumed outside the household is not always well collected. Therefore the value of food consumed/acquired over the reference period may be wrongly estimated.
- Habitual food consumption may not be captured well. There could be shortcomings in the survey or questionnaire design (e.g., food consumption is not collected over the year; list of food products is not exhaustive enough to fully reflect habitual consumption of the household; food consumption may be collected through interview with long recall periods; use of many units of measurement when collecting quantities of food consumed/acquired).
- The quality of the food matching between reported foods and those of the FCT. On the one hand, the higher the percentage of exact matches means the higher the quality of the dietary energy estimation. On the other hand, the higher the proportion of foods which cannot be converted to grams EP means the lower the quality of the estimate of dietary energy consumed/acquired.
- The quality of the food composition data. The FCT used should be adequate for the country, of high quality, and complete. There should be no missing data because they would lead to an underestimation of the energy values. In addition, the higher the proportion of foods for which no specific nutrient values can be attributed means the lower the quality of the energy and nutrient estimations.
- Treatment of outliers (i.e., implausible under- and overconsumption). Procedures to treat for outliers are not included in this book.

Estimation of Food and Total Consumption Expenditures and Income

If the data are reliable, total income is calculated as the sum of income of all household members. Otherwise, it can be approximated by the total household expenditure, which is equal to the sum of total consumption expenditure plus nonconsumption expenditures.

Total consumption expenditure includes the following:

- Food
- Clothing and footwear

- Gross rent, fuel, and power
- Furniture
- Medical care and health expenses
- Transport and communications
- Recreation, entertainment, education, and cultural services
- Miscellaneous (personal care, package tours, etc.)

Nonconsumption expenditures include direct and indirect taxes, insurance premiums, charity donations, social security contributions, and remittances or gifts to other households.

Adjustment to Account for Temporal Variability of Prices

As already discussed, the period usually covered by NHS is one year to account for the seasonal variations of food consumption and income. In this way, households report the acquired food over different months within a year. The monetary value of food commodities may vary not only among regions within a country due to extra costs as part of the regional trade chain, but also over the survey period due to price fluctuations or economic factors. Variations in the monetary values because of the geographical distribution of households are not removed for food security analysis because they are indicative of price differentials on an item within the country. However, in the estimation of food expenditure, total consumption expenditure, and income, it is important to consider inflation and deflation.

If food expenditures, consumption expenditures, and income have not been deflated before executing the ADePT-FSM, it can be done within the program by adjusting monetary values using monthly deflators. The deflators are calculated based on monthly food and consumer price indexes (FPI and CPI, respectively) associated with each household according to the month and year in which the household was surveyed. The deflators used to adjust food expenditure values are obtained as the ratio of the monthly FPI and the survey midperiod FPI, which is estimated as the average of all the monthly FPI during the survey period. The deflators used to adjust total consumption expenditure and income are obtained as the ratio of the monthly CPI and the survey midperiod CPI, which is estimated as the average of all the monthly CPI during the survey period.

Annex 2D shows an example of the calculation of food and total price deflators.

Table 2.4: Summary Table on Procedures of Standardization in ADePT-FSM

Conversion into dietary energy	Procedure 1	Steps 1 to 2	Manual
		Steps 3 to 6	Automatic
	Procedure 2	Steps 1 to 4	Automatic
Calculation of total expenditures			Automatic
Temporal adjustment			Automatic
Conversion in per person			Automatic
National and subnational inference			Automatic

Conversion in per Person per Day

The indicators are standardized and expressed in terms of per person per day, to remove variations due to household size and time period of data collection. Most of the data from household surveys do not allow for an analysis of the intrahousehold distribution of food consumption and expenditure. Therefore, it is assumed that both of them are equally distributed among household members. Some surveys collect information on the number of people who participated in the meal (partakers). When data on partakers are available food consumption statistics (excluding food expenditure) are calculated using the number of food partakers instead of the household size.

Inference at National and Subnational Levels

The users of food security statistics are interested in having the information disaggregated by population groups within the country. Therefore, the statistics estimated for the sampled households are adjusted to infer statistics at national and subnational levels; to do so, population statistical weights are applied to the data. The population weight is the household weight multiplied by the number of household members. The household weight is corrected for nonresponses, and it is calculated as the inverse of the probability of the household to be selected multiplied by the expansion factor.

Table 2.4 summarizes all the procedures that are automatic in ADePT-FSM and those that need to be undertaken manually during the preparation of the datasets prior to executing the software.

Indicators on Food Security

This section presents the food security indicators generated by ADePT-FSM and their respective methods of estimation. As discussed in the section on standardization, the indicators produced by ADePT-FSM are standardized in per person per day and are representative at the national and subnational levels according to the survey sampling design.

Food Insecurity Indicators Produced by ADePT-FSM

Groups of Analysis

The food security indicators are derived at national and subnational levels. The subnational levels are subsamples of households in terms of geographic, demographic, or socioeconomic factors. Statistics are provided not only for groups of population but also for food groups or food commodities. The statistics derived using a parametric approach, such as prevalence of undernourishment, can be produced only for the population groups for which the survey sample is representative.

Category of Population Groups   ADePT-FSM allows for the analysis of food security indicators derived by population groups. These population groups include households' geographical location and household heads' socioeconomic or demographic characteristics. Table 2.5 presents all the population groups that can be analyzed using ADePT-FSM.

Food Commodity Groups   The food commodity groups are defined by the user. Table 2.6 is an example of the classification used by the Statistics

Table 2.5: Population Groups

National
Regional
Urban and rural areas
Quintile of income
Household size
Gender of the household's head
Age of the household's head
Economic activity of the household's head
Education level of the household's head
Occupation of the household's head
Population group 1 defined by the user (e.g., marital status of household's head)
Population group 2 defined by the user (e.g., type of access to drinkable water)
Population group 3 defined by the user (e.g., does or does not receive institutional food aid)
Population group 4 defined by the user (e.g., refugee or not)
Population group 5 defined by the user (e.g., ethnicity)

Table 2.6: FAO Food Commodity Groups' Classification to Process Household Surveys

1	Cereals and derived products
2	Roots and tubers, and derived products
3	Sugar crops and sweeteners and derived products
4	Pulses and derived products
5	Nuts and derived products
6	Oil-bearing crops and derived products
7	Vegetables and derived products
8	Fruits and derived products
9	Stimulant crops and derived products
10	Spices
11	Alcoholic beverages
12	Meat (including poultry and pork) and derived products
13	Eggs
14	Seafood and derived products
15	Milk, cheese, and derived products
16	Vegetable oils and fats
17	Animal oils and fats
18	Nonalcoholic beverages
19	Miscellaneous and prepared food

Division of the FAO, which reflects the main food groups used for the food balance sheets.

Food Commodity Items The food commodity items analyzed are those listed in the NHS and are well-defined, such as fresh milk; long-grained rice; tomatoes; boneless, frozen mutton, etc. The list and number of food commodities are country- and survey-specific.

Indicators Produced by ADePT-FSM

The indicators listed in table 2.7 are derived for each category of population group (LCU refers to local currency). Indicators produced only at national, urban/rural areas, or regional levels are indicated with a asterisk (*).

The indicators listed in table 2.8 are derived for each food commodity group.

The indicators listed in table 2.9 are derived for each food item of the NHS.

Indicators and Methods of Estimation

The various indicators and related methods of estimation are presented below.

Table 2.7: Food Security Statistics Produced for Each Category of Population Groups

General	Number of sampled households
	Average household size
	Estimated population

Access to diet and quality of diet

Dietary energy	Average dietary energy consumption (kcal/person/day)
and macro-	Average protein consumption (g/person/day)
nutrients	Average carbohydrates consumption (g/person/day)
	Average fats consumption (g/person/day)
	Average availability of vitamin A, retinol, and beta-carotene (mcg RAE/person/day)
	Average availability of vitamins B1, B2, B6, and C, calcium (mg/person/day), and vitamin B12 (mcg/person/day)
Micronutrients	Average availability of animal, nonanimal, heme, and nonheme iron (mg/person/day)
	Ratio of vitamins A and B12 available to required (%)
	Ratio of vitamins A, B1, B2, B6, B12, and C, and calcium available to recommended safe intake (%)
Amino acids	Average availability of essential amino acids: isoleucine, leucine, lysine, methionine, phenylalanine, threonine, tryptophan, valine, histidine, cystine, and tyrosine (g/person/day)
Quality of diet	Share of dietary energy consumption from protein (%)
	Share of dietary energy consumption from carbohydrates (%)
	Share of dietary energy consumption from fats (%)
	Share of animal protein in total protein consumption (%)

Economic access to food

Monetary	Average food consumption (LCU/person/day)
value	Average total consumption (LCU/person/day)
	Average income (LCU/person/day)
Price	Average dietary energy unit value (LCU/1,000 kcal)
Sources of	Share of purchased food in total food consumption (in dietary energy) (%)
acquisition	Share of own produced food in total food consumption (in dietary energy) (%)
	Share of food consumed away from home in total food consumption (in dietary energy) (%)
	Share of food from other sources in total food consumption (in dietary energy) (%)
	Share of purchased food in total food consumption (in monetary value) (%)
	Share of own produced food in total food consumption (in monetary value) (%)
	Share of food consumed away from home in total food consumption (in monetary value) (%)
	Share of food from other sources in total food consumption (in monetary value) (%)
	Share of food consumption in total income (%) (Engel ratio)
Responsiveness	Income demand elasticity of dietary energy consumption
of demand to	Income demand elasticity of food consumption in monetary value
income	Income demand elasticity of Engel ratio
inequality	Dispersion ratio of food consumption in dietary energy (80/20)
	Dispersion ratio of food consumption in monetary value (80/20)
	Dispersion ratio of total consumption expenditure (80/20)
Food	Minimum and average dietary energy requirements (kcal/person/day)
inadequacy	Prevalence of undernourishment (%) (*)
	Depth of food deficit (kcal/person/day) (*)

Dietary Energy and Macronutrient Consumption

The average daily calories consumed by a representative individual in a population group of analysis are estimated as follows:

$$Calories\ per\ person\ per\ day = \frac{\sum_{h=1}^{H} (hh\_wgt_h * DEC_h)}{\sum_{h=1}^{H} (hh\_size_h * hh\_wgt_h * num\_days_h)}$$

Table 2.8: Food Security Statistics Produced for Each Food Commodity Group

Access to diet and quality of diet	
Dietary energy and macronutrients	Average dietary energy consumption (kcal/person/day)
	Average protein consumption (g/person/day)
	Average carbohydrates consumption (g/person/day)
	Average fats consumption (g/person/day)
Quality of diet	Contribution of food groups to total dietary energy consumption (%)
	Contribution of food groups to total protein consumption (%)
	Contribution of food groups to total carbohydrates consumption (%)
	Contribution of food groups to total fats consumption (%)
	Average protein consumption per kcal (g/1,000 kcal)
	Average carbohydrates consumption per kcal (g/1,000 kcal)
	Average fats consumption per kcal (g/1,000 kcal)
Micronutrients	Average availability of vitamin A, retinol, and beta-carotene (mcg RAE/person/day)
	Average availability of vitamins B1, B2, B6, and C, and calcium (mg/person/day), and vitamin B12 (mcg/person/day)
	Average availability of animal, nonanimal, heme, and nonheme iron (mg/person/day)
	Contribution of food groups to micronutrient availability (%)
Amino acids	Average availability of essential amino acids: isoleucine, leucine, lysine, methionine, phenylalanine, threonine, tryptophan, valine, histidine, cystine, and tyrosine (g/person/day)
	Contribution of food groups to amino acid availability (%)
Economic access to food	
Monetary value	Average food consumption (LCU/person/day)
Price	Average dietary energy unit value (LCU/1,000 kcal)
	Average protein unit value (LCU/100 g)
	Average carbohydrates unit value (LCU/100 g)
	Average fats unit value (LCU/100 g)

Table 2.9: Food Security Statistics Produced for Each Food Commodity

Access to diet and quality of diet	
Dietary energy and macronutrients	Average edible food quantity (g/person/day)
	Average dietary energy consumption (kcal/person/day)
	Average protein consumption (g/person/day)
Micronutrients	Average availability of vitamin A, retinol, and beta-carotene (mcg RAE/person/day)
	Average availability of vitamins B1, B2, B6, and C, and calcium (mg/person/day), and vitamin B12 (mcg/person/day)
	Average availability of animal, nonanimal, heme, and nonheme iron (mg/person/day)
Amino acids	Average availability of essential amino acids: isoleucine, leucine, lysine, methionine, phenylalanine, threonine, tryptophan, valine, histidine, cystine, and tyrosine (g/person/day)
Economic access to food	
Monetary value	Average food consumption (LCU/person/day)
Price	Dietary energy unit value (LCU/1000 kcal)

$$DEC_h = \sum_{j=1}^{ag} DEC_{hj} + \sum_{j=1}^{k} DEC_{hj}$$

The average daily macronutrients (protein, carbohydrates, and fat) consumed by a representative individual in a population group is estimated as follows:

$$Macronutrients\ per\ person\ per\ day = \frac{\sum_{h=1}^{H}(hh\_wgt_h * Nutrient_h)}{\sum_{h=1}^{H}(hh\_size_h * hh\_wgt_h * num\_days_h)}$$

$$Nutrient_h = \sum_{j=1}^{g} Nutrient_{hj} + \sum_{j=1}^{k} Nutrient_{hj}$$

$$Nutrient_{jh} = \left(\left(\frac{fq_{jh} * lg_j}{100}\right) * \left(1 - \frac{refuse_j}{100}\right)\right)$$

where H is the total number of sampled households belonging to the population group of analysis; hh_wgt_h is the household weight (expansion factor divided by the probability of the household to be sampled) of household h; hh_size_h is the total number of members (household size) in household h; num_days_h is the number of days of the food data reference period for household h; DEC_{hj} refers to the calories consumed of food item j by household h; g is the number of food items in household h, for which the nutrient content is estimated applying procedure 1; k is the number of food items in household h, for which the nutrient content is estimated applying procedure 2; $Nutrient_h$ is the total amount of macronutrients in household h; $Nutrient_{hj}$ is the amount of macronutrients in food item j in household h; fq_{jh} is the quantity of the food item j consumed/acquired by household h and expressed in grams "as purchased" (includes the nonedible part); lg_j refers to the grams of micronutrients per 100 grams edible portion of the food item j (as in FCT); and $refuse_j$ is the refuse factor (nonedible part) of the food item j expressed in percentage.

Micronutrient Availability

A proper intake of macronutrients in terms of a balanced diet is not enough for human beings to conduct a healthy life if they do not consume adequate amounts of minerals, vitamins (micronutrients), and indispensable amino acids. The micronutrients analyzed by the ADePT-Food Security Module are the A vitamins, ascorbic acid, thiamine, riboflavin, B6, cobalamin, and the minerals calcium and iron. The indispensable amino acids analyzed are isoleucine, leucine, lysine, threonine, tryptophan, valine, histidine, methionine and cystine, and phenylalanine and tyrosine.

Most NHS collect data on food acquisition rather than consumption. Further, the content of micronutrients in food may vary from the moment of its acquisition to its consumption because of several reasons including storage conditions and the way the food is processed. Moreover, the presence of other substances in the food may inhibit or enhance nutrient absorption.[11] Therefore, the derived estimates are indicative, and they should not be interpreted as a result of the evaluation of intake by individuals in the population groups. That is why the term *availability* is used instead of *consumption*.

In the micronutrients assessment, neither supplementation nor fortification is taken into consideration because such information usually is not collected in the surveys.

The equation applied to estimate the micronutrients available for consumption is given below:

$$Micronutrients\ per\ person\ per\ day = \frac{\sum_{h=1}^{H}(hh\_wgt_h * Nutrient_h)}{\sum_{h=1}^{H}(hh\_size_h * hh\_wgt_h * num\_days_h)}$$

$$Nutrient_h = \sum_{j=1}^{n} Nutrient_{hj}$$

$$Nutrient_j = \left(\left(\frac{fq_{jh} * lg_j}{100}\right) * \left(1 - \frac{refuse_j}{100}\right)\right)$$

where H is the total number of sampled households belonging to the population group of analysis; hh_wgt_h is the household weight (expansion factor divided by the probability of the household to be sampled) of household h; hh_size_h is the total number of members (household size) in household h; num_days_h is the number of days of the food data reference period for household h; n *is* the total number of food items (excluding those consumed away from home[12]) in household h; $Nutrient_h$ is the amount of micronutrients available in household h (excluding those consumed away from home); $Nutrient_{hj}$ is the amount of micronutrients available in food item j in household h; fq_{jh} is the quantity of the food item j consumed/acquired by household h and expressed in grams "as purchased" (includes the nonedible part); lg_j refers to the grams of micronutrients in 100 edible grams of the food item j

(as in FCT); and *refuse$_j$* is the refuse factor (nonedible part) of the food item *j* expressed in percentage.

For the micronutrients' ADePT-FSM analysis, it is worth clarifying some concepts on vitamin A and iron.

More than one unit of measurement can be found in the literature when referring to vitamin A. The ADePT-FSM was developed to express the availability of vitamin A in terms of retinol activity equivalent (RAE). The use of µg RAE rather than µg retinol equivalent (RE) or international units (IU) is preferred when calculating and reporting the amount of the total vitamin A in mixed foods or assessing the amount of dietary and supplemental vitamin A consumed (see National Academy of Sciences [NAS] 2001). According to NAS the conversion of retinol and pro-vitamin A carotenoids into vitamin A is as follows:

$$Vitamin\ A\ in\ \text{µg RAE} = \text{µg retinol} + \frac{\text{µg βcarotene}}{12}$$

$$+ \frac{\text{µg αcarotene or βcryptoxanthin}}{24}$$

Regarding iron, it can be distinguished as animal or nonanimal. The first refers to meat, fish, eggs, milk, and cheese, and their derived products. Another type of iron classification is with respect to the mechanism of its absorption: heme and nonheme. The latter is present in food of both animal and nonanimal origin, whereas the former can be found only in meat and fish (as it is derived from hemoglobin and myoglobin).[13]

Amino Acids

Amino acids are the building blocks of proteins. Some of their functions are building cells, protecting the body from viruses or bacteria, repairing damaged tissue, providing nitrogen, and carrying oxygen throughout the body. They can be classified as dispensable or indispensable. The latter are also called essential amino acids (EAA) and cannot be synthesized by the human body. Therefore, they should be supplied to the body through the consumption of protein in food.[14]

The indispensable amino acids analyzed in ADePT-FSM are isoleucine, leucine, lysine, threonine, tryptophan, valine, histidine, methionine and cystine, and phenylalanine and tyrosine. ADePT-FSM estimates the average daily per person grams of indispensable amino acids available for consumption and the equations used are:

$$Amino\ acid\ per\ person\ per\ day = \frac{\sum_{h=1}^{H} (hh\_wgt_h * AA_h)}{\sum_{h=1}^{H} (hh\_size_h * hh\_wgt_h * num\_days_h)}$$

$$AA_h = \sum_{j=1}^{n} AA_{jh}$$

$$AA_{jh} = \left(\left(\frac{fq_{jh} * lg_j}{100} \right) * \left(1 - \frac{ref}{100} \right) * \left(\frac{pd}{100} \right) \right)$$

where H is the total number of sampled households belonging to the population group of analysis; hh_wgt_h is the household weight (expansion factor divided by the probability of the household to be sampled) of household h; hh_size_h is the total number of members (household size) in household h; num_days_h is the number of days of the food data reference period for household h; n is the total number of food items (excluding those consumed away from home[15]) in household h; AA_h is the amount of amino acid available in household h (excluding those consumed away from home); AA_{jh} is the amount of amino acid available in food item j in household h; fq_{jh} is the quantity of the food item j consumed/acquired by household h and expressed in grams "as purchased" (includes the nonedible part); lg_j refers to the grams of amino acid in 100 edible grams of the food item j (as in FCT); ref is the refuse factor (nonedible part) of the food item j expressed in percentage; and pd is the protein digestibility of the food item j expressed in percentage.

Balanced Diet

A balanced diet is a diet that provides energy and all essential nutrients for growth and a healthy and active life. Since few foods contain all the nutrients required to permit the normal growth, maintenance, and functioning of the human body, a variety of food is needed to cover a person's macro- and micronutrient needs. Any combination of foods that provides the correct amount of dietary energy and all essential nutrients in optimal amounts and proportions is a balanced diet (CFS 2012).

A joint WHO/FAO expert group established guidelines for a balanced diet (WHO 2003). These guidelines are related to effects on the chronic nondeficiency diseases. According to expert opinion, a balanced diet exists when the following conditions are met:

- The proportion of dietary energy provided by protein is in the range of 10–15 percent.
- The proportion of dietary energy provided by fats is in the range of 15–30 percent.
- The proportion of total dietary energy available derived from carbohydrates is in the range of 55–75 percent.

From surveys collecting food consumption or acquisition, it is not possible to assess if a population group consumes a balanced diet, because there is no information about how people combine the food they consume or about intrahousehold differences in food consumption. However, from the data collected it is possible to infer whether or not households have access to a balanced diet.

Monetary Values

The average daily food expenditure of a representative individual in a population group is estimated as follows:

$$Food\ monetary\ value\ per\ person\ per\ day = \frac{\sum_{h=1}^{H}(hh\_wgt_h * FMV_h)}{\sum_{h=1}^{H}(hh\_size_h * hh\_wgt_h * num\_days_h)}$$

$$FMV_h = \sum_{j=1}^{n} FMV_{jh}$$

where H is the total number of sampled households belonging to the population group of analysis; hh_wgt_h is the household weight (expansion factor divided by the probability of the household to be sampled) of household h; hh_size_h is the total number of members (household size) in household h; num_days_h is the number of days of the food data reference period for household h; n is the total number of food items (including those consumed away from home) in household h; FMV_h is the food monetary value of household h; and FMV_{jh} is the food monetary value of food item j in household h.

A similar formula is applied to estimate the average daily total consumption expenditure and income of a representative individual in a population group.

Price

Food prices are important determinants of food security. ADePT-FSM calculates the calorie unit value of dietary energy expressed in monetary value per 1,000 kcal. At the population group level, the software computes the calorie unit value at household level and then estimates the correspondent mean. At food item and food group levels, because some food items or food groups may present only a few cases, the median calorie unit value is used instead of the mean. Finally, the calorie unit values do not include the cost of the energy required to cook food.

In addition to the monetary value of 1,000 kcal, macronutrient unit monetary values are also provided, and they are expressed in monetary terms per 100 grams of nutrients.

Responsiveness of Food Demand to Income

The income elasticity of the demand of food is measured through the responsiveness of dietary energy, food expenditure, or the Engel ratio to a variation in income. In other words, this relative responsiveness depicts the relationship between acquired food and income, described by the Engel curve. The estimates assume that substitution among food commodities occurs for different income levels and that *food commodity prices are constant*.

For a given country, it is assumed that household dietary energy consumption per person can be linked to household income per person by the following regression equation (FAO 1996):

$$x_h = \beta_0 + \beta_1 * \ln(V_h) + u_h$$

where β_0 and β_1 are parameters of the equation; x_h is the demand of food expressed in terms of dietary energy, food expenditure, or Engel ratio of household h on a per person basis; V_h is the income per person in household h; and u_h is the random variation of food demand across households.

In ADePT-FSM the individual household data are grouped by income decile classes, and the average food consumption and income per person in each income decile class is inferred and used to estimate the parameters of the equation. Therefore the equation becomes:

$$\overline{x}_J = \alpha_0 + \alpha_1 * \ln(\overline{V}_j) + u_j$$

where α_0 and α_1 are parameters of the equation; and $\overline{x}_J$ is the inferred demand of food expressed in terms of dietary energy, food expenditure, or Engel ratio of the income class j on a per person basis.

$$\overline{x}_J = \frac{\sum_{h=1}^{H_j}(f_h * x_h)}{pop_j}$$

$\overline{V}_J$ is the inferred per person income of the income class j.

$$\overline{V}_j = \frac{\sum_{h=1}^{H_j}(f_h * V_h)}{pop_j}$$

H_h refers to the total number of sampled households in income decile j; x_h is the demand of food expressed in terms of dietary energy, food expenditure, or Engel ratio of household h; and pop_j is the inferred total population in the income decile j.

$$pop_j = \sum_{h=1}^{H_j}(hh\_size * hh\_wgt_h)$$

f_h is the inferred total number of people represented by household h.

$$f_h = (hh\_size * hh\_wgt_h)$$

hh_size_h is the total number of members (household size) in household h; hh_wgt_h is the household weight (expansion factor divided by the probability of the household to be sampled) of household h; and u_j is the random variation of the average food demand across income decile classes.

Figure 2.1 shows an example of the demand of food consumption as a function of income. This example is from real country data and represents the average values of food demand (in terms of dietary energy and food expenditure) by average values of income (estimated for income decile groups of the population).

43

Figure 2.1: Example of Food Consumption Demand as Function of Income

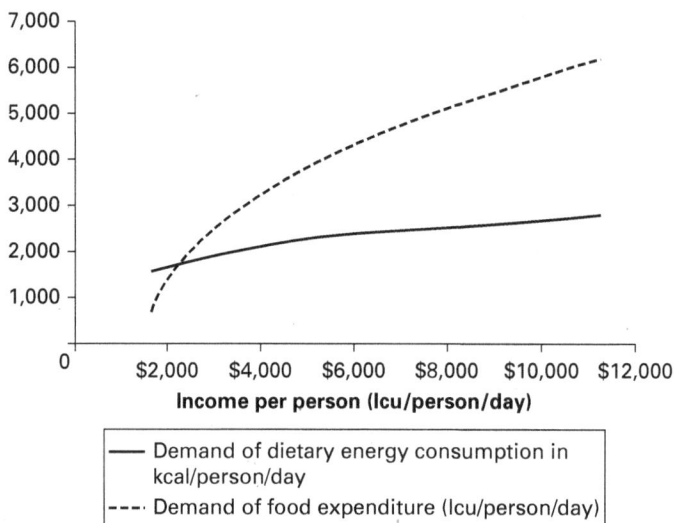

The elasticity of food consumption with respect to income is:

$$\eta = \left(\frac{\partial x}{\partial V} \right) * \frac{V}{x} = \frac{\alpha_1}{V} * \frac{V}{x} = \frac{\alpha_1}{x}$$

Therefore, the income elasticity (η) of food demand (represented by the mean per person μ) can be estimated as:

$$\eta = \frac{\alpha_1}{\mu}$$

Reviewing: This expression of elasticity allows the estimation of the elasticity by income deciles.

$$\eta_j = \left(\frac{\hat{\alpha}_1}{\hat{x}_j} \right) = \left(\frac{\hat{\alpha}_1}{\hat{\alpha}_0 + \hat{\alpha}_1 * \ln(\bar{V}_j)} \right)$$

where $\hat{\alpha}_1$ is the estimated slope of the Engel function; and $\hat{x}_j$ corresponds to the estimated fitted mean of dietary energy, food expenditure, or Engel ratio of the j_{th} income decile.

Food Consumption Statistics by Sources of Acquisition

As discussed previously, households acquire food from different sources, including purchases, own production, aid, and as payment for labor. The ADePT-FSM analyzes four main sources of food acquisition: purchases (excluding food consumed away from home), own production, consumed away from home, and all other sources. The latter includes food received as aid, gift or payment for labor, hunting, and wild harvesting.

The contribution of each food source to total food consumption in both monetary and dietary energy terms varies depending on the population group of analysis. For instance, it is expected that the share of food consumption from own production in rural households is higher than that in urban households.

The share of food expenditure in total income is also called the Engel ratio. Low-income households spend a large percentage of their total consumption expenditure on food. With higher income, the food ratio declines following Engel's law, which states that the proportion of income spent on food decreases with increasing income, because food is a basic primary need.

Measures of Inequality

Dispersion Ratios   The dispersion ratios measure inequality between the two extreme income quintile groups. They are calculated using as reference the average values corresponding to the first quintile. For instance, one ratio is defined as the average food consumption (in terms of dietary energy or monetary values) in the highest income quintile divided by the correspondent average food consumption in the lowest one.

Coefficient of Variation   The coefficient of variation (CV) is a relative measure of inequality in a given distribution. In principle, a *direct* estimate of the variability in the distribution of dietary energy consumption (DEC) could be obtained through a measure of the empirical dispersion of individuals' consumption from a survey. There are, however, several reasons why this may be problematic. Household food consumption data (collected in surveys) on a per person basis are very likely to be more dispersed than the actual per person yearly average of food consumption in the population. This is because of the presence of "spurious" variability (introduced both systematically through features of survey design and accidentally due to nonsampling errors) related to the following:

- *Survey rounds of data collections usually spread over the year.* This is done to avoid introducing biases in the estimation of mean consumption, when consumption of food is known to be varying over the seasons. Unfortunately, spreading data collection over the seasons means that seasonal *variability* in consumption (which should not be considered in estimating the variability of the average year consumption in the population) is still present.
- *Missing data and outliers.* For example, nonsampling errors that are associated with errors in recall, under- or overreporting, incompleteness of data collection forms, especially with reference to food consumed away from home, interview effects, etc.
- *Surveys collecting food acquisition instead of food consumption.* Food acquisition surveys may overestimate the distribution of calories across households because the variability *within* households will be confounded with the variability *between households*. Calories can be acquired through durable foods such as cereals to be stocked and consumed over a long period of time and not during the reference food collection period.
- *Expected variability.* During the year, there is an expected variability in adequately nourished households, for instance, the result of a party given by the households. This variability is considered as an excess variability, since we are interested in capturing the habitual food consumption.

All these factors might induce a systematic positive bias in the estimate of the *variability* parameter of the distribution. This bias is difficult to reduce once survey data have been collected. Cleaning the data to identify outliers and missing values can help reduce the potential bias, but this may introduce a certain degree of subjectivity in the analysis that should not go unnoticed. In addition, when the distribution in the population is skewed, as seen in two-stage sampling (commonly used in household income expenditure surveys), a systemic bias in the estimate of variability indicators can result.

All these considerations raise reservations about the possibility of obtaining a reliable estimate of DEC variability through the observed empirical variance of individual household data in a survey. Therefore, the estimation of the CV of DEC can be derived as the combination of two sources of variability of DEC: one due to income and the other due to other factors. Indeed, while the role of income in explaining DEC and its variability within a population is at the heart of all theories of poverty and economic development, there are many other factors inducing variability in DEC. These factors have to be considered physiological in a population, and should therefore be tolerated.

The overall value of the CV is then obtained following the steps described below:

Step 1: Estimation of the CV of DEC Tabulated by Income   Individual households are grouped by classes of income decile, and the average per person food consumption in each class of income is inferred. By averaging within an income class, most of the variations in the level of DEC because of factors that are not strongly correlated with income are clearly netted out. The resulting measure of CV should thus properly be interpreted as an estimate of the component of the total variability of DEC in the population tabulated by income, which we term $CV_{x/v}(x)$.

The coefficient of variation of DEC tabulated by income is defined as:

$$CV_{(x/v)} = \frac{\sigma_{(x/v)}}{\mu_x}$$

where $\sigma_{(x/v)}$ is the standard deviation of the distribution of the average per person dietary energy consumption of income decile groups and is derived from the formula:

$$\sigma_{(x/v)} = \sqrt{\frac{\left[\left[\sum_{j=1}^{10}(f_j * x_j^2) - \frac{\left(\sum_{j=1}^{10} f_j * x_j\right)^2}{pop}\right]\right]}{pop-1}}$$

μ_x is the average per person dietary energy consumption at the income decile level and is derived from the formula:

$$\mu_x = \frac{\sum_{j=1}^{10}\left(f_j * \overline{x_j}\right)}{pop} = \frac{\sum_{h=1}^{H}\left(f_h * x_h\right)}{pop}$$

where j refers to income decile group; h refers to household; H is the total number of sampled households in the survey; Hj is the total number of sampled households in income decile j; $\bar{x}_j$ is the average per person dietary energy consumption of income decile j; x_h is the average per person dietary energy consumption of household h; and *pop* is the inferred total population.

$$pop = \sum_{h=1}^{H} (hh\_size_h * hh\_wgt_h)$$

f_j is the inference total number of people in income decile j.

$$f_i = \sum_{h=1}^{H_j} (hh\_size * hh\_wgt)_h$$

f_h is the inference total number of people represented by household h.

$$f_h = (hh\_size * hh\_wgt)_h$$

hh_size_h is the total number of members (household size) in household h; and hh_wgt_h is the household weight (expansion factor divided by the probability of the household to be sampled) of household h.

Step 2: Estimation of CV of DEC Because of Other Factors If it is true that people tend to consume according to their respective dietary energy requirements (DER), and as long as there is an interindividual variation in DER, there will be variation in DEC due to physiological factors. For this reason, a component reflecting the variability of DEC induced by the factors determining the variability of DER, $CV_{x/r}(x) = CV(r)$ is also considered to estimate the total CV. This variation of dietary energy due to requirements is estimated taking into account the coefficient of variation of three components: body weight, physical activity level (PAL), and measurement error. The coefficient of variations due to body weight and PAL are estimated under the assumption of the lognormality. The regression equations used for estimating the basal metabolic rate (BMR) given a body weight are subject to a prediction error corresponding to a CV of about 0.08. Since this variation is of a random nature, it is not considered in deriving the dietary energy requirements. However, in this context, where the variation in energy requirement is used for estimating the variation in energy intake, the variation owing to error in estimating the BMR is taken into account (FAO 2002). For more details on the estimation of the CV of DEC due to physiological factors refer to annex 2E.

Step 3: Aggregation Finally, the CV of DEC is derived as the sum of the square of the two CVs as estimated in steps 1 and 2.

$$CV(x) = \sqrt{(CV_{x/v}(x))^2 + (CV_{x/r}(x))^2}$$

Step 4: Selection of the CV In ADePT-FSM, the coefficient of variation of dietary energy consumption corresponds to the CV whose value is the lowest between the CV from the empirical distribution and the CV obtained as a combination of the two sources of variability.

Measures of Asymmetry

The skewness measures the asymmetry of a distribution. As opposed to income that can increase infinitely when the mean increases (corresponding to a long tail to the right), the dietary energy of food consumed is limited by biological constraints.

The method to estimate the value of the skewness depends on how the coefficient of variation of calories is derived. On one hand, when the final CV is obtained from the empirical distribution of calories across individuals, the value of the skewness is the one obtained from the empirical distribution, and a flexible distributional form is used for the calculation of the prevalance of undernourishment (PoU), known as the skewed-normal distribution. On the other hand, when the CV is derived as the sum of two components, the distribution is assumed to be lognormal and the skewness is given by:[16]

$$Skewness = (CV^2 + 3) * CV$$

Note that prior to the methodological improvements resulting from the choice of the CV, the addition of the skewness and the functional form of the log-normal distribution was always used for the calculation of the PoU. For this reason, the user has been left with the option of calculating the distribution according to the old or improved methodology by selecting either the log-normal or skewed-normal distribution, respectively.

Dietary Energy Requirements

The most common levels of dietary energy requirements found in the literature are the minimum and the average. They are derived from the consideration that food energy requirements can be safely defined only in terms of a *distribution within a given class or population group*, not at the individual level (FAO/WHO/UNU 2001). Nevertheless, a minimum or average level of dietary energy intake that is compatible with a healthy and productive life can be meaningfully defined *statistically* with reference to the representative individual in a group or class. As for the estimation of both requirements, the Food and Agriculture Organization (FAO) has devised an indirect procedure based on expert recommendations on what the acceptable ranges of DER would be in groups of individuals of the same sex and age, and on the observed sex/age composition of the countries.

Minimum Dietary Energy Requirement The minimum dietary energy requirement (MDER) is estimated for each sex/age class of individuals based on the energy requirement (based on the basal metabolic rate) for the lowest acceptable body weight for that sex/age combination, adjusted for a minimal physical activity level compatible with a healthy life. Then a weighted average (the weights used are the proportions of the population in the corresponding sex/age groups) of the minimum DERs of each sex/age class is computed. Finally, the extra energy required by pregnant women is added to the weighted average to derive the minimum dietary energy requirement of a representative individual of the population.

Therefore, the information needed to estimate the MDER through the equations suggested by the joint FAO/WHO/UNU expert consultation held in 2001 is the following:

- Country birth ratio in the year of the survey (exogenous parameter)
- Structure of the population in the country by specific sex/age groups (from the survey)

Children Less Than 10 Years Old
- Body mass index (BMI) (50th percentile) (exogenous parameter)[17]
- Height of people in the country for specific sex/age groups (cm) (from demographic and health surveys [DHS] or literature)
- Weight gain per age (grams per day) (50th percentile) (exogenous parameter)[18]
- Energy per gram of weight gain (kcals) (exogenous parameter)[19]

- Country under-five mortality rate (U5MR) in the survey year (per 1,000 live births) (exogenous parameter)

Adolescents and Adults
- Body mass index (fifth percentile) (exogenous parameter)
- Height of people in the country for specific sex/age groups (cm) (from DHS or literature)
- The parameter used for adjusting the requirements due to the level of activity is the PAL. A PAL of 1.55 corresponds to sedentary physical activity (exogenous parameter).[20]

The BMI is used to estimate the weight in kilograms for the attained height, while the U5MR value defines which equations should be applied to estimate the energy requirements of children less than two years old. The birth ratio is used to estimate the extra energy requirement for pregnant women. For more details refer to annex 2F.

Average Dietary Energy Requirement   The formulas to estimate the average dietary energy requirement (ADER) are equal to those used in the estimation of MDER; however, some parameters are different. The ADER refers to the amount of energy considered adequate to meet the energy needs for normative average acceptable weight for an attained height while performing moderate physical activity in good health. Therefore, only the 50th percentile of the BMI is applied to all the equations. The PAL parameter to estimate the average energy requirement is 1.85 and corresponds to a moderate level of physical activity.

While no large variation is expected to exist between the metabolic rate of people in different countries within the same sex/age group (though differences across latitude could be important), the sex/age composition of the population changes over time, and so the estimated dietary energy requirements have to be adjusted to reflect this change in demographic structure.

Micronutrients Availability versus Recommended or Required Intakes

The so-called "hidden hunger" refers to a deficiency of micronutrients; it is a health threat, particularly for children and pregnant women. For an individual, the amount of micronutrients supplied in the diet should be in line with his or her required levels of mineral and vitamins. To minimize the risk of nutrient deficit or excess, a joint FAO/WHO expert group defined the dietary requirement for a micronutrient as an intake level that meets specified criteria for adequacy. This dietary requirement is expressed in terms of an estimated average requirement (EAR) and a recommended nutrient intake (RNI). EAR is the average daily nutrient intake level that meets the needs of 50 percent of the "healthy" individuals in a particular age and sex group. RNI is the daily intake, set at the EAR plus two standard deviations, which meets the nutrient requirements of almost all apparently healthy individuals in an age and sex specific population group (FAO/WHO 2004). Therefore, to express nutrient requirements and recommended intakes for population groups, the requirements applied separately to each individual belonging to the population of analysis are summed. The individual requirements were defined for sex/age population groups by a FAO/WHO group of experts in 1998 (FAO/WHO 2004).

Despite having the micronutrient content of food acquired or consumed by households, it is not possible to talk about micronutrient consumption but availability at the household level. The reason for this is that from the moment households acquire the food to the time they eat it the content of nutrients in the food has changed. The nutrient content varies with food storage practices and processing and preparation methods (NAS 2000). For example, (1) high temperature processing can affect the vitamin content, e.g., vitamin C; and (2) discarding of water used in cooking will lead to the loss of water-soluble food components (e.g., B vitamins, vitamin C, and certain bioactive components) (FAO/INFOODS 2012).

According to the National Academy of Sciences (NAS) (2000), the household nutrient requirement estimated as the sum of the needs[21] of the household members cannot be used as an EAR because intake and requirement are not correlated for most nutrients. When a diet provides the amount of nutrient needed by household members, it is likely that food (and so the nutrient) will be distributed in proportion to energy needs of the individuals, not to nutrient requirement needs. Therefore, it is suggested to estimate the required nutrient density of a household diet, such that when the diet is shared in proportion to calories, it is likely that the nutrient requirements of all the individuals will be met. The required nutrient density of the household is the highest nutrient density among household members (FAO/WHO 1970). Note that if the dietary energy consumed is not enough for the total household, it cannot be assured that food (and nutrient consumption) is distributed in proportion to the calories required by household members. Therefore, this approach is meaningful when households have a consumption of calories at least equal to their requirements.

The NAS also stated that the calculation of required nutrient density is not as simple as computing the ratio of the estimated average requirement for the nutrient to the average energy requirement.[22] On the one hand, the calculations must take into account variability of the nutrient requirement, expected variability of the nutrient density in ingested diets, and assurance of adequacy for the targeted individual. On the other hand, the recommended nutrient intake, which meets the nutrient requirements of almost all individuals (when requirement in the group has a normal distribution), should not be used as a cutoff point for assessing nutrient intakes of a population group because it would result in an overestimation of the proportion of people at risk of inadequacy.

Currently, ADePT-FSM generates statistics that compare levels of mean nutrient availability with both mean nutrient requirements and recommended intakes. These statistics, which are described below, will be reconsidered in light of the NAS report for future ADePT-FSM releases.

Ratio of Micronutrient Available to Required   For a given population group, the average amount of available micronutrients (to be consumed by a representative individual of the population) is divided by the estimated average requirement. The available amount for consumption is the numerator, and the EAR is the denominator of the ratio. In comparing the average availability with a measure of average requirement, micronutrient distribution across the population is unaccounted.[23]

Ratio of Micronutrient Available to Recommended   For a given population group, the average amount of micronutrients available (to be consumed by a representative individual of the population) is divided by the recommended nutrient intake. The available amount for consumption is the numerator, and the RNI is the denominator of the ratio. For most micronutrients, if the mean intake equals the RNI, a substantial proportion of the population will have intakes less than their own requirements.

Other Ratios   The development of Food-Based Dietary Guidelines (FBDG) focuses on how a combination of foods can meet nutrient requirements rather than on how each specific nutrient is provided in adequate amounts.

In contrast to recommended intakes (RI), FBDG are based on the fact that people eat food, not nutrients. Defining nutrient intakes alone is only part of the task of dealing with nutritional adequacy. The notion of nutrient density is helpful for defining FBDG and evaluating the adequacy of diets. Unlike RI, FBDG can be used to educate the public through the mass media and provide a practical guide to selecting foods by defining dietary adequacy (FAO/WHO 2004).

Food items can have a high or low nutrient density. Nutrient dense foods are those providing substantial amounts of vitamins and minerals and relatively few calories. For instance, fruits and vegetables are nutrient dense commodities. On the other hand, food items with low nutrient density supply calories but a relatively small or null amount of micronutrients. This is the case of added sugars, fats, and alcohol (USHHS/USDA 2005).

For some vitamins and minerals, ADePT-FSM estimates nutrient densities in the diet as the amount of micronutrients per 1,000 kcal provided by the food; it also estimates required/recommended nutrient densities that are estimated as the EAR/RNI of the nutrients per 1,000 required calories. The 1,000 required calories are based on the average dietary energy requirements for a representative individual of the population. Then, for these vitamins and minerals, the software computes ratios of nutrient densities in the diet to required/recommended nutrient densities.

Prevalence of Undernourishment

Since the beginning of its history FAO put emphasis on the problem of undernourishment and studied the problem in depth to reach a good estimation of the number of undernourished people in the world. The first publication on this subject was the "World Food Survey." Starting in 1946, every five or seven years it depicted the situation of global undernourishment. Subsequently, there has been substantial improvement in the methodology used to produce this estimation and in the many experts working on that issue (especially P. Sukhatme and L. Naiken). In 1996 the first FAO World Food Summit was held, and it was decided to have a yearly publication, *The State of Food Insecurity in the World* (SOFI), which provides the latest estimates of the number of chronically hungry people in the world and introduces the first comparable estimates ever made of the number of people who go hungry. This and subsequent editions of SOFI serve as regular progress reports on global and national efforts to reach the goal set by the World Food Summit in 1996: to reduce the number of undernourished people in the world by half by the year 2015 (FAO 1999). The term *undernourishment* indicates the condition of not consuming, on average over an extended period of time (usually a year), an amount of dietary energy sufficient to cover the minimum requirements for a healthy life.

The calculation is an exercise in model-based statistical inference. A probability distribution model is assumed for the annual average dietary energy intake of a representative individual in the population, and its parameters are estimated on the basis of the best available data. Required data include (1) the average food consumption, (2) information on the distribution of food access within the population (variability and asymmetry), (3) the demographic structure of the population (by age and sex population groups), and (4) anthropometric data. Once the probability distribution is characterized and the threshold is set, the proportion of the population that is likely suffering from chronic food deprivation, PoU, is estimated as the probability mass that falls below the threshold.

Formally, the PoU expresses the probability that, by randomly selecting one individual from the population, a person will be found to consume (on average and over a period of time) a level of food energy below the minimum required to maintain a healthy life. The operational definition of food insecurity that is embedded in this indicator is best labeled as "chronic undernourishment in a population."

The probability distribution framework is:

$$PoU = P(x < r_L) = \int_{x < r_L} f_x(x)\, dx = F_x(x_{r_L})$$

where *PoU* represents the probability that an individual randomly selected within a population is found to be undernourished; x represents the daily habitual dietary energy consumption within a year of a "representative individual" in the population; r_L is the daily minimum dietary energy requirements of a "representative individual" in the population; and $f(x)$ represents the distribution of yearly habitual dietary energy consumption across individuals, or, equivalently, the probability distribution of the habitual food intake levels for the population's "representative" individual. See figure 2.2.

Figure 2.2: Graphical Representation of the Model

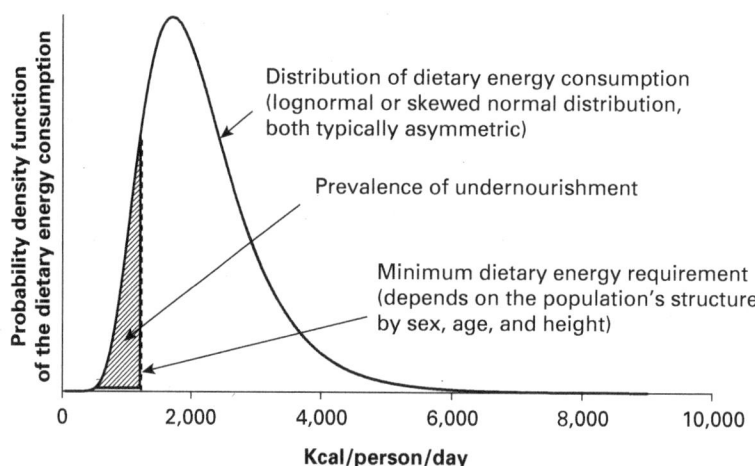

The major limitations of this methodology are the following:

- Though the concept relates to an individual condition, the indicator is designed to measure hunger at the level of a population. Its calculation neither depends on the possibility of collecting data on individuals, nor is the indicator intended to be used to assess the undernourishment condition of any specific individual or group of individuals in a reference population. Therefore, it does not capture possible idiosyncratic, individual problems in accessing food. However, the method can be applied to subnational populations, provided subgroups are representative of the population and data pertaining to such subpopulations are available (Sibrián 2008).
- By focusing on food access, it does not reflect cases of *malnutrition* associated with factors related to the efficient utilization of food.
- Similarly, it misses the "quality" dimension of food security, for example, micronutrient deficiency and related morbidity.
- Finally, by focusing on a determined period, the indicator misses the dimension of risk and vulnerability associated with the (in)stability in the access to food.

Implementing the statistical concept just described to NHS data requires a set of *ancillary assumptions*, mostly driven by feasibility and data availability constraints. The current practice at FAO is based on the following:

1. Food intake is approximated by quantities *available* for consumption at the household level, with no consideration of household level food waste.
2. The distribution of food available for consumption is analyzed between households. Therefore, possible unequal distribution of food within the household is ignored.
3. The minimum dietary energy requirement is defined at the population and not at the individual level.
4. An assumption needs to be made regarding the distribution of the usual intake of a typical person from the population.

The first two assumptions are conditioned by data availability. Though measures of actual intake could be obtained from nutrition surveys, the vast majority of available datasets on food consumption do not allow for a precise estimation of household food waste. Similarly, data from very few and recent surveys could allow for an analysis of the intrahousehold distribution of food consumption.

Assumption 3 is more substantial. It is derived from the consideration that food energy requirements can be safely defined only in terms of a *distribution within a given class or population group*, not at the individual level (FAO/WHO/UNU 2001). This implies that classification of single individuals as undernourished based on a comparison of the level of habitual food intake with their individual requirements is problematic, because the latter cannot usually be estimated with sufficient precision. A minimum level of dietary energy intake that is compatible with a healthy and productive life can nevertheless be meaningfully defined in a *statistical sense* with reference to the representative individual in a group or class.

Assumption 4 regards the statistical model used to conduct the inference at the population level. Originally, the log-normal distribution was chosen due to some desirable characteristics. For example, it is positive valued and with an elongated right tail, and the number of parameters needed for its characterization (only two: one for location and one for dispersion). Concerns were raised that the log-normal model may be not flexible enough to capture changes in the distribution of food access, especially if such changes affect the two "tails" of the distribution in opposite ways. For this reason, in 2011, FAO's Statistics Division explored alternative models that afford greater flexibility in representing the distribution of food consumption.

Therefore, a more flexible model (the skew-normal introduced by Azzalini in 1980) has been deemed more appropriate to represent the distribution of habitual food consumption in the population; a major advantage compared to the log-normal distribution is that this model can now capture changes in the asymmetry of the distribution of food consumption.

Estimation of PoU in ADePT

ADePT-FSM provides estimates of undernourishment (derived from NHS data) at the national level, for urban and rural areas, and regions provided that these population groups have representativeness in the survey sample.

MDG 1.9 Indicator of Prevalence of Food Deprivation

In addition to the estimation of the PoU using NHS data, with ADePT-FSM it is possible to estimate, at the year of the survey, the value of the prevalence of undernourishment used to compute the MDG 1.9 indicator published yearly by FAO in SOFI. Indeed, one of FAO's mandates is to provide a global estimate of the prevalence of undernourishment to monitor progress toward reduction of global hunger by half by 2015 compared to the level of 1990–92. To publish estimates of the prevalence of undernourishment for about 180 countries back to 1990–92, FAO is using the dietary energy supply (DES) as derived from the food balance sheets and corrected for losses at the retail level as the mean of the distribution.

The MDG 1.9 indicator is computed as a three-year weighted average of the number of people undernourished using total population as weights. The PoU for a specific year used in the three-year average can be reproduced using ADePT-FSM if data[24] on the DES, adjusted by losses at the retail level, CV, skewness, and MDER, are used as exogenous parameters in ADePT.

Besides the MDG 1.9 indicator, ADePT-FSM also computes the PoU by region, urban, and rural areas. In these cases the values of CV and skewness remain the same while the DES adjusted by losses, and MDER are calculated by the program applying the formulas:

$$DES_{Sub} = DES_{Nat} * \frac{DEC_{SubHS}}{DEC_{NatHS}}$$

$$MDER_{Sub} = MDER_{SOFI} * \frac{MDER_{SubHS}}{MDER_{NatHS}}$$

where DES_{Sub} is the individual daily dietary energy supply (corrected for losses[25]) at the regional or area level; DES_{Nat} is the individual daily dietary energy supply (corrected for losses[26]) at the national level; DEC_{NatHS} is the daily dietary energy consumption per person at the national level obtained from the NHS data; DEC_{SubHS} is the daily dietary energy consumption per person at the regional or area level obtained from the NHS data; $MDER_{Sub}$ is the daily minimum dietary energy requirement per person at the regional or area level; $MDER_{SOFI}$ is the daily minimum dietary energy requirement per person at the national level as used in SOFI; $MDER_{NatHS}$ is the daily minimum dietary energy requirement per person at the national level obtained from the NHS data; and $MDER_{SubHS}$ is the daily minimum dietary energy requirement per person at the regional or area level obtained from the NHS data.

Depth of the Food Deficit

The depth of the food deficit indicates how many calories would be needed to lift the undernourished from their status, everything else being constant. The average intensity of food deprivation of the undernourished, estimated as the difference between the average dietary energy requirement and the average dietary energy consumption of the undernourished population, is multiplied by the number of undernourished to provide an estimate of the total food deficit in the country, which is then normalized by the total population.

For each category of the population groups, the depth of the food deficit has to be estimated as the absolute difference between the average calories consumed by the deprived population and the average dietary energy requirements multiplied by the prevalence of undernourishment.

The average consumption of the undernourished population can be computed by taking the average consumption corresponding to the part of the distribution of dietary energy consumption below the minimum dietary energy requirement, as follows:

$$\mu_u = \frac{\int_0^{MDER} xf(x)\,dx}{\int_0^{MDER} f(x)\,dx}$$

where μ_u is the average dietary energy consumption of the food-deprived population; $f(x)$ is the density function of dietary energy consumption; and MDER is the minimum dietary energy requirement.

Absolute food deficit from average dietary energy requirements (ADER) in food-deprived population

$$Food\ Deficit \left(\dfrac{\dfrac{Kcal}{person}}{day} \right) = ADER - \mu_u$$

Depth of food deficit is then estimated as:

$$Depth\ of\ food\ deficit \left(\dfrac{\dfrac{Kcal}{person}}{day} \right) = (ADER - \mu_u) * PoU$$

where PoU refers to the prevalence of undernourishment.

Annexes

Annex 2A

Table 2A.1: Example of Different Units of Measurement in Which Food Data Are Collected and Respective Conversion into Metric Units

Food item in survey	Unit of measurement of the food quantity in survey	Unit equivalent to convert unit of measurement into (A)	Food item quantity collected in survey (B)	Density coefficient (gram/milliliter) (C)	Extra factor (D)	Food item quantity standardized in (E = A*B*C*D)
		Kilogram or liter				*Kilogram*
Flour of wheat	Kilogram	1	2.5	1	1	2.5
Flour of wheat	Gram	0.001	500	1	1	0.5
Beer	Liter	1	3	1.007	1	3
Beer	Milliliter	0.001	1,500	1.007	1	1.5
Egg	Unit of 50 grams	0.05	12	1	1	0.6
Rice	Bag of 5 kilograms	5	1	1	1	5
Crackers	Packet of 500 grams	0.5	2	1	1	1
Tuna	Pound	0.45359	0.5	1	1	0.23
		Gram or milliliter				*Gram*
Flour of wheat	Kilogram	1,000	2.5	1	1	2,500
Flour of wheat	Gram	1	500	1	1	500
Beer	Liter	1,000	3	1.007	1	3,021
Beer	Milliliter	1	1,500	1.007	1	1,500
Egg	Unit of 50 grams	50	12	1	1	600
Rice	Bag of 5 kilograms	5,000	1	1	1	5,000
Crackers	Packet of 500 grams	500	2	1	1	1,000
Tuna	Pound	453.59	0.5	1	1	226.8
		Gram or milliliter				*Pound*
Flour of wheat	Kilogram	1,000	2.5	1	0.0022046	5.51
Flour of wheat	Gram	1	500	1	0.0022046	1.1
Beer	Liter	1,000	3	1.007	0.0022046	6.66
Beer	Milliliter	1	1,500	1.007	0.0022046	3.31
Egg	Unit of 50 grams	50	12	1	0.0022046	1.32
Rice	Bag of 5 kilograms	5,000	1	1	0.0022046	11.02
Crackers	Packet of 500 grams	500	2	1	0.0022046	2.2
Tuna	Pound	453.59	0.5	1	0.0022046	0.5

Annex 2B

Procedure 1: Estimation of Nutrients and Calories from Food Quantities

Table 2B.1: Procedure 1: Steps 3 to 4

Item	Food quantity as acquired (grams)	Refuse factor (%)	House-hold size	Reference period (number of days)	Edible quantity (g/person/day)	Conversion factors from food composition table					After applying conversion factors from food composition table (g/person/day)				
						Protein	Fats	Available carbo-hydrates	Fibers	Alcohol	Protein	Fats	Available carbo-hydrates	Fibers	Alcohol
Rice	9,660	0	3	14	230.0	6.50	0.52	76.35	2.80	0.00	14.95	1.20	175.61	6.44	0.00
Macaroni	1,764	0	3	14	42.0	14.63	1.40	75.03	8.30	0.00	6.14	0.59	31.51	3.49	0.00
Eggs	477	12	3	14	10.0	12.56	9.51	0.72	0.00	0.00	1.26	0.95	0.07	0.00	0.00
Milk	3,738	0	3	14	89.0	3.15	3.25	4.80	0.00	0.00	2.80	2.89	4.27	0.00	0.00
Yogurt	504	0	3	14	12.0	3.47	3.25	4.66	0.00	0.00	0.42	0.39	0.56	0.00	0.00
Potatoes	2,240	25	3	14	40.0	1.68	0.10	13.31	2.40	0.00	0.67	0.04	5.32	0.96	0.00
Onions	560	10	3	14	12.0	1.10	0.10	7.64	1.70	0.00	0.13	0.01	0.92	0.20	0.00
Garlic	29	13	3	14	0.6	6.36	0.50	30.96	2.10	0.00	0.04	0.00	0.19	0.01	0.00
Tomatoes	1,615	9	3	14	35.0	0.98	0.26	2.91	0.70	0.00	0.34	0.09	1.02	0.25	0.00
Oranges	1,323	27	3	14	23.0	0.94	0.12	9.35	2.40	0.00	0.22	0.03	2.15	0.55	0.00
Fresh Fish	4,141	29	3	14	70.0	18.60	13.89	0.00	0.00	0.00	13.02	9.72	0.00	0.00	0.00
Chicken	5,904	31	3	14	97.0	18.33	14.83	0.13	0.00	0.00	17.78	14.39	0.13	0.00	0.00
Minced meat	1,470	0	3	14	35.0	19.82	17.88	0.00	0.00	0.00	6.94	6.26	0.00	0.00	0.00
Salt	25	0	3	14	0.6	0.00	0.00	0.00	0.00	0.00	0.00	0.00	0.00	0.00	0.00
Sugar	210	0	3	14	5.0	0.00	0.00	99.98	0.00	0.00	0.00	0.00	5.00	0.00	0.00
Oil	840	0	3	14	20.0	0.00	100.00	0.00	0.00	0.00	0.00	20.00	0.00	0.00	0.00
Tea beverage	42	0	3	14	1.0	0.00	0.00	0.30	0.00	0.00	0.00	0.00	0.00	0.00	0.00
Beer outside home	1,260	0	3	14	30.0	0.46	0.00	3.55	0.00	3.90	0.14	0.00	1.07	0.00	1.17
Restaurant meal	..	..	3	14	..	..	..	..	..	..	..	..	..	..	..

Table 2B.2: Procedure 1: Steps 5 to 6

| HH ID | From food items having food quantities expressed in standard units and valid nutrient conversion factors (g/person/day) | | | | | Calories (kcal/person/day) from the following: | | | | | Calories from food items having valid quantities and nutrient conversion factors (kcal/person/day) |
| | Protein | Fats | Available carbohydrates | Fiber | Alcohol | Protein B*4 | Fats C*9 | Available carbohydrates D*4 | Fiber E*2 | Alcohol F*7 | Kcal = G + H + I + J + K |
	B	C	D	E	F	G	H	I	J	K	L
1	74	63	530	28	0	296	566	2,119	57	0	3,038
2	28	29	304	51	0	110	258	1,215	103	0	1,686
3	72	83	646	100	0	288	751	2,584	199	0	3,822
4	29	45	332	38	0	115	403	1,328	76	0	1,922
5	15	52	157	22	0	60	466	629	43	0	1,199
6	19	50	245	17	0	77	447	981	34	0	1,539
7	68	58	274	38	0	270	518	1,095	75	0	1,959
8	35	62	479	42	0	138	560	1,917	84	0	2,699
9	41	37	203	38	0	164	329	813	76	0	1,382
10	67	103	448	25	0	267	924	1,790	51	0	3,032
11	33	84	248	44	0	134	757	993	87	0	1,971
12	42	62	354	28	0	168	556	1,415	56	0	2,194
13	21	39	329	72	0	83	349	1,317	144	0	1,893
14	31	57	462	32	0	124	509	1,848	63	0	2,543
15	30	87	537	31	0	122	785	2,148	62	0	3,117
16	39	57	534	56	0	154	515	2,137	111	0	2,918
17	44	49	276	21	0	176	438	1,104	42	0	1,759
18	35	46	277	84	0	140	411	1,106	168	0	1,825
19	25	57	381	34	0	99	513	1,522	67	0	2,202

Annex 2C

Procedure 2: Estimation of Nutrients and Calories from Food Expenditure

Table 2C.1: Procedure 2: Steps 1 to 2

HH ID	Calories (kcal/person/day)	Proportion of calories from protein 100*G/L	Proportion of calories from fats 100*H/L	Food expenditure (lcu/person/day)	Household calorie price (lc/kcal)	Region	Area	Income quintile	Average calorie price ($/Kcal) of Region 1, urban area and income quintile 2	Food expenditure associated to missing calories (lcu/person/day)	Estimated missing calories (Kcal/person/day)
	L	M	N								O
1	3,038	10	19	2.4	0.0008	1	Urban	2	0.00083	1.8	2,147
2	1,686	7	15	1.2	0.0007	1	Urban	2	0.00083	1.3	1,604
3	4,947	8	20	3.3	0.0009	1	Urban	2	0.00083	1.2	1,448
4	1,922	6	21	1.2	0.0006	1	Urban	2	0.00083	0.8	1,001
5	1,199	5	39	1.2	0.0010	1	Urban	2	0.00083	1.1	1,339
6	1,539	5	29	0.7	0.0005	1	Urban	2	0.00083	0.9	1,122
7	1,959	14	26	2.6	0.0013	1	Urban	2	0.00083	0.4	531
8	2,699	5	21	6.6	0.0024	1	Urban	2	0.00083	0.9	1,074
9	1,382	12	24	2.3	0.0016	1	Urban	2	0.00083	0.5	639
10	3,032	9	30	2.1	0.0007	1	Urban	2	0.00083	0.7	808
11	1,971	7	38	1.4	0.0007	1	Urban	2	0.00083	1.3	1,604
12	2,194	8	25	1.4	0.0006	1	Urban	2	0.00083	0.7	808
13	1,893	4	18	1.4	0.0008	1	Urban	2	0.00083	0.5	639
14	2,543	5	20	1.2	0.0005	1	Urban	2	0.00083	0.6	663
15	3,117	4	25	1.6	0.0005	1	Urban	2	0.00083	0.5	639
16	2,918	5	18	1.5	0.0005	1	Urban	2	0.00083	0.4	434
17	1,759	10	25	1.7	0.0010	1	Urban	2	0.00083	0.5	627
18	1,825	8	23	1.6	0.0009	1	Urban	2	0.00083	0.5	603
19	2,202	4	23	1.0	0.0005	1	Urban	2	0.00083	0.5	603

Food items having food quantities expressed in standard units and valid nutrient conversion factors

Table 2C.2: Procedure 2: Steps 3 to 5

HH ID	Estimated missing calories (kcal/person/day) from		Estimated missing calories (kcal/person/day) from carbohydrates (including fiber and alcohol)	Estimated missing grams (person/day)		
	Protein	Fats		Protein	Fats	Carbohydrates (including fiber and alcohol)
	P	Q	R	S	T	U
	O*M/100	O*N/100	O – P – Q	P/4	Q/9	R/4
1	209	400	1,538	52	44	384
2	105	246	1,254	26	27	313
3	109	284	1,054	27	32	264
4	60	210	731	15	23	183
5	67	521	751	17	58	188
6	56	326	740	14	36	185
7	73	140	317	18	16	79
8	55	223	796	14	25	199
9	76	152	411	19	17	103
10	71	246	491	18	27	123
11	109	617	879	27	69	220
12	62	205	542	15	23	135
13	28	118	494	7	13	123
14	32	133	499	8	15	125
15	25	161	453	6	18	113
16	23	77	335	6	9	84
17	63	156	409	16	17	102
18	46	136	421	12	15	105
19	27	141	435	7	16	109

Annex 2D

Table 2D.1: Example of Calculation of Food and Total Price Temporal Deflators

Month	Year	Price indexes		Deflators	
		Food price index (FPI)	Consumer price index (CPI)	Food monetary values deflator (FPI/average FPI)	Total consumption and income deflator (CPI/average CPI)
9	2004	121.91	122.44	0.962	0.958
10	2004	123.04	123.80	0.971	0.968
11	2004	123.74	124.73	0.977	0.976
12	2004	123.85	124.62	0.978	0.975
1	2005	124.61	125.30	0.984	0.980
2	2005	125.54	126.35	0.991	0.988
3	2005	126.61	127.69	0.999	0.999
4	2005	127.77	129.14	1.009	1.010
5	2005	129.79	131.33	1.024	1.027
6	2005	131.75	134.01	1.040	1.048
7	2005	131.56	133.66	1.038	1.046
8	2005	130.10	131.02	1.027	1.025
Average		126.69	127.84		

Annex 2E

Table 2E.1: Estimation of the Coefficient of Variation of Dietary Energy Consumption Due to Other Factors

$CV^2_{x/r} = CV^2_{PAL} + CV^2_{wh} + CV^2_{err}$	
Where Ln refers to Neperian Logarithm, and normsinv(p) is the function which returns the value Z such that, with probability p, a standard normal random variable takes on a value that is less than or equal to Z.	
(CV_{PAL}) Coefficient of variation of dietary energy requirement due to physical activity level (PAL)	
Standard deviation of PAL – Maximum (MXSDP)	$(Ln(2.4)-Ln(1.4))/(normsinv(0.95) - normsinv(0.05))$
Standard deviation of PAL – Minimum (MNSDP)	$(Ln(2.4)-Ln(1.4))/(normsinv(0.975) - normsinv(0.025))$
CV of PAL – Maximum	$= \sqrt{(e^{MXSDP^2}) - 1}$
CV of PAL – Minimum	$= \sqrt{(e^{MNSDP^2}) - 1}$
If the proportion of labor force in the primary sector is more than 49%	
CV of dietary energy requirement due to PAL	Maximum CV of PAL * proportion of labor force in the primary sector
If the proportion of labor force in the primary sector is less than 50%	
CV of dietary energy requirement due to PAL	Minimum CV of PAL * proportion of labor force in the primary sector
(CV_{wh}) Coefficient of variation of dietary energy requirement due to body weight	

For each sex/age population group	Weight in Kg using the 5th percentile of the BMI and the median height in cm (W5th)	$BMI_{5th} * \left(\dfrac{height}{100}\right)^2$
	Weight in Kg using the 95th percentile of the BMI and the median height in cm (W95th)	$BMI_{95th} * \left(\dfrac{height}{100}\right)^2$
	Variance of the distribution of body weight	$(Ln(W95th)-Ln(W5th))/(normsinv(0.95)-normsinv(0.05))^2$

Population weighted average value of the variance (VARBW)	$\displaystyle\sum_{i-1}^{31} (f_i * \delta_i^2)$	Where *i* refers to the sex/age group; *f* is the proportion of the population belonging to the *ith* group; and δ is the standard deviation of the distribution of body weight of the *ith* group.
CV of dietary energy requirement due to body weight	$\sqrt[2]{(e^{VARBW}) - 1}$	
(CV_{err}) Coefficient of cariation due to error		
CV of dietary energy requirement due to error	0.08	

Annex 2F

Table 2F.1: Estimation of the Minimum Dietary Energy Requirement

Where TEE refers to total energy expenditure (kcal); U5MR refers to under-five mortality rate; the probability per 1,000 that a newborn baby will die before reaching age 5, if subject to current age-specific mortality rates; KG refers to BMI * (height/100)^2; height is in cm; WG refers to weight gain for age (g/day); ERwg is the energy required per gram of weight gain (kcal); and PAL refers to 1.55 for sedentary physical activity.

Years: Less than 1/Class group: 1			Note
Male and female	Country with high children undernutrition and infection (U5MR proxy high)		50th percentile for BMI and WG
	if U5MR > 10‰	TEE = (−99.4 + 88.6 * KG) + 2 * WG * ERwg	
	Country with low children undernutrition and infection (U5MR low)		
	if U5MR <= 10‰	TEE = (−99.4 + 88.6 * KG) + WG * ERwg	

Years: From 1 to 1.9/Class group: 2			Note
	Country with high children undernutrition and infection (U5MR proxy high)		50th percentile for BMI and WG
Male	if U5MR > 10‰	TEE = 0.93 * (310.2 + 63.3 * KG − 0.263 * KG^2) + 2 * WG * ERwg	
Female	if U5MR > 10‰	TEE = 0.93 * (263.4 + 65.3 * KG − 0.454 * KG^2) + 2 * WG * ERwg	
	Country with low children undernutrition and infection (U5MR low)		
Male	if U5MR <= 10‰	TEE = 0.93 * (310.2 + 63.3 * KG − 0.263 * KG^2) + WG * ERwg	
Female	if U5MR <= 10‰	TEE = 0.93 * (263.4 + 65.3 * KG − 0.454 * KG^2) + WG * ERwg	

Years: From 2 to 9.9/Class group: From 3 to 10		Note
Male	TEE = (310.2 + 63.3 * KG − 0.263 * KG^2) + WG * ERwg	50th percentile for BMI and WG
Female	TEE = (263.4 + 65.3 * KG − 0.454 * KG^2) + WG * ERwg	

Years: From 10 to 17.9/Class group: From 11 to 18		Note
Male	TEE = 0.85 * (310.2 + 63.3 KG − 0.263 KG^2) + WG * ERwg	5th percentile for BMI and WG
Female	TEE = 0.85 * (263.4 + 65.3 KG − 0.454 KG^2) + WG * ERwg	

Years: From 18 to 29.9/Class group: From 19 to 22		Note
Male	TEE = PAL * (692.2 + 15.057 KG)	5th percentile for BMI
Female	TEE = PAL * (486.6 + 14.818 KG)	

Years: From 30 to 59.9/Class group: From 23 to 28		Note
Male	TEE = PAL * (873.1 + 11.472 KG)	5th percentile for BMI
Female	TEE = PAL * (845.6 + 8.126 KG)	

Years: More than 59.9/Class group: From 29 to 31		Note
Male	TEE = PAL * (587.7 + 11.711 KG)	5th percentile for BMI
Female	TEE = PAL * (658.5 + 9.082 KG)	

Pregnancy allowance
Energy extra = Birth ratio * 210

Notes

1. Expressed as per person per day.
2. Further information in forthcoming *Assessment of the Reliability and Relevance of the Food Data Collected in National Household Consumption and Expenditure Surveys.*
3. Note that tobacco and narcotics are not considered as food and are excluded from the analysis.
4. For more information on food matching, see the FAO/INFOODS *Guidelines for Food Matching, Version 1.2* (2012). The *Guidelines for Food Matching* include a quality scheme for the food matches. They should be recorded and used in the assessment of the quality of the estimated energy and nutrient intake and food security estimations. Food composition data are not just values that can be used without previous knowledge on food composition. If done so, there is a high risk of applying the data wrongly. Therefore, it is highly recommended to complete the FAO/INFOODS e-Learning Course on Food Composition Data (available free-of-charge at the INFOODS website).
5. For converting amounts of total foods (including inedible part) to EP, see the FAO/INFOODS *Guidelines for Converting Units, Denominators and Expressions Version 1.0* (2012).
6. Density values for liquids or semiliquids can be found in the FAO/ INFOODS Density Database Version 2.0: http://www.fao.org/infoods /infoods/tables-and-databases/faoinfoods-databases/en/.
7. If the data were corrected for outliers the median should be close to the mean.
8. Density values of solids to be applied in this analysis are equal to 1.
9. *Guidelines for Converting Units, Denominators and Expressions* is available at http://www.fao.org/infoods/infoods/standards-guidelines/en/.
10. Unless it is a nutritional dietary survey that measures direct individual food intake.
11. For instance, ascorbic acid enhances iron absorption.
12. When estimating the available micronutrients for consumption, ADePT-FSM excludes from the analysis those provided by food consumed away from home.
13. Heme iron accounts for a minor part of total iron intake, especially in developing countries where the consumption of meat and fish is usually low. Thus, nonheme iron is the main source of dietary iron intake

(Hallberg 1981). Still, not all the nonheme iron consumed is absorbed by the human body because this process is influenced either positively or negatively by many factors, such as the presence of certain substances in the diet.

14. The indispensable amino acids are not present in all food items. For instance, lysine, threonine, and tryptophan are marginal in cereals. Whereas the former (lysine) is lacking especially in wheat, the latter (tryptophan) is lacking in maize. Methionine and cysteine, which are equally abundant in cereal and animal proteins, are marginal in legume proteins (WHO 2007).

15. When estimating the available amino acids for consumption, ADePT-FSM excludes from the analysis those provided by food consumed away from home.

16. As the log-normal distribution is fully characterized by only two parameters (μ and σ), the skewness coefficient is a simple monotonic transformation of the standard deviation $SK = (e^{\sigma^2} + 2)\sqrt{e^{\sigma^2} - 1}$, and it can also be conveniently expressed as a function of the coefficient of variation, according to the formula

$$\text{skewness} = (CV^2 + 3) \times CV.$$

17. See WHO Child Growth Standards: BMI for age tables. WHO. Geneva. http://www.who.int/childgrowth/standards/bmi_for_age/en/index.html. In addition, see WHO 2007, WHO Growth reference 5–19 years: BMI for age tables. WHO. Geneva. http://www.who.int/growthref/who2007_bmi_for_age/en/index.html.

18. For further information see WHO (1983).

19. For further information see FAO/WHO/UNU (2001).

20. For further information see FAO/WHO/UNU (2001).

21. The sum of the needs is determined by using the average of needs of similar individuals.

22. Based on a publication FAO/WHO/UNU (1985).

23. The prevalence of inadequacy depends on the shape and variation of the usual intake distribution, not on mean intake. See NAS (2000).

24. See the FAO statistics website: http://www.fao.org/economic/ess/ess-fs/fs-methods/adept-fsn/en/.

25. The losses are at the retail level and exclude losses within households.

26. Based on a publication FAO/WHO/UNU (1985).

References

CFS (Committee on World Food Security). 2012. "Coming to Terms with Terminology." Final report 2012/39, Rome, October 15–20.

FAO (Food and Agriculture Organization). 1999. *The State of Food Insecurity in the World.* Rome: FAO. http://www.fao.org/docrep/007/x3114e/x3114e00.htm.

———. 2002. "Food Energy: Methods of Analysis and Conversion Factors." FAO Food and Nutrition Paper 77. FAO, Rome. http://www.fao.org/docrep/006/Y5022E/Y5022E00.HTM.

———. 2002. "Measurement and Assessment of Food Deprivation and Undernutrition." Proceedings of the Food and Agriculture Organization symposium "International Scientific Symposium on Measurement and Assessment of Food Deprivation and Undernutrition," Rome, June 28–30. http://www.fao.org/docrep/005/Y4249E/y4249e00.htm.

FAO, and INFOODS (International Network of Food Data Systems). 2011. E-Learning Course on Food Composition Data. Rome: FAO. http://www.fao.org/infoods/infoods/training/en/.

———. 2012. *Guidelines for Converting Units, Denominators and Expressions Version 1.0.* Rome: FAO. http://www.fao.org/infoods/infoods/standards-guidelines/en/.

———. 2012. *Guidelines for Food Matching Version 1.2.* Rome: FAO. http://www.fao.org/infoods/infoods/standards-guidelines/en/.

FAO, and WHO (World Health Organization). 1970. *Requirements of Ascorbic Acid, Vitamin D, Vitamin B12, Folate, and Iron.* WHO Technical Report Series No. 452 and FAO Nutrition Meetings Report Series No. 47. Geneva: WHO.

———. 2004. *Vitamin and Mineral Requirements in Human Nutrition,* 2nd ed. Rome: FAO.

FAO, WHO, and UNU (United Nations University). 1985. *Energy and Protein Requirements.* Technical Report Series 724. Geneva: WHO. http://www.fao.org/docrep/003/aa040e/aa040e00.HTM.

———. 2001. *Human Energy Requirements.* Report of a joint FAO/WHO/UNU Expert Consultation, Rome, October 17–24. http://www.fao.org/docrep/007/y5686e/y5686e00.htm.

Hallberg, L. 1981. "Bioavailability of Dietary Iron in Man." *Annual Review of Nutrition* (1): 123–47.

NAS (National Academy of Sciences). 2000. *Dietary Reference Intakes: Applications in Dietary Assessment.* Washington, DC: National Academy Press. http://www.nap.edu/catalog/9956.html.

————. 2001. *Dietary Reference Intake.* Food and Nutrition Board, Institute of Medicine. Washington, DC: National Academy Press.

Sibrián, R. L., ed. 2008. *Deriving Food Security Information from National Household Budget Surveys: Experiences, Achievements, Challenges.* Rome: FAO. http://www.fao.org/docrep/011/i0430e/i0430e00.htm.

USHHS (U.S. Department of Health and Human Services), and USDA (U.S. Department of Agriculture). 2005. *Dietary Guidelines for Americans 2005,* 6th ed. Washington, DC: U.S. Government Printing Office.

WHO. 1983. *Measuring Change in Nutritional Status.* Geneva: WHO.

————. 2003. *Diet, Nutrition and the Prevention of Chronic Diseases.* Report of a Joint WHO and FAO Expert Consultation, Geneva, January 28–February 1, WHO Technical Report Series 961, Geneva: WHO.

————. 2007. *Protein and Amino Acid Requirements in Human Nutrition.* Report of a Joint WHO, FAO, and UNU Expert Consultation, WHO Technical Report Series 935, Geneva: WHO.

Bibliography

Cafiero, C. 2011. "Measuring Food Insecurity: Meaningful Concepts and Indicators for Evidence-Based Policy Making." Paper prepared for the Committee on World Food Security (CFS) conference "Round Table on Monitoring Food Security," FAO, Rome, September 12–13.

FAO (Food and Agriculture Organization). 1996. *The Sixth World Food Survey.* Rome: FAO.

Naken, L. 2002. "FAO Methodology for Estimating the Prevalence of Undernourishment." Paper presented at the International Scientific Symposium "Measurement and Assessment of Food Deprivation and Undernutrition," Rome, June 26–28. http://www.fao.org/docrep/005/Y4249E/y4249e00.htm.

————. 2007. "The Probability Distribution Framework for Estimating the Prevalence of Undernourishment: Exploding the Myth of the Bivariate Distribution." FAO Statistics Division Working Paper Series

ESS/ESSG/009e, FAO, Rome. http://www.fao.org/fileadmin/templates/ess/documents/food_security_statistics/working_paper_series/WP009e.pdf.

Sibrián, R. 2007. "Indicators on Food Deprivation and Income Deprivation at National and Sub-national Levels: Methodological Issues." Paper presented at the FAO Statistics Division, "Fourth International Conference on Agriculture Statistics (ICAS-4)," Beijing, October 25.

Sibrián, R., S. Ramasawmy, and J. Mernies. 2008. "Measuring Hunger at Subnational Levels from Household Surveys Using the FAO Approach." FAO Statistics Division Working Paper Series ESS/ESSA/005e. FAO, Rome. http://www.fao.org/fileadmin/templates/ess/documents/food_security_statistics/working_paper_series/WP005e.pdf.

Sukhatme, P. V. 1961. "The World's Hunger and Future Needs in Food Supplies." *Journal of the Royal Statistical Society.* Series A (124): 463–525.

Chapter 3

Guide to Output Tables

Ana Moltedo, Chiara Brunelli, Nathalie Troubat

Introduction

Food security as a *multidimensional* phenomenon covers four dimensions: food availability, food access, food utilization, and vulnerability to food insecurity. The ADePT-Food Security Module produces a suite of food security indicators that encompasses some of these dimensions. To better understand food consumption patterns and better target groups of a population in a situation of food insecurity, indicators are disaggregated by the following:

- Socioeconomic, demographic, and geographical characteristics of the household such as region, household size, gender, level of education, and occupation of the head of the household (28 Excel tables)
- Groups of food commodities[1] (22 Excel tables)
- Food commodity (15 Excel tables)

These indicators include statistics on dietary energy, value of food expenditures, and cost of the diet, as well as statistics related to the composition of the food available in terms of macro- and micronutrients, amino acids, and vitamins. The purpose of this chapter is to present each output table produced by ADePT-FSM and to provide a brief interpretation of the indicators that are displayed in the tables. The same indicator may appear in different tables depending at which level of disaggregation (by population group, food commodity group, or food commodity) it is shown. To avoid repeating the interpretation of the indicator after each table, all indicators are described in the glossary of indicators that follows the section presenting the output tables. Indicators are presented in alphabetical order to assist the reader when using the glossary.

Output Tables

Food Consumption (Dietary Energy, Macronutrients, and Monetary Values)

Disaggregated by Population Group: Tables 1.1 to 1.14

Table 1.1: Prevalence of Undernourishment Using Mainly Survey Data This table shows estimates of the prevalence of undernourishment[2] (PoU), using the methodology of the Food and Agriculture Organization (FAO), along with all the parameters used for its computation (i.e., dietary energy consumption, the minimum dietary energy requirement, coefficient of variation, and skewness). The PoU is computed at national, regional, and urban/rural levels under the assumption that the survey sample is representative for such geographic domains. If this is the case, the total number of people undernourished calculated as the sum from each region or from urban/rural is expected to be close to the one at the national level.

The minimum and average dietary energy requirements at the national[3] level are those used to estimate the Millennium Development Goal (MDG)

Table 1.1: Prevalence of Undernourishment Using Mainly Survey Data

	Population ('000s)	Average dietary energy consumption (kcal/person/day)	Coefficient of variation of dietary energy consumption (%)	Skewness of dietary energy consumption	Minimum dietary energy requirement (kcal/person/day)	Prevalence of undernourishment (%)	Average dietary energy requirement (kcal/person/day)	Depth of food deficit (kcal/person/day)
Total	31,906.9	2,199.5	29.07	0.90	1,694.0	23.8	2,108.0	146.1
Area								
Capital city	1,845.3	2,063.6	39.13	1.23	1,784.6	N/A	2,258.2	N/A
Other urban areas	4,406.6	2,179.3	32.18	1.00	1,728.5	N/A	2,168.3	N/A
Rural areas	25,655.0	2,212.7	29.64	0.92	1,681.6	23.1	2,086.8	138.8
Region								
Region1	1,778.4	2,401.1	23.94	0.73	1,665.9	6.9	2,061.6	37.4
Region2	2,031.7	1,947.9	28.59	0.88	1,697.4	38.8	2,108.8	261.3
Region3	1,178.8	2,053.4	31.86	0.99	1,712.5	37.1	2,136.2	256.5
Region4	1,647.1	2,162.7	29.20	0.90	1,723.7	28.2	2,148.5	182.3
Region5	1,652.8	2,269.9	30.21	0.93	1,718.8	23.7	2,151.1	149.5
Region6	761.4	1,997.6	33.75	1.05	1,712.3	N/A	2,143.4	N/A

1.9 indicator and depth of food deficit, respectively, published with *The State of Food Insecurity in the world* (SOFI). The statistics of dietary energy consumption, coefficient of variation, and skewness are derived from the survey data.

When a N/A value appears, this means the value of skewness is higher than 1. A skewness higher than 1 indicates that there is a large number of food quantity outliers (or an excessive variability in the consumption/acquisition distribution), and so a more careful food consumption data analysis has to be done.

Table 1.2: Prevalence of Undernourishment Using Mainly External Sources
This table shows estimates of the prevalence of undernourishment[4], using the FAO methodology, along with all the parameters used for its computation. The PoU is computed at the national, regional, and urban/rural levels under the assumption that the survey sample is representative for such geographic domains. If this is the case, the total number of people undernourished calculated as the sum from each region or from urban/rural areas is expected to be close to the one at the national level.

When a N/A value appears, this means the value of skewness is higher than 1. A skewness higher than 1 indicates that there is a large number

Table 1.2: Prevalence of Undernourishment Using Mainly External Sources

	Population ('000s)	Dietary energy supply adjusted for losses (kcal/ person/day)	Coefficient of variation of dietary energy consump-tion (%)	Skewness of dietary energy consump-tion	Minimum dietary energy require-ment (kcal/ person/ day)	Preva-lence of under-nourish-ment (%)	Average dietary energy requirement (kcal/ person/day)	Depth of food deficit (kcal/ person/ day)
MDG 1.9 indicator (SOFI)		1,970.5	32.17	0.99	1,694.0	40.7	2,108.0	285.7
Total	31,906.9	1,970.5	29.07	0.90	1,694.0	37.6	2,108.0	252.6
Area								
Capital city	1,845.3	1,848.7	39.13	1.23	1,784.6	N/A	2,258.2	N/A
Other urban areas	4,406.6	1,952.4	32.18	1.00	1,728.5	N/A	2,168.3	N/A
Rural areas	25,655.0	1,982.4	29.64	0.92	1,681.6	36.6	2,086.8	240.9
Region								
Region1	1,778.4	2,151.1	23.94	0.73	1,665.9	16.8	2,061.6	95.2
Region2	2,031.7	1,745.1	28.59	0.88	1,697.4	53.3	2,108.8	391.7
Region3	1,178.8	1,839.6	31.86	0.99	1,712.5	49.5	2,136.2	376.1
Region4	1,647.1	1,937.5	29.20	0.90	1,723.7	42.1	2,148.5	298.3
Region5	1,652.8	2,033.5	30.21	0.93	1,718.8	36.8	2,151.1	255.5
Region6	761.4	1,789.6	33.75	1.05	1,712.3	N/A	2,143.4	N/A

of food quantity outliers (or an excessive variability in the consumption/ acquisition distribution), and so a more careful food consumption data analysis has to be done.

The first row of the table shows the MDG 1.9 indicator as published in the latest edition of SOFI corresponding to the same year of the survey and the parameters used (published in the Statistics Division of the FAO website[5]). These are the parameters:

- Average dietary energy supply
- Losses that occurred at the retail level
- Coefficient of variation of dietary energy consumption
- Skewness of dietary energy consumption
- Average dietary energy requirement
- Minimum dietary energy requirement

To estimate the statistics at the subnational level (regions and urban/ rural areas):

- The coefficient of variation and skewness are derived from the survey data.
- The region- and area-specific dietary energy supplies adjusted for losses are estimated following the relationship of the dietary energy consumption in the subpopulation group with respect to the national calories.
- The region- and area-specific minimum and average dietary energy requirements are estimated following the relationship of the requirements of the subpopulation group with respect to the calorie requirements as from SOFI.

Example for area of residence: First, the software computes the dietary energy consumption (DEC) at the national, urban, and rural levels using national household survey (NHS) data. Then it calculates the ratio between (1) urban and national DEC and (2) rural and national DEC; the ratios are applied to the national dietary energy supply (DES), adjusted for losses to compute the DES at the urban and rural levels. The software estimates the national DES adjusted for losses from the two exogenous parameters, which are the DES as from the food balance sheets (FBS) and the share of losses at the retail level.

Second, the software computes the minimum dietary energy requirement (MDER) at the national, urban, and rural levels using the NHS data. Then it calculates the ratio between (1) urban and national MDER and (2) rural and national MDER. The ratios are applied to the minimum national dietary energy requirement (as in SOFI and introduced as an exogenous parameter) to compute the MDER at the urban and rural levels. The difference in value between the MDER as in SOFI and the one computed from the NHS data is due to a different structure of the population used by sex and age groups. Also, because the reference height values by sex and age classes for the calculation of the MDER are taken from other sources (e.g., demographic health surveys), differences between heights recorded from the survey and the reference height values can lead to differences in the MDER.

The table below shows an example of how SOFI parameters are calculated at the subnational level using information from the survey.

	Dietary energy consumption (DEC) derived from the survey (kcal/person/day)	Ratio of subnational DEC/national DEC	Dietary energy supply adjusted for losses (kcal/person/day)	Minimum dietary energy requirement (MDER) derived from the survey (kcal/person/day)	Ratio of subnational MDER/national MDER	Minimum dietary energy requirement (kcal/person/day)
National	2084	1.000	2360 (*)	1824	1.000	1830 (*)
Urban	2130	1.022	2412	1805	0.992	1815
Rural	2035	0.976	2305	1834	1.008	1844

Note: (*) used to estimate MDG 1.9.

Table 1.3: Selected Food Consumption Statistics by Population Groups This table shows some food consumption statistics expressed in dietary energy and monetary values, as well as the average unit value cost of 1,000 kcal and the minimum dietary energy required of a representative individual in the population group. The minimum energy requirement is computed using the age/sex structure of the population as derived from the survey. See glossary and chapter 2 for more details on the calculation of the minimum dietary energy consumption.

Table 1.4: Selected Food Consumption Statistics of Population Groups by Income Deciles This table presents average values for food and total consumption as well as income disaggregated by income deciles. The first decile refers to the poorest group of the population while the tenth refers to the wealthiest one. As poor populations have lower values of income and consumption as compared to rich ones, the values of the statistics shown in this table are expected to increase from the first to the last income group.

Table 1.3: Selected Food Consumption Statistics by Population Groups

	Number of sampled households	Average household size	Average dietary energy consumption (kcal/person/day)	Minimum dietary energy requirement (kcal/person/day)	Average food consumption in monetary value (LCU/person/day)	Average dietary energy unit value (LCU/1000 kcals)	Average total consumption in monetary value (LCU/person/day)
Total	22175	4.9	2199	1691	220.97	100.46	352.71
Quintiles of income							
Lowest quintile	2714	6.6	1596	1640	101.64	63.68	142.49
2	3236	5.6	2043	1676	166.18	81.33	241.69
3	4110	5.0	2250	1690	218.23	97.00	333.62
4	5002	4.2	2604	1719	299.82	115.12	480.80
Highest quintile	7113	3.4	3051	1782	448.89	147.13	812.53
Area							
Capital city	1225	4.3	2064	1782	395.73	191.77	726.83
Other urban areas	13382	4.5	2179	1726	291.85	133.92	494.62
Rural areas	7568	5.1	2213	1679	196.22	88.68	301.42
Household size							
One person	2503	1.0	3667	2022	529.04	144.28	924.86
Between 2 and 3 people	5676	2.6	2667	1784	307.82	115.40	501.16
Between 4 and 5 people	6226	4.5	2253	1672	237.00	105.19	380.89
Between 6 and 7 people	4141	6.4	2097	1656	198.68	94.76	309.84
More than 7	3629	10.3	1951	1677	170.34	87.30	266.79
Gender of the household head							
Male	16751	5.2	2207	1700	219.40	99.41	351.14
Female	5424	4.0	2167	1655	227.75	105.10	359.49
Age of the household head							
Less than 35	7133	3.9	2310	1635	240.19	103.99	388.01
Between 35 and 45	6728	5.3	2155	1681	222.74	103.37	360.31
Between 46 and 60	5433	5.8	2206	1745	212.94	96.55	340.93
More than 60	2881	5.0	2089	1708	198.75	95.13	296.83

Table 1.4: Selected Food Consumption Statistics of Population Groups by Income Deciles

	Number of sampled households	Average household size	Estimated population	Average dietary energy consumption (kcal/person/day)	Average dietary energy unit value (LCU/1000kcals)	Average food consumption in monetary value (LCU/person/day)	Average total consumption in monetary value (LCU/person/day)	Average income (LCU/person/day)
Total								
1	1344	7.2	4624421	1439	59.03	84.96	115.49	122.00
2	1370	5.9	3851732	1784	68.18	121.66	174.91	188.26
3	1634	5.9	3825344	2050	75.83	155.46	223.84	240.31
4	1602	5.2	3384098	2035	87.59	178.29	261.86	294.60
5	1858	5.1	3293406	2235	90.56	202.39	306.42	355.73
6	2252	4.9	3130354	2265	103.69	234.89	362.24	436.89
7	2311	4.4	2858068	2557	107.09	273.83	437.51	539.38
8	2691	4.0	2569153	2657	123.72	328.73	528.95	698.55
9	3064	3.6	2335255	2905	134.94	391.95	674.51	1001.65
10	4049	3.2	2035056	3219	159.74	514.23	970.90	2927.19
Area								
Capital city								
1	7	3.7	18622	778	151.03	117.54	126.09	127.09
2	29	6.5	67083	983	121.82	119.69	174.57	185.05
3	36	5.9	79524	1109	140.47	155.79	236.00	243.00
4	37	7.3	78240	1345	146.93	197.66	290.41	300.12
5	65	6.0	198849	1316	152.92	201.27	344.05	357.19
6	86	5.6	184519	1560	162.38	253.34	414.75	439.84
7	132	4.7	201667	1744	167.35	291.78	499.91	540.86
8	174	4.4	279204	2050	185.18	379.69	659.03	720.97
9	277	4.0	361336	2422	196.12	474.99	859.09	1030.48
10	382	3.1	376271	3150	226.89	714.69	1449.77	2999.53
Other urban areas								
1	471	6.7	243508	1244	70.35	87.52	119.72	126.87
2	592	6.4	282113	1413	92.55	130.81	180.39	189.23
3	792	5.8	325095	1569	96.73	151.80	221.52	239.95
4	825	5.7	328223	1699	104.03	176.79	267.95	296.18
5	1033	5.3	377364	1829	110.06	201.27	319.24	356.85
6	1394	5.2	550613	1879	124.83	234.53	371.24	436.92
7	1460	4.6	538197	2290	119.43	273.46	459.15	544.31
8	1773	4.4	636163	2528	133.78	338.14	567.13	708.65
9	2119	3.5	515264	2679	157.24	421.25	724.13	1000.35
10	2923	3.1	610035	3095	177.98	550.86	1038.77	3228.57

Particularly in this table, the number of sampled households used to produce the estimates by income deciles has to be analyzed to assess the reliability of the estimates. For instance, in table 1.4 the estimates of the first income decile group in the capital city are considered unreliable due to the low number of households used to derive the estimates (7 households). In general, a statistic obtained with data from fewer than 30 households is considered unreliable.

Table 1.5: Shares of Food Consumption by Food Sources (in Dietary Energy) Households acquire food in different ways, the main ones being through purchases, own production, gifts/aid, bartering, and in-kind

Table 1.5: Shares of Food Consumption by Food Sources (in Dietary Energy)

	Number of sampled households	Share of purchased food in total food consumption (%)	Share of own produced food in total food consumption (%)	Share of food consumed away from home in total food consumption (%)	Share of food from other sources in total food consumption (%)
Total	22175	52.56	40.01	3.38	4.06
Quintiles of income					
Lowest quintile	2714	40.31	53.34	1.82	4.54
2	3236	42.01	51.83	2.11	4.06
3	4110	51.34	41.80	2.62	4.25
4	5002	62.10	30.64	3.37	3.88
Highest quintile	7113	67.84	21.44	7.19	3.54
Area					
Capital city	1225	84.15	0.45	13.27	2.13
Other urban areas	13382	79.69	12.58	4.69	3.04
Rural areas	7568	45.85	47.31	2.49	4.36
Household size					
One person	2503	56.62	19.60	18.00	5.78
Between 2 and 3 people	5676	55.02	36.36	3.52	5.10
Between 4 and 5 people	6226	53.90	39.13	3.16	3.81
Between 6 and 7 people	4141	52.26	40.60	2.83	4.31
More than 7	3629	49.63	44.72	2.39	3.26
Gender of the household head					
Male	16751	52.66	39.88	3.56	3.89
Female	5424	52.10	40.59	2.55	4.76
Age of the household head					
Less than 35	7133	53.61	37.69	4.59	4.11
Between 35 and 45	6728	55.88	37.31	3.23	3.58
Between 46 and 60	5433	50.43	42.97	2.69	3.91
More than 60	2881	47.48	44.51	2.72	5.29

payment. In addition, household members consume food at sit-down and fast food restaurants and from street vendors. For the purpose of the analysis, food sources are classified in four main categories according to the type of acquisition: (1) purchase (excluding food consumed away from home), (2) own production, (3) consumed away from home, and (4) others (including gifts/aid, in-kind payment, etc.).

This table shows the proportion of total dietary energy provided by each of the four food sources. This information is useful, for instance, to assess how much households rely on the following:

- Food purchases (illustrating potential vulnerability to food price shocks)
- Own production (illustrating potential vulnerability to natural shocks such as drought or flood)

Table 1.6: Shares of Food Consumption by Food Sources (in Dietary Energy) by Income Deciles   This table shows the proportion of total dietary energy provided by each of the four food sources: purchases to be consumed inside the home, own production, consumption away from home, and other sources combined. The data are disaggregated by income decile groups.

Particularly in this table, the number of sampled households used to produce the estimates at income decile levels has to be analyzed to assess the reliability of the estimates. For instance, in table 1.6 the estimates of the first income decile group in the capital city are considered unreliable due to the low number of households used to derive the estimates (7 households). In general, a statistic obtained with data from fewer than 30 households is considered unreliable.

Table 1.7: Shares of Food Consumption by Food Sources (in Monetary Value)   This table shows the proportion of total food expenditure that each of the four food sources (purchases to be consumed inside the home, own production, consumption away from home, and other sources combined) represents. The share of money spent to purchase food in total household food expenditure is an indirect measure of a household's vulnerability to market food crises. In general, the higher the proportion of food consumed from purchases, the higher the risk of households being affected by food price shocks. As well, the percentage of food from own production gives an idea of the dependency a household has on its own agricultural outcome. Households that practice farming are highly

Table 1.6: Shares of Food Consumption by Food Sources (in Dietary Energy) by Income Deciles

	Number of sampled households	Average income (LCU/person/day)	Share of purchased food in total food consumption (%)	Share of own produced food in total food consumption (%)	Share of food consumed away from home in total food consumption (%)	Share of food from other sources in total food consumption (%)
Total						
1	1344	122.00	40.44	52.96	1.69	4.91
2	1370	188.26	40.17	53.71	1.93	4.19
3	1634	240.31	40.30	53.70	1.89	4.11
4	1602	294.60	43.96	49.69	2.35	3.99
5	1858	355.73	50.55	43.32	2.26	3.88
6	2252	436.89	52.16	40.22	3.00	4.63
7	2311	539.38	60.39	33.26	2.48	3.88
8	2691	698.55	63.94	27.84	4.33	3.89
9	3064	1001.65	66.28	25.27	4.71	3.74
10	4049	2927.19	69.45	17.47	9.75	3.33
Area						
Capital city						
1	7	127.09	86.64	0.57	4.41	8.37
2	29	185.05	87.37	4.62	3.34	4.67
3	36	243.00	87.23	1.06	8.65	3.06
4	37	300.12	88.49	0.91	5.63	4.97
5	65	357.19	93.55	0.30	4.83	1.33
6	86	439.84	90.83	0.36	7.13	1.68
7	132	540.86	91.20	0.06	7.77	0.97
8	174	720.97	85.37	0.06	12.36	2.20
9	277	1030.48	85.82	0.14	12.51	1.53
10	382	2999.53	75.71	0.72	20.93	2.64
Other urban areas						
1	471	126.87	76.95	17.30	1.87	3.88
2	592	189.23	76.75	16.94	2.05	4.26
3	792	239.95	72.18	21.67	2.16	4.00
4	825	296.18	74.26	17.58	2.95	5.21
5	1033	356.85	76.54	18.56	2.09	2.81
6	1394	436.92	80.10	13.72	2.48	3.69
7	1460	544.31	81.90	11.99	3.26	2.85
8	1773	708.65	80.51	12.52	4.86	2.11
9	2119	1000.35	82.08	10.42	4.55	2.95
10	2923	3228.57	81.40	6.19	9.96	2.45
Rural areas						
1	866	121.71	38.59	54.78	1.68	4.95
2	749	188.25	37.41	56.50	1.91	4.18
3	806	240.28	37.48	56.60	1.79	4.13
4	740	294.28	40.49	53.39	2.25	3.87
5	760	355.47	45.99	47.74	2.17	4.10
6	772	436.65	45.22	46.96	2.88	4.94
7	719	537.98	53.87	39.88	1.98	4.28
8	744	690.88	55.56	36.57	3.16	4.72
9	668	994.97	57.68	34.66	3.25	4.40
10	744	2725.93	60.83	29.31	5.81	4.04

Table 1.7: Shares of Food Consumption by Food Sources (in Monetary Value)

	Number of sampled households	Share of food consumption in total income (%) (Engel ratio)	Share of purchased food in total food consumption (%)	Share of own produced food in total food consumption (%)	Share of food consumed away from home in total food consumption (%)	Share of food from other sources in total food consumption (%)
Total	22175	40.57	65.38	26.38	4.24	4.01
Quintiles of income						
Lowest quintile	2714	66.82	50.15	42.89	1.84	5.12
2	3236	62.52	53.50	40.11	2.19	4.20
3	4110	55.21	62.04	30.88	2.76	4.33
4	5002	48.77	71.56	20.92	3.79	3.73
Highest quintile	7113	23.65	76.58	12.06	7.96	3.40
Area						
Capital city	1225	36.13	83.70	0.45	13.25	2.59
Other urban areas	13382	33.29	85.16	6.96	5.00	2.88
Rural areas	7568	43.80	57.67	35.10	2.73	4.50
Household size						
One person	2503	30.01	62.30	12.56	20.58	4.56
Between 2 and 3 people	5676	38.97	68.19	23.30	4.15	4.36
Between 4 and 5 people	6226	41.27	67.47	25.13	3.71	3.69
Between 6 and 7 people	4141	41.35	64.87	27.19	3.39	4.55
More than 7	3629	43.07	61.79	31.93	2.79	3.49
Gender of the household head						
Male	16751	39.46	65.27	26.48	4.51	3.74
Female	5424	46.00	65.85	25.94	3.08	5.13
Age of the household head						
Less than 35	7133	35.90	66.61	23.04	6.12	4.22
Between 35 and 45	6728	40.20	68.76	23.79	3.95	3.49
Between 46 and 60	5433	43.09	63.00	30.05	3.18	3.77
More than 60	2881	49.40	59.53	32.10	3.09	5.28

exposed to natural shocks, so they are particularly vulnerable in disaster-prone countries where recurrent natural shocks damage household agricultural production.

Table 1.7 also shows the Engel ratio defined as the percentage of total income dedicated to acquire food. Engel's law states that the proportion of income spent on food decreases when income increases. This does not mean that food expenditure decreases as income increases; on the contrary, while food intake has an upper limit due to biological factors, food expenditure does not. However, the relative importance of food expenditure tends to be greater among the poor households since they focus their acquisition on primary need goods (thus limiting the expenses on the other items). The share of food expenditure tends to be lower among the wealthier households because they spend a greater proportion of their income on nonfood items. However, it should be noted that "while the share of food expenditure in total expenditure may be a good starting-point for assessing vulnerability, it is not sufficient within a given economic environment and the same food expenditure share would not necessarily represent the same level of vulnerability across different economic environments" (Schmidhuber 2003).

Table 1.8: Shares of Food Consumption by Food Sources (in Monetary Value) by Income Deciles   This table shows the proportion of total food expenditure that each of the four food sources represents (purchases to be consumed

Table 1.8: Shares of Food Consumption by Food Sources (in Monetary Value) by Income Deciles

	Number of sampled households	Average income (LCU/ person/ day)	Share of food consumption in total income (%) (Engel ratio)	Share of purchased food in total food consumption (%)	Share of own produced food in total food consumption (%)	Share of food consumed away from home in total food consumption (%)	Share of food from other sources in total food consumption (%)
Total							
1	1344	122.00	69.63	49.85	42.61	1.91	5.63
2	1370	188.26	64.62	50.41	43.12	1.79	4.69
3	1634	240.31	64.69	51.68	41.89	2.08	4.34
4	1602	294.60	60.52	55.29	38.35	2.30	4.07
5	1858	355.73	56.89	60.70	32.58	2.51	4.21
6	2252	436.89	53.77	63.26	29.33	2.98	4.43
7	2311	539.38	50.77	70.26	23.02	2.83	3.90
8	2691	698.55	47.06	72.77	18.97	4.69	3.57
9	3064	1001.65	39.13	75.65	15.17	5.50	3.68
10	4049	2927.19	17.57	77.40	9.35	10.11	3.15
Area							
Capital city							
1	7	127.09	92.48	88.09	1.23	3.63	7.05
2	29	185.05	64.68	89.21	3.61	3.41	3.77
3	36	243.00	64.11	86.64	1.20	9.26	2.90
4	37	300.12	65.86	89.66	1.71	5.77	2.86
5	65	357.19	56.35	93.24	0.24	5.03	1.48
6	86	439.84	57.60	90.56	0.38	7.00	2.05
7	132	540.86	53.95	90.38	0.09	8.34	1.19
8	174	720.97	52.66	86.12	0.13	12.00	1.75
9	277	1030.48	46.09	82.61	0.18	12.75	4.45
10	382	2999.53	23.83	78.70	0.66	18.44	2.21

inside the home, own production, consumption away from home, and other sources combined). The data are disaggregated by income decile groups.

Particularly in this table, the number of sampled households used to produce the estimates at income decile levels has to be analyzed to assess the reliability of the estimates. For instance, in table 1.8 the estimates of the first income decile group in the capital city are considered unreliable due to the low number of households used to derive the estimates (7 households). In general, a statistic obtained with data from fewer than 30 households is considered unreliable.

Table 1.9: Food Consumption in Dietary Energy, Monetary, and Nutrient Content by Population Groups   The human body requires energy for different purposes including metabolic processes, muscular activity, growth, and

Table 1.9: **Food Consumption in Dietary Energy, Monetary, and Nutrient Content by Population Groups**

	Average dietary energy consumption (kcal/person/day)	Average food consumption in monetary value (LCU/person/day)	Average protein consumption (g/person/day)	Average fat consumption (g/person/day)	Average carbohydrates consumption (g/person/day)
Total	2199	220.97	57.0	38.8	359.1
Quintiles of income					
Lowest quintile	1596	101.64	41.7	21.1	280.3
2	2043	166.18	53.8	32.0	340.9
3	2250	218.23	57.9	39.2	367.8
4	2604	299.82	65.9	50.3	412.3
Highest quintile	3051	448.89	79.8	69.5	462.9
Area					
Capital city	2064	395.73	53.4	52.1	328.0
Other urban areas	2179	291.85	55.8	48.9	347.2
Rural areas	2213	196.22	57.5	36.1	363.4
Household size					
One person	3667	529.04	95.7	76.4	512.7
Between 2 and 3 people	2667	307.82	69.1	51.4	413.9
Between 4 and 5 people	2253	237.00	58.8	40.5	364.0
Between 6 and 7 people	2097	198.68	53.2	35.0	349.6
More than 7	1951	170.34	51.2	32.8	330.1
Gender of the household head					
Male	2207	219.40	57.1	38.6	359.5
Female	2167	227.75	56.8	39.7	357.4
Age of the household head					
Less than 35	2310	240.19	60.2	42.0	375.5
Between 35 and 45	2155	222.74	55.5	38.1	352.1
Between 46 and 60	2206	212.94	57.2	38.8	360.0
More than 60	2089	198.75	54.6	34.5	343.4

synthesis of new tissues. Humans obtain the required energy through the intake of energy-yielding macronutrients from food consumption. These macronutrients are protein, fats, total carbohydrates (including fiber), and alcohol. Each of them contributes to the total dietary energy but in different proportions. Because available carbohydrates are estimated as the difference between total carbohydrates and fiber combined with the use of the Atwater[6] factors, the energy densities of the nutrients comprise the following:

- Four calories per gram of protein
- Nine calories per gram of fats
- Four calories per gram of available carbohydrates
- Two calories per gram of fiber
- Seven calories per gram of alcohol

This table shows protein, fats, and carbohydrates consumption expressed in grams per person per day. Note that the carbohydrates values, reported in table 1.9 (last column), are those corresponding to available carbohydrates. On average worldwide, people consume more carbohydrates per day than protein or fats. It is expected that macronutrient consumption increases with income, since food consumption is positively correlated with income. However, the pattern of the increase in macronutrient consumption varies among population groups because households with higher income can afford a more diverse diet (e.g., more protein from meat) than those with lower income.

Table 1.10: Nutrient Contribution to Dietary Energy Consumption This table shows the proportion of dietary energy provided by each macronutrient. The proportion of calories from protein and fats are estimated as their respective consumption in grams times 4 and 9, respectively. Then the calories from total carbohydrates and alcohol are estimated as the difference between total dietary energy consumption and the calories coming from protein and fats.

The concept of a balanced diet is applied in more than one of the ADePT-FSM output tables. A joint WHO/FAO group of experts established guidelines for a "balanced diet," described in terms of the proportions of total dietary energy provided by diverse sources of energy (WHO 2003). These guidelines are related to the effects of chronic

Table 1.10: Nutrient Contribution to Dietary Energy Consumption

	Average dietary energy consumption (kcal/person/day)	Share of DEC from protein (%)	Share of DEC from fat (%)	Share of DEC from total carbohydrates and alcohol (%)
Total	2199	10.37	15.87	73.75
Quintiles of income				
Lowest quintile	1596	10.46	11.88	77.66
2	2043	10.53	14.08	75.39
3	2250	10.30	15.67	74.03
4	2604	10.13	17.40	72.47
Highest quintile	3051	10.45	20.50	69.02
Area				
Capital city	2064	10.36	22.72	66.89
Other urban areas	2179	10.24	20.19	69.53
Rural areas	2213	10.40	14.68	74.92
Household size				
One person	3667	10.42	18.70	70.78
Between 2 and 3 people	2667	10.36	17.34	72.28
Between 4 and 5 people	2253	10.45	16.16	73.39
Between 6 and 7 people	2097	10.15	15.04	74.81
More than 7	1951	10.50	15.14	74.36
Gender of the household head				
Male	2207	10.35	15.73	73.91
Female	2167	10.48	16.48	73.04
Age of the household head				
Less than 35	2310	10.42	16.36	73.20
Between 35 and 45	2155	10.30	15.93	73.76
Between 46 and 60	2206	10.37	15.84	73.79
More than 60	2089	10.46	14.85	74.69

nondeficiency diseases. So, according to the experts, a diet is determined to be balanced when

- The proportion of dietary energy provided by protein is in the range of 10–15 percent
- The proportion of dietary energy provided by fats is in the range of 15–30 percent
- The proportion of total dietary energy provided by the remaining macronutrients is in the range of 55–75 percent

Table 1.11: Nutrient Contribution to Dietary Energy Consumption at Income Quintile Levels This table indicates whether households classified by income quintile groups have access to a balanced diet. The main sources of dietary energy are protein, fats, and total carbohydrates. Households have

Table 1.11: Nutrient Contribution to Dietary Energy Consumption at Income Quintile Levels

	Average dietary energy consumption (kcal/person/ day)	Share of DEC from protein (%)	Share of DEC from fat (%)	Share of DEC from total carbohydrates and alcohol (%)	Within range of population protein intake goal: 10%–15%	Within range of population fat intake goal: 15%–30%	Within range of population total carbohydrates and alcohol intake goal: 55%–75%
Total							
Quantiles of income							
Lowest quintile	1596	10.46	11.88	77.66	OK	LOW	HIGH
2	2043	10.53	14.08	75.39	OK	LOW	HIGH
3	2250	10.30	15.67	74.03	OK	OK	OK
4	2604	10.13	17.40	72.47	OK	OK	OK
Highest quintile	3051	10.45	20.50	69.02	OK	OK	OK
Area							
Capital city							
Lowest quintile	938	9.86	15.51	74.63	LOW	OK	OK
2	1226	9.99	16.37	73.64	LOW	OK	OK
3	1434	10.02	20.45	69.52	OK	OK	OK
4	1922	10.32	22.47	67.21	OK	OK	OK
Highest quintile	2793	10.52	24.31	65.12	OK	OK	OK
Other urban areas							
Lowest quintile	1335	10.17	15.94	73.89	OK	OK	OK
2	1635	10.06	16.42	73.51	OK	OK	OK
3	1858	10.22	18.16	71.62	OK	OK	OK
4	2419	9.95	19.41	70.61	LOW	OK	OK
Highest quintile	2905	10.59	24.08	65.26	OK	OK	OK
Rural areas							
Lowest quintile	1621	10.48	11.63	77.89	OK	LOW	HIGH
2	2105	10.57	13.86	75.57	OK	LOW	HIGH
3	2382	10.32	15.10	74.57	OK	OK	OK
4	2749	10.16	16.39	73.45	OK	OK	OK
Highest quintile	3193	10.38	18.06	71.55	OK	OK	OK

access to a balanced diet if the proportion of dietary energy from each macronutrient is within the experts' recommendations.[7] When OK appears for the three calorie-yielding macronutrients, we can consider that households in that population have access to a balanced diet. However, little else is known about households' consuming a balanced diet because there is no information about how people combine the food they consume or about intrahousehold allocation of food.

Table 1.12: Nutrient Density per 1,000 Kcal   This table shows the grams of protein, carbohydrates, and fats per 1,000 kcals (kilocalories) of households' consumption (macronutrient density).

Table 1.12: Nutrient Density per 1,000 Kcal

	Average dietary energy consumption (kcal/person/ day)	Average protein consumption (g/1000 kcal)	Average carbohydrates consumption (g/1000 kcal)	Average fat consumption (g/1000 kcal)
Total	2199	25.9	163.2	17.6
Quintiles of income				
Lowest quintile	1596	26.1	175.6	13.2
2	2043	26.3	166.8	15.6
3	2250	25.7	163.5	17.4
4	2604	25.3	158.3	19.3
Highest quintile	3051	26.1	151.7	22.8
Area				
Capital city	2064	25.9	158.9	25.2
Other urban areas	2179	25.6	159.3	22.4
Rural areas	2213	26.0	164.2	16.3
Household size				
One person	3667	26.1	139.5	20.8
Between 2 and 3 people	2667	25.9	155.2	19.3
Between 4 and 5 people	2253	26.1	161.6	18.0
Between 6 and 7 people	2097	25.4	166.7	16.7
More than 7	1951	26.3	169.2	16.8
Gender of the household head				
Male	2207	25.9	162.9	17.5
Female	2167	26.2	164.9	18.3
Age of the household head				
Less than 35	2310	26.1	162.5	18.2
Between 35 and 45	2155	25.7	163.4	17.7
Between 46 and 60	2206	25.9	163.2	17.6
More than 60	2089	26.2	164.4	16.5

Table 1.13: Share of Animal Protein in Total Protein Consumption This table shows the proportion of protein consumption coming from food of animal origin (animal proteins). The food commodities considered to be of animal origin are meat (red and white), fish, eggs, milk, and cheese. When households are classified by income quintiles, an increasing trend in the proportion of protein of animal origin consumed as one moves from the first to the last income quintile is expected. This is mainly because richer households can afford more expensive food products such as meat and fish. However, such a trend probably is not present in pastoral regions where poor

Table 1.13: Share of Animal Protein in Total Protein Consumption

	Share of animal protein in total protein consumption (%)
Total	21.2
Quintiles of income	
Lowest quintile	16.0
2	18.3
3	20.8
4	23.4
Highest quintile	28.0
Area	
Capital city	25.3
Other urban areas	24.2
Rural areas	20.5
Household size	
One person	26.1
Between 2 and 3 people	23.1
Between 4 and 5 people	21.4
Between 6 and 7 people	19.7
More than 7	20.8
Gender of the household head	
Male	21.3
Female	21.0
Age of the household head	
Less than 35	21.6
Between 35 and 45	21.9
Between 46 and 60	20.5
More than 60	20.7

communities/households derive a sizeable part of their consumption from livestock products (i.e., milk and cheese).

Table 1.14: Within-Region Differences in Nutrient Consumption, by Regional Income Quintiles This table shows the average macronutrients consumption by region and income quintile providing information on the intraregional differences. Such disaggregation can be used to explore income-based disparities on macronutrient consumption within each region and identify regions where disparities due to income are more pronounced. Note that the first row of the table for each region corresponds to table 1.9.

Table 1.14: Within-Region Differences in Nutrient Consumption, by Regional Income Quintiles

	Average protein consumption (g/person/day)	Average fat consumption (g/person/day)	Average carbohydrates consumption (g/person/day)
Region			
Region 1			
Total	69.11	43.87	372.61
Lowest quintile	58.41	28.75	340.23
2	65.74	39.17	354.78
3	66.16	41.44	345.70
4	78.96	55.96	414.48
Highest quintile	81.41	61.05	428.31
Region 2			
Total	52.38	39.78	316.28
Lowest quintile	40.42	21.95	267.46
2	45.01	29.18	273.65
3	49.31	34.52	289.86
4	62.47	52.19	380.20
Highest quintile	72.66	75.11	404.26
Region 3			
Total	46.13	41.07	310.79
Lowest quintile	31.13	19.66	232.15
2	36.71	31.13	263.27
3	45.50	38.97	313.15
4	53.25	50.73	349.16
Highest quintile	73.79	76.22	438.10
Region 4			
Total	50.35	37.53	380.04

Disaggregated by Food Commodity Group: Tables 2.1 to 2.9

The output tables showing statistics on consumption (grams/person/day) of protein, fats, and carbohydrates by food commodity group are useful in providing a picture of the consumption pattern. Note that this information also helps to identify which food commodity group contributes the most to the consumption of a given macronutrient. Note as well that the values of carbohydrates refer to available carbohydrates.[8]

Table 2.1: Food Consumption by Food Commodity Group This table shows the macronutrients (expressed in grams) and the food consumption (in dietary energy and monetary values) at the *national level* disaggregated by food commodity groups.

Table 2.1: Food Consumption by Food Commodity Groups

Food group	Average food consumption in monetary value (LCU/person/day)	Average dietary energy consumption (kcal/person/day)	Average protein consumption (g/person/day)	Average carbohydrates consumption (g/person/day)	Average fat consumption (g/person/day)
Cereals	67.4	1201	29.5	231.0	12.6
Roots and tubers	14.9	258	2.6	58.7	0.5
Sugars and syrups	12.7	89	0.0	22.3	0.0
Pulses	12.5	73	5.5	9.8	0.3
Tree nuts	0.1	3	0.1	0.0	0.2
Oil crops	4.9	79	2.6	1.1	6.8
Vegetables	18.6	30	1.7	4.0	0.3
Fruits	10.2	69	0.6	15.4	0.2
Stimulants	2.0	5	0.1	0.9	0.1
Spices	2.9	2	0.0	0.2	0.0
Alcoholic beverages	7.8	114	0.1	1.7	0.0
Meat	23.1	71	5.3	0.0	5.5
Eggs	0.8	1	0.1	0.0	0.1
Fish	15.1	27	5.4	0.0	0.6
Milk and cheese	7.2	24	1.3	1.8	1.3
Oils and fats (vegetable)	8.4	76	0.0	0.0	8.4
Oils and fats (animal)	0.3	2	0.0	0.0	0.2
Nonalcoholic beverages	2.8	2	0.0	0.5	0.0
Miscellaneous and prepared food	9.4	74	2.0	11.8	1.5

Table 2.2: Contribution of Food Commodity Groups to Total Nutrient Consumption This table shows the contribution (in percentage) of each food commodity group to the total dietary energy, protein, available carbohydrates, and fats consumed by the households at the *national level*. The disaggregation of these statistics by food commodity groups helps identify which food commodity groups are the main sources of calories, protein, total carbohydrates, and fats.

Table 2.3: Food Consumption by Food Commodity Group and Income Quintile This table has the same indicators as table 2.1 except that the statistics are disaggregated by income quintile. This table helps to identify the food item groups that contribute the most in terms of calories and macronutrients to the diet of population groups segmented according to their income level.

Table 2.4: Food Consumption by Food Commodity Group and Area This table shows the *urban/rural* food consumption statistics in terms of

Table 2.2: Contribution of Food Commodity Groups to Total Nutrient Consumption

	Share of total dietary energy consumption (%)	Share of total protein consumption (%)	Share of total carbohydrates consumption (%)	Share of total fat consumption (%)
Food group				
Cereals	54.6	51.6	64.3	32.5
Roots and tubers	11.7	4.6	16.4	1.3
Sugars and syrups	4.1	0.0	6.2	0.0
Pulses	3.3	9.7	2.7	0.8
Tree nuts	0.1	0.2	0.0	0.6
Oil crops	3.6	4.6	0.3	17.5
Vegetables	1.3	3.0	1.1	0.8
Fruits	3.1	1.1	4.3	0.5
Stimulants	0.2	0.2	0.2	0.2
Spices	0.1	0.1	0.1	0.1
Alcoholic beverages	5.2	0.3	0.5	0.0
Meat	3.2	9.4	0.0	14.3
Eggs	0.1	0.2	0.0	0.2
Fish	1.2	9.5	0.0	1.7
Milk and cheese	1.1	2.3	0.5	3.5
Oils and fats (vegetable)	3.5	0.0	0.0	21.8
Oils and fats (animal)	0.1	0.0	0.0	0.5
Nonalcoholic beverages	0.1	0.0	0.1	0.0
Miscellaneous and prepared food	3.4	3.5	3.3	3.8

Table 2.3: Food Consumption by Food Commodity Group and Income Quintile

	Average food consumption in monetary value (LCU/ person/day)	Average dietary energy consumption (kcal/person/ day)	Average protein consumption (g/person/day)	Average carbohydrates consumption (g/person/day)	Average fat consumption (g/person/day)
Quintiles of income					
Lowest quintile					
Cereals	35.75	987	24.6	188.5	10.5
Roots and tubers	11.62	267	2.6	60.9	0.5
Sugars and syrups	3.50	25	0.0	6.2	0.0
Pulses	6.76	53	4.0	7.1	0.2
Tree nuts	0.08	2	0.1	0.0	0.2
Oil crops	1.76	34	1.3	0.5	2.9
Vegetables	10.25	23	1.3	3.0	0.2
Fruits	3.34	30	0.3	6.8	0.1
Stimulants	0.47	2	0.0	0.4	0.0
Spices	1.61	0	0.0	0.0	0.0
Alcoholic beverages	2.25	59	0.1	0.8	0.0
Meat	8.06	29	2.4	0.0	2.2
Eggs	0.12	0	0.0	0.0	0.0
Fish	8.21	18	3.5	0.0	0.4
Milk and cheese	3.49	15	0.8	1.1	0.8

(continued)

Table 2.3: Food Consumption by Food Commodity Group and Income Quintile (continued)

	Average food consumption in monetary value (LCU/person/day)	Average dietary energy consumption (kcal/person/day)	Average protein consumption (g/person/day)	Average carbohydrates consumption (g/person/day)	Average fat consumption (g/person/day)
Oils and fats (vegetable)	2.20	21	0.0	0.0	2.4
Oils and fats (animal)	0.08	1	0.0	0.0	0.1
Nonalcoholic beverages	0.22	0	0.0	0.0	0.0
Miscellaneous and prepared food	1.87	29	0.8	4.9	0.5
Quintile 2					
Cereals	57.42	1192	29.4	228.9	12.4
Roots and tubers	14.53	265	2.6	60.6	0.5
Sugars and syrups	8.23	57	0.0	14.3	0.0
Pulses	10.63	65	4.9	8.7	0.3

Table 2.4: Food Consumption by Food Commodity Group and Area

	Average food consumption in monetary value (LCU/person/day)	Average dietary energy consumption (kcal/person/day)	Average protein consumption (g/person/day)	Average carbohydrates consumption (g/person/day)	Average fat consumption (g/person/day)
Area					
Capital city					
Cereals	110.12	1029	24.7	200.2	10.6
Roots and tubers	8.95	50	0.7	11.2	0.1
Sugars and syrups	22.55	184	0.0	46.1	0.0
Pulses	15.27	51	3.8	6.8	0.2
Tree nuts	0.10	1	0.0	0.0	0.1
Oil crops	10.86	105	1.5	1.8	9.6
Vegetables	33.88	24	1.2	3.5	0.2
Fruits	19.88	44	0.4	9.8	0.1
Stimulants	3.63	5	0.1	1.0	0.1
Spices	2.94	4	0.1	0.5	0.1
Alcoholic beverages	12.99	8	0.0	0.4	0.0
Meat	40.76	91	6.2	0.0	7.3
Eggs	2.99	3	0.2	0.0	0.2
Fish	23.49	34	6.5	0.0	0.9
Milk and cheese	7.52	11	0.6	0.8	0.6
Oils and fats (vegetable)	14.71	132	0.0	0.0	14.6
Oils and fats (animal)	1.32	6	0.0	0.0	0.6
Nonalcoholic beverages	11.32	9	0.0	2.3	0.0
Miscellaneous and prepared food	52.44	274	7.3	43.6	6.6
Other urban areas					
Cereals	87.62	1217	29.4	234.3	13.1
Roots and tubers	11.06	134	1.6	30.2	0.3
Sugars and syrups	20.73	148	0.0	36.9	0.0
Pulses	12.87	57	4.2	7.6	0.3

macronutrients,[9] dietary energy, and monetary values disaggregated by food commodity groups. This table allows the analyst to explore the macronutrient consumption patterns in urban and rural areas and detect differences, if any.

Table 2.5: Contribution of Food Commodity Groups to Total Nutrient Consumption by Area   This table shows the contribution (in percentage) of each food commodity group to the total dietary energy, protein, available carbohydrates,[10] and fats consumed by the households in *rural and urban areas*. The disaggregation of these statistics by food commodity groups helps to identify which food commodity group(s) are the main sources of calories, protein, available carbohydrates, and fats within urban and rural areas and highlights urban/rural-based differences.

Table 2.6: Food Consumption by Food Commodity Group and Region   This table shows, for the *first income quintile of each region*, the food consumption statistics in terms of macronutrients, dietary energy, and monetary values disaggregated by food commodity groups. Because the food consumption pattern varies among regions, the analysis of the first income quintile group by region is important to identify the main sources of each macronutrient for the poorest population.

Table 2.7: Food Consumption by Food Commodity Group and Region in the First Quintile   This table shows, for the *first income quintile of each region*, the food consumption statistics in terms of macronutrients,[11] dietary energy, and monetary values disaggregated by food commodity groups. Because the first income quintile refers to the poorest population and the food consumption pattern varies among regions, the analysis is important in helping to identify regional differences within the poorest part of the population.

Table 2.8: Nutrient Costs by Food Commodity Group   This table shows the unit value of dietary energy, protein, available carbohydrates,[12] and fats disaggregated by *food commodity groups*. The objective of this table is to identify the food commodity groups that are low-cost sources of dietary energy, protein, carbohydrates, or fats.

The unit values are estimated using expenditures of each food commodity group as well as their contribution to total calories or nutrient content

Table 2.5: Contribution of Food Commodity Groups to Total Nutrient Consumption by Area

	Share of total dietary energy consumption (%)	Share of total protein consumption (%)	Share of total carbohydrates consumption (%)	Share of total fat consumption (%)
Area				
Capital city				
Cereals	49.8	46.3	61.0	20.4
Roots and tubers	2.4	1.3	3.4	0.2
Sugars and syrups	8.9	0.0	14.0	0.0
Pulses	2.5	7.1	2.1	0.4
Tree nuts	0.1	0.1	0.0	0.2
Oil crops	5.1	2.8	0.5	18.5
Vegetables	1.1	2.3	1.1	0.4
Fruits	2.2	0.8	3.0	0.2
Stimulants	0.2	0.2	0.3	0.2
Spices	0.2	0.2	0.2	0.2
Alcoholic beverages	0.4	0.1	0.1	0.0
Meat	4.4	11.6	0.0	14.0
Eggs	0.1	0.4	0.0	0.4
Fish	1.7	12.1	0.0	1.7
Milk and cheese	0.5	1.0	0.2	1.1
Oils and fats (vegetable)	6.4	0.0	0.0	28.1
Oils and fats (animal)	0.3	0.0	0.0	1.2
Nonalcoholic beverages	0.5	0.0	0.7	0.0
Miscellaneous and prepared food	13.3	13.6	13.3	12.6
Other urban areas				
Cereals	55.8	52.7	67.5	26.9
Roots and tubers	6.2	2.9	8.7	0.5
Sugars and syrups	6.8	0.0	10.6	0.0
Pulses	2.6	7.6	2.2	0.5

(in kcal or grams, respectively). Then the dietary energy unit value is expressed in local currency per 1,000 kcal, while the cost of each macronutrient is expressed in local currency per 100 grams of the respective nutrient. Each time N/A replaces a unit value, it means that the dietary energy or nutrient content provided by the food commodity group is very low or null, or there was no acquisition of that food group.

Table 2.9: Food Consumption by Food Commodity Group and Food Sources (in Dietary Energy)   This table shows the contribution of each food source to the dietary energy consumption for each food commodity group.

In table 2.9, own production contributes 47 percent to the total dietary energy consumption coming from cereals while most of the dietary energy consumption provided by vegetable oils and fats are coming from purchases (93.4 percent). This table makes it possible to identify the main sources of acquisition of the food group commodity being consumed.

Table 2.6: Food Consumption by Food Commodity Group and Region

	Average food consumption in monetary value (LCU/person/day)	Average dietary energy consumption (kcal/person/day)	Average protein consumption (g/person/day)	Average carbohydrates consumption (g/person/day)	Average fat consumption (g/person/day)
Region					
Region 1					
Cereals	69.53	1614	41.6	307.5	16.5
Roots and tubers	5.67	41	0.7	9.1	0.1
Sugars and syrups	9.62	67	0.0	16.7	0.0
Pulses	12.22	93	7.1	12.3	0.4
Tree nuts	0.05	1	0.0	0.0	0.1
Oil crops	5.36	124	5.2	1.6	10.3
Vegetables	22.22	47	2.7	5.6	0.5
Fruits	4.56	18	0.3	3.4	0.1
Stimulants	1.35	4	0.1	0.8	0.1
Spices	2.72	1	0.0	0.2	0.0
Alcoholic beverages	7.13	145	0.2	2.1	0.0
Meat	19.85	66	4.9	0.0	5.2
Eggs	0.65	1	0.1	0.0	0.1
Fish	6.53	12	2.4	0.0	0.3
Milk and cheese	7.53	33	1.8	2.4	1.8
Oils and fats (vegetable)	7.59	63	0.0	0.0	6.9
Oils and fats (animal)	0.22	1	0.0	0.0	0.1
Nonalcoholic beverages	1.24	1	0.0	0.2	0.0
Miscellaneous and prepared food	6.13	69	2.0	10.8	1.3
Region 2					
Cereals	73.76	1275	31.9	241.3	14.7
Roots and tubers	6.45	40	0.8	8.4	0.1
Sugars and syrups	16.91	113	0.0	28.3	0.0
Pulses	11.50	54	4.0	7.3	0.3

Table 2.7: Food Consumption by Food Commodity Group and Region in the First Quintile

	Average food consumption in monetary value (LCU/person/day)	Average dietary energy consumption (kcal/person/day)	Average protein consumption (g/person/day)	Average carbohydrates consumption (g/person/day)	Average fat consumption (g/person/day)
Region					
Region 1					
Cereals	44.76	1584	42.0	301.2	15.7
Roots and tubers	2.93	31	0.4	6.9	0.1
Sugars and syrups	2.66	19	0.0	4.7	0.0
Pulses	5.83	56	4.3	7.4	0.2
Tree nuts	0.00	0	0.0	0.0	0.0
Oil crops	3.67	74	3.2	1.0	6.2
Vegetables	18.62	47	2.7	5.6	0.5
Fruits	2.14	10	0.2	1.7	0.1

(continued)

Table 2.7: Food Consumption by Food Commodity Group and Region in the First Quintile (continued)

	Average food consumption in monetary value (LCU/person/day)	Average dietary energy consumption (kcal/person/day)	Average protein consumption (g/person/day)	Average carbohydrates consumption (g/person/day)	Average fat consumption (g/person/day)
Stimulants	0.65	9	0.1	1.9	0.1
Spices	1.60	0	0.0	0.1	0.0
Alcoholic beverages	3.66	98	0.1	1.4	0.0
Meat	5.31	20	1.5	0.0	1.6
Eggs	0.37	0	0.0	0.0	0.0
Fish	2.89	7	1.3	0.0	0.2
Milk and cheese	5.44	25	1.3	1.8	1.4
Oils and fats (vegetable)	2.52	20	0.0	0.0	2.2
Oils and fats (animal)	0.01	0	0.0	0.0	0.0
Nonalcoholic beverages	0.06	0	0.0	0.0	0.0
Miscellaneous and prepared food	1.96	41	1.2	6.6	0.6
Region 2					
Cereals	46.80	1264	31.9	236.4	15.5
Roots and tubers	3.08	21	0.4	4.7	0.0
Sugars and syrups	4.09	30	0.0	7.6	0.0
Pulses	5.90	35	2.6	4.7	0.2

Table 2.8: Nutrient Costs by Food Commodity Group

	Average dietary energy unit value (LCU/1000 kcal)	Average protein unit value (LCU/100 g)	Average carbohydrates unit value (LCU/100 g)	Average fat unit value (LCU/100 g)
Food group				
Cereals	56.11	228.83	29.19	534.81
Roots and tubers	57.88	567.85	25.40	N/A
Sugars and syrups	142.73	N/A	57.10	
Pulses	169.82	225.32	127.47	N/A
Tree nuts	49.99	146.84	343.23	58.57
Oil crops	61.88	186.93	431.55	71.81
Vegetables	626.42	N/A	462.75	N/A
Fruits	147.45	N/A	66.18	N/A
Stimulants	432.40	N/A	225.33	N/A
Spices	N/A	N/A	N/A	N/A
Alcoholic beverages	68.81	N/A	462.77	
Meat	324.50	433.27	N/A	417.05
Eggs	683.22	814.44	N/A	N/A
Fish	551.73	279.98		N/A
Milk and cheese	294.66	554.64	404.89	534.26
Oils and fats (vegetable)	110.11			99.10
Oils and fats (animal)	169.17	N/A		152.70
Nonalcoholic beverages	N/A	N/A	574.81	
Miscellaneous and prepared food	126.07	469.16	79.66	635.46

Note: N/A: very low or no nutrient content or no consumption.

Table 2.9: Food Consumption by Food Commodity Group and Food Sources (in Dietary Energy)

Food group	Purchases		Own Production		Food consumed away from home		Other sources	
	Average dietary energy consumption (kcal/person/ day)	Share in food commodity group's total consumption (%)	Average dietary energy consumption (kcal/person/ day)	Share in food commodity group's total consumption (%)	Average dietary energy consumption (kcal/person/ day)	Share in food commodity group's total consumption (%)	Average dietary energy consumption (kcal/person/ day)	Share in food commodity group's total consumption (%)
Cereals	593.8	49.4	565.5	47.1		0.0	42.0	3.5
Roots and tubers	90.8	35.2	157.7	61.2		0.0	9.2	3.6
Sugars and syrups	85.5	95.9	0.8	0.9		0.0	2.8	3.2
Pulses	35.2	48.0	35.0	47.7		0.0	3.2	4.3
Tree nuts	1.2	44.5	1.1	40.4		0.0	0.4	15.1
Oil crops	43.0	54.7	30.9	39.3		0.0	4.7	6.0
Vegetables	11.8	39.8	16.7	56.4		0.0	1.1	3.8
Fruits	27.8	40.2	36.4	52.7		0.0	4.9	7.1
Stimulants	3.0	65.7	0.8	18.1		0.0	0.7	16.2
Spices	1.4	88.5	0.1	8.4		0.0	0.0	3.0
Alcoholic beverages	93.9	82.7	6.6	5.8		0.0	13.1	11.5
Meat	57.3	80.4	10.2	14.4		0.0	3.7	5.2
Eggs	0.7	64.1	0.3	30.7		0.0	0.1	5.2
Fish	25.8	94.3	0.7	2.6		0.0	0.9	3.1
Milk and cheese	10.3	42.3	13.1	53.6		0.0	1.0	4.1
Oils and fats (vegetable)	70.9	93.4	3.8	5.1		0.0	1.2	1.6
Oils and fats (animal)	1.6	86.4	0.2	10.9		0.0	0.1	2.7
Nonalcoholic beverages	1.8	89.7	0.0	0.2		0.0	0.2	10.1
Miscellaneous and prepared food		0.0	0.0	0.0	74.8	100.0	0.2	0.0

Disaggregated by Food Commodity: Tables 3.1 to 3.9

The food commodities analyzed are those collected in the survey excluding those consumed away from home. Therefore, the total protein consumed from the listed commodities is underestimated. The food commodity quantities refer to edible portions, which mean that they exclude the nonedible parts (peels, bones, etc.).

Table 3.1: Consumption Statistics for Each Food Item at National Level   This table shows *national* food consumption statistics by food commodities. The statistics comprise food commodity edible quantities and their respective monetary value, the calories they provide, and the calorie costs.

This table is useful to identify the food commodities providing more calories to the households' consumption at the national level and how much an individual living in the country has to pay to acquire those calories. Moreover, it enables one to do a comparison between food availability and food consumption. For instance, one could look for differences between daily calories[13] consumption per person (third column) obtained from NHS and those available obtained from the FBS.

Table 3.2: Food Item Protein Consumption at National Level   This table shows *national* food consumption statistics by food commodities. The statistics comprise food commodity edible quantities and their respective monetary value, the amount of protein they provide, and the protein costs.

This table is useful to identify the food commodities providing more protein to the households' consumption at the national level and how much an individual living in the country has to pay to acquire that amount of protein. Moreover, it enables one to do a comparison between food availability as compiled in the FBS and food consumption as collected in NHS. For instance, one could look for differences between daily protein consumption per person (third column) obtained from NHS and those available obtained from the FBS.

Table 3.3: Consumption Statistics for Each Food Item by Area   This table shows *urban/rural* food consumption statistics by food commodity. The statistics comprise food commodity edible quantities and their respective monetary value, the calories they provide, and the calorie costs. This table is useful to identify differences between urban and rural areas with respect to calorie consumption patterns and unit values.

Table 3.1: Consumption Statistics for Each Food Item at National Level

Food item	Average edible quantity consumed (g/person/day)	Average food consumption in monetary value (LCU/person/day)	Average dietary energy consumption (kcal/person/day)	Average dietary energy unit value (LCU/1000 kcals)
Rice paddy or rough	6.12	0.98	21.37	45.78
Rice husked	48.14	18.65	169.44	110.07
Maize cob fresh	9.29	1.71	6.10	279.42
Maize grain	72.72	7.01	263.81	26.57
Maize flour	163.94	27.63	586.57	47.10
Millet whole grain dried	1.68	0.33	5.34	62.75
Millet foxtail Italian whole grain	1.17	0.43	3.70	116.10
Sorghum whole grain brown	7.91	0.88	28.09	31.35
Sorghum average of all variety	20.38	2.68	72.43	36.97
Wheat durum whole grain	0.46	0.11	1.66	66.89
Wheat meal or flour unspecified wheat	4.41	1.54	14.90	103.16
Wheat	1.30	0.20	4.68	42.37
Bread	3.11	1.65	8.22	201.08
Baby cereals	0.09	0.04	0.33	128.53
Biscuits wheat from Europe	0.15	0.27	0.65	409.68
Buns cakes	3.25	3.10	10.50	295.24
Macaroni spaghetti	0.27	0.16	0.95	171.61
Oats	2.31	1.63	8.61	188.93
Cassava sweet roots raw	28.98	2.96	45.53	64.95
Cassava sweet roots dried	14.31	1.30	45.20	28.84
Cassava flour	35.67	4.18	112.69	37.12
Sweet potato	50.00	3.93	35.65	110.37
Coco yam tuber	5.45	0.65	5.76	112.69
Potatoes tubers raw	9.00	1.58	5.03	314.51
Banana cooking	42.28	5.41	52.93	102.12
Starch	2.17	0.31	7.93	39.20
Sugar refined white	21.67	12.21	86.60	141.02
Honey local product	0.58	0.17	1.92	88.47
Lemon sweet	0.22	0.34	0.62	551.97
Peas dry	4.15	1.13	13.34	84.99
Beans dry	36.36	9.40	38.36	244.94
Lentil seed dried whole	7.39	1.75	20.67	84.75
Pulse product	1.04	0.18	1.02	177.34

Table 3.4: Food Item Protein Consumption by Area This table shows *urban/rural* food consumption statistics by food commodity. The statistics comprise food commodity edible quantities and their respective monetary value, the amount of protein they provide, and the protein costs. This table is useful to identify differences between rural and urban areas with respect to protein consumption and protein unit values.

Table 3.5: Consumption Statistics for Each Food Item by Region This table shows *regional* food consumption statistics by food commodity. The statistics comprise food commodity edible quantities and their respective monetary

Table 3.2: Food Item Protein Consumption at National Level

Food item	Average edible quantity consumed (g/person/day)	Average food consumption in monetary value (LCU/person/day)	Average protein consumption (g/person/day)	Average protein unit value (LCU/100 g)
Rice paddy or rough	6.12	0.98	0.40	241.71
Rice husked	48.14	18.65	3.61	516.60
Maize cob fresh	9.29	1.71	0.17	1019.90
Maize grain	72.72	7.01	6.85	102.33
Maize flour	163.94	27.63	13.28	208.07
Millet whole grain dried	1.68	0.33	0.20	171.37
Millet foxtail Italian whole grain	1.17	0.43	0.08	556.05
Sorghum whole grain brown	7.91	0.88	0.89	98.58
Sorghum average of all varieties	20.38	2.68	2.30	116.25
Wheat durum whole grain	0.46	0.11	0.06	176.74
Wheat meal or flour unspecified wheat	4.41	1.54	0.60	254.43
Wheat	1.30	0.20	0.30	66.05
Bread	3.11	1.65	0.27	603.70
Baby cereals	0.09	0.04	0.01	345.18
Biscuits wheat from Europe	0.15	0.27	0.01	1886.31
Buns cakes	3.25	3.10	0.15	2027.08
Macaroni spaghetti	0.27	0.16	0.03	582.82
Oats	2.31	1.63	0.39	417.84
Cassava sweet roots raw	28.98	2.96	0.41	728.87
Cassava sweet roots dried	14.31	1.30	0.37	350.35
Cassava flour	35.67	4.18	0.93	451.02
Sweet potato	50.00	3.93	0.60	655.78
Coco yam tuber	5.45	0.65	0.08	793.35
Potatoes tubers raw	9.00	1.58	0.23	676.19
Banana cooking	42.28	5.41	0.34	1598.24
Starch	2.17	0.31	0.01	4775.90
Sugar refined white	21.67	12.21	0.00	

Table 3.3: Consumption Statistics for Each Food Item by Area

Area	Average edible quantity consumed (g/person/day)	Average food consumption in monetary value (LCU/person/day)	Average dietary energy consumption (kcal/person/day)	Average dietary energy unit value (LCU/1000 kcals)
Capital city				
Rice paddy or rough	0.60	0.12	2.11	58.75
Rice husked	108.34	43.98	381.34	115.32
Maize cob fresh	0.68	0.27	0.45	594.81
Maize grain	7.68	1.35	27.86	48.48
Maize flour	125.27	28.35	448.23	63.24
Millet whole grain dried	0.42	0.19	1.32	145.65
Millet foxtail Italian whole grain	0.71	0.49	2.23	220.35
Sorghum whole grain brown	0.13	0.05	0.46	98.48
Sorghum average of all varieties	0.04	0.01	0.15	58.51
Wheat durum whole grain	0.24	0.08	0.87	92.83

(continued)

Table 3.3: Consumption Statistics for Each Food Item by Area (continued)

	Average edible quantity consumed (g/person/day)	Average food consumption in monetary value (LCU/person/day)	Average dietary energy consumption (kcal/person/day)	Average dietary energy unit value (LCU/1000 kcals)
Wheat meal or flour unspecified wheat	10.40	3.22	35.14	91.71
Wheat	0.21	0.09	0.77	115.73
Bread	16.83	9.18	44.46	206.59
Baby cereals	0.04	0.06	0.14	427.80
Biscuits wheat from Europe	0.50	0.78	2.13	365.65
Buns cakes	10.44	9.75	33.69	289.34
Macaroni spaghetti	2.18	1.30	7.79	167.22
Oats	10.69	11.05	39.93	276.67
Cassava sweet roots raw	13.06	2.24	20.52	109.14
Cassava sweet roots dried	1.09	0.13	3.43	38.41
Cassava flour	0.83	0.15	2.64	55.26
Sweet potato	13.23	2.20	9.43	233.14
Coco yam tuber	2.45	0.54	2.59	210.14
Potatoes tubers raw	10.96	3.26	6.12	531.81
Banana cooking	13.80	5.55	17.27	321.50

Table 3.4: Food Item Protein Consumption by Area

	Average edible quantity consumed (g/person/day)	Average food consumption in monetary value (LCU/person/day)	Average protein consumption (g/person/day)	Average protein unit value (LCU/100 g)
Area				
Capital city				
Rice paddy or rough	0.60	0.12	0.04	310.22
Rice husked	108.34	43.98	8.13	541.26
Maize cob fresh	0.68	0.27	0.01	2171.06
Maize grain	7.68	1.35	0.72	186.70
Maize flour	125.27	28.35	10.15	279.37
Millet whole grain dried	0.42	0.19	0.05	397.77
Millet foxtail Italian whole grain	0.71	0.49	0.05	1055.33
Sorghum whole grain brown	0.13	0.05	0.01	309.64
Sorghum average of all varieties	0.04	0.01	0.00	183.97
Wheat durum whole grain	0.24	0.08	0.03	245.30
Wheat meal or flour unspecified wheat	10.40	3.22	1.42	226.19
Wheat	0.21	0.09	0.05	180.40
Bread	16.83	9.18	1.48	620.23
Baby cereals	0.04	0.06	0.01	1148.95
Biscuits wheat from Europe	0.50	0.78	0.05	1683.56
Buns cakes	10.44	9.75	0.49	1986.58
Macaroni spaghetti	2.18	1.30	0.23	567.92
Oats	10.69	11.05	1.81	611.88
Cassava sweet roots raw	13.06	2.24	0.18	1224.71
Cassava sweet roots dried	1.09	0.13	0.03	466.67
Cassava flour	0.83	0.15	0.02	671.35
Sweet potato	13.23	2.20	0.16	1385.23
Coco yam tuber	2.45	0.54	0.04	1479.39
Potatoes tubers raw	10.96	3.26	0.28	1143.39
Banana cooking	13.80	5.55	0.11	5031.45

Table 3.5: Consumption Statistics for Each Food Item by Region

	Average edible quantity consumed (g/person/day)	Average food consumption in monetary value (LCU/person/day)	Average dietary energy consumption (kcal/person/day)	Average dietary energy unit value (LCU/1000 kcals)
Region				
Region 1				
Rice paddy or rough	0.29	0.06	1.02	60.51
Rice husked	26.25	10.63	92.39	115.08
Maize cob fresh	11.73	2.57	7.70	333.78
Maize grain	50.15	4.09	181.92	22.47
Maize flour	240.10	33.01	859.08	38.43
Millet whole grain dried	1.68	0.26	5.32	48.86
Millet foxtail Italian whole grain	1.67	1.11	5.28	210.73
Sorghum whole grain brown	20.07	1.84	71.29	25.80
Sorghum average of all varieties	102.41	12.41	363.88	34.12
Wheat durum whole grain	0.05	0.02	0.19	110.07
Wheat meal or flour unspecified wheat	3.35	1.17	11.30	103.09
Wheat	1.40	0.24	5.05	48.00
Bread	1.07	0.70	2.84	247.73
Baby cereals	0.04	0.01	0.13	52.66
Biscuits wheat from Europe	0.09	0.17	0.40	428.68
Buns cakes	2.69	2.38	8.67	274.66
Macaroni spaghetti	0.12	0.10	0.43	225.61
Oats	1.38	1.28	5.15	249.02
Cassava sweet roots raw	11.73	1.63	18.42	88.51
Cassava sweet roots dried	0.16	0.03	0.50	63.99
Cassava flour	0.29	0.06	0.91	64.02
Sweet potato	22.52	2.32	16.06	144.43
Coco yam tuber	0.24	0.05	0.25	197.18
Potatoes tubers raw	7.74	1.52	4.33	351.12
Banana cooking	2.33	0.52	2.92	179.39

value, the calories they provide, and the calorie costs. This table is useful to identify differences across regions with respect to calorie consumption and unit values.

Table 3.6: Food Item Protein Consumption by Region This table shows *regional* food consumption statistics by food commodity. The statistics comprise food commodity edible quantities and their respective monetary value, the amount of protein they provide, and the protein costs. This table is useful to identify differences across regions with respect to protein consumption and unit values.

Table 3.7: Food Item Quantities by Food Source For food fortification programs, the distinction of the food source plays an important role. Food that is home-produced is assumed not to have been fortified and

Table 3.6: Food Item Protein Consumption by Region

Region	Average edible quantity consumed (g/person/day)	Average food consumption in monetary value (LCU/person/day)	Average protein consumption (g/person/day)	Average protein unit value (LCU/100 g)
Region 1				
Rice paddy or rough	0.29	0.06	0	319.53
Rice husked	26.25	10.63	2	540.13
Maize cob fresh	11.73	2.57	0	1218.31
Maize grain	50.15	4.09	5	86.53
Maize flour	240.10	33.01	19	169.75
Millet whole grain dried	1.68	0.26	0	133.43
Millet foxtail Italian whole grain	1.67	1.11	0	1009.28
Sorghum whole grain brown	20.07	1.84	2	81.11
Sorghum average of all varieties	102.41	12.41	12	107.27
Wheat durum whole grain	0.05	0.02	0	290.83
Wheat meal or flour unspecified wheat	3.35	1.17	0	254.26
Wheat	1.40	0.24	0	74.82
Bread	1.07	0.70	0	743.74
Baby cereals	0.04	0.01	0	141.42
Biscuits wheat from Europe	0.09	0.17	0	1973.79
Buns cakes	2.69	2.38	0	1885.79
Macaroni spaghetti	0.12	0.10	0	766.22
Oats	1.38	1.28	0	550.72
Cassava sweet roots raw	11.73	1.63	0	993.23
Cassava sweet roots dried	0.16	0.03	0	777.43
Cassava flour	0.29	0.06	0	777.84
Sweet potato	22.52	2.32	0	858.17
Coco yam tuber	0.24	0.05	0	1388.15
Potatoes tubers raw	7.74	1.52	0	754.90
Banana cooking	2.33	0.52	0	2807.42

Table 3.7: Food Item Quantities by Food Source

	Purchases		Own production		Other sources	
	Quantity "as purchased," g/person/day	Proportion of households in total households (%)	Quantity "as produced," g/person/day	Proportion of households in total households (%)	Quantity "as received," g/person/day	Proportion of households in total households (%)
Food item						
Rice husked	56.1	67.4	63.7	14.4	19.2	8.9
Maize grain	134.6	30.6	82.1	25.9	73.6	5.0
Maize flour	113.3	52.7	189.3	52.2	29.8	11.3
Buns cakes	6.0	51.6	2.8	1.2	1.2	7.2
Oats	5.4	30.7	18.6	2.1	1.4	4.8
Sweet potato	48.7	28.4	124.2	24.0	25.4	6.5
Sugar refined white	28.4	72.5	5.2	1.5	8.6	7.2
Beans dry	30.2	66.8	40.5	34.3	14.6	9.0
Groundnuts shelled	7.8	31.0	15.7	15.5	4.1	5.1
Onion garden	8.8	70.8	5.1	5.8	2.5	5.0

(continued)

Table 3.7: Food Item Quantities by Food Source (continued)

Food item	Purchases		Own production		Other sources	
	Quantity "as purchased," g/person/ day	Proportion of households in total households (%)	Quantity "as produced," g/person/ day	Proportion of households in total households (%)	Quantity "as received," g/person/ day	Proportion of households in total households (%)
Spinach raw	12.9	43.4	10.9	24.9	5.6	4.0
Tomato raw ripe whole	23.7	73.8	12.2	11.7	7.5	7.6
Cattle meat	25.5	63.9	18.2	2.4	9.1	7.7
Fish average of all kinds raw	32.3	34.7	24.4	3.0	13.6	4.9
Sardine salted dried	17.0	77.7	4.6	3.8	4.9	8.4
Milk cow fluid whole	39.1	30.8	90.3	9.0	16.2	5.0
Cooking oil other	9.9	43.8	6.7	2.0	2.8	2.4
Salt	12.3	85.4	6.5	2.3	4.2	4.4
Tea common dried black	1.0	47.0	0.9	0.7	0.3	1.9
Soft drinks	15.7	28.7	3.6	0.3	6.4	7.4

not to be fortifiable. In assessing the potential coverage of a fortified or fortifiable food, only food that is purchased should be included in the analysis. Information on the proportion of households purchasing a food commodity is also relevant for food fortification programs. For instance, in some cases processed staple foods (e.g., flour) are purchased by households in larger quantities than the respective unprocessed food commodity (e.g., grain). So, from a fortification policy perspective, the processed food can be as important as, or more important, than the staple (Fiedler 2009).

Table 3.7 shows information for the 20 food commodities most purchased by households at the *national level*. The information comprises (1) the food quantities acquired from purchases (i.e., at the market, from street vendors, at shops, etc.) and the percentage of households that purchased these food quantities; (2) the food quantities from own production and the percentage of households that reported own production; and (3) the food quantities from other sources and the percentage of households that reported other sources.[14]

Note that the sum of the proportion of households that acquired the product through purchase, or received in kind, or from own consumption does not necessarily equal 100 percent because not all households might have consumed the food.

Table 3.8: Food Item Quantities by Food Source and Area   This table shows information for the 20 food commodities most purchased by households by *rural and urban* areas separately. The information comprises (1) the food quantities acquired from purchases (i.e., at the market, from street vendors, at shops, etc.) and the percentage of households that purchased these food quantities; (2) the food quantities from own production and the percentage of households that reported own production; and (3) the food quantities from other sources and the percentage of households that reported other sources.[15]

Note that the sum of the proportion of households that acquired the product through purchase, or received in kind, or from own consumption does not necessarily equal 100 percent because not all households might have consumed the food.

Table 3.9: Food Item Quantities by Food Source and Region   This table shows information for the 20 food commodities most purchased by households at the *regional* level. The information comprises (1) the food quantities acquired from purchases (i.e., at the market, from street vendors, at shops, etc.) and the percentage of households that purchased these food quantities; (2) the food quantities from own production and the percentage of households that reported own production; and (3) the food quantities from other sources and the percentage of households that reported other sources.[16]

Note that the sum of the proportion of households that acquired the product through purchase, or received in kind, or from own consumption does not necessarily equal 100 percent because not all households might have consumed the food.

Inequality

The dispersion ratios measure inequality between the two extreme income quintile groups. They are calculated using as reference the average values corresponding to the first quintile. The following tables show dispersion ratios related to food and nonfood consumption, as well as between *each income quintile* and the *first quintile*. Since consumption is positively correlated with income, when the *first* income quintile is used as reference, all the ratios are expected to be greater than 1. In this case, a higher ratio value implies higher inequality between the poorest and the richest groups. For instance, a dietary energy dispersion ratio of

Table 3.8: Food Item Quantities by Food Source and Area

Area	Purchases			Own production			Other sources		
	Quantity "as purchased," g/person/day	Proportion of households in total households (%)		Quantity "as produced," g/person/day	Proportion of households in total households (%)		Quantity "as received," g/person/day	Proportion of households in total households (%)	
Capital city									
Rice husked	110.6	90.6		44.9	0.5		43.2	6.9	
Maize flour	128.8	91.1		18.4	1.3		35.6	6.9	
Bread	20.9	74.0		5.7	0.5		4.1	1.6	
Buns cakes	11.7	86.2		1.0	0.8		1.7	5.1	
Oats	13.4	78.9		1.8	1.3		1.8	5.2	
Potatoes tubers raw	22.8	56.9		3.4	0.1		17.7	1.2	
Sugar refined white	44.8	93.2		3.2	1.0		22.0	4.0	
Beans dry	32.1	86.6		4.3	0.2		8.4	3.8	
Coconut mature kernel	52.7	77.7		44.8	0.6		16.2	3.0	
Onion garden common	12.5	88.2		0.5	0.7		3.8	2.8	
Spinach raw	18.4	78.8		4.7	1.7		5.6	3.4	
Tomato raw ripe whole	45.5	92.2		5.0	1.0		10.9	3.3	
Cattle meat	34.2	83.1		16.0	0.1		9.4	2.4	
Fish dried	10.7	56.9		5.1	0.1		1.6	0.8	
Sardine salted dried	9.3	67.1		12.6	0.3		4.3	2.0	
Cooking oil other	15.2	73.0		0.7	0.9		2.4	1.5	
Salt	9.9	77.2		3.3	0.3		2.1	1.0	
Tea common dried black	1.1	78.2		0.0	0.5		0.1	0.4	
Soft drinks	33.4	66.0		3.6	0.3		9.1	12.8	
Orange sweet juice fresh	17.8	56.5		0.6	0.1		6.6	6.6	
Other urban areas									
Rice husked	81.6	90.2		64.6	6.8		20.6	10.6	
Maize flour	116.4	70.6		159.4	25.1		27.5	7.0	

Table 3.9: Food Item Quantities by Food Source and Region

	Purchases		Own production		Other sources	
Region	Quantity "as purchased," g/person/day	Proportion of households in total households (%)	Quantity "as produced," g/person/day	Proportion of households in total households (%)	Quantity "as received," g/person/day	Proportion of households in total households (%)
Region 1						
Rice husked	46.1	54.1	16.8	6.0	9.9	5.2
Maize flour	167.9	35.7	244.5	71.2	29.6	13.7
Buns cakes	5.6	44.3	2.2	1.0	0.6	6.9
Sweet potato	34.7	32.4	49.4	15.1	13.6	6.1
Potatoes tubers raw	26.2	25.4	38.7	4.1	14.6	5.4
Sugar refined white	23.8	59.1	4.8	2.6	7.4	6.5
Beans dry	25.5	63.6	26.1	22.7	8.0	8.2
Groundnuts shelled	12.2	31.5	18.8	34.7	4.9	6.8
Onion garden common	7.2	65.9	9.3	7.1	2.6	8.7
Spinach raw	9.3	32.0	9.2	23.4	4.5	3.5
Tomato raw ripe whole	17.0	59.8	10.6	15.0	2.8	8.0
Other fruit	38.0	27.4	11.0	3.5	21.3	9.5
Cattle meat	22.6	68.4	8.4	4.6	9.0	15.2
Sardine salted dried	8.9	71.4	4.0	2.1	1.8	7.8
Milk cow fluid whole	35.0	25.3	56.0	10.3	21.4	11.3
Yogurt made from whole milk	28.4	34.6	85.5	16.0	28.7	22.7
Oil sunflower seed	6.2	33.9	2.2	0.8	2.0	2.8
Cooking oil other	7.9	46.8	0.5	3.9	2.6	1.7
Salt	12.6	77.9	3.8	2.3	4.5	6.3
Tea common dried black	0.9	30.0	0.3	1.8	0.2	1.4
Region 2						
Rice husked	53.8	70.3	15.3	3.1	14.0	3.8
Maize grain	160.0	67.0	155.5	35.7	105.7	13.9

2 (between the fifth and first income groups) indicates that households belonging to the highest income quintile consume twice as many calories as those in the lowest quintile. As the first income quintile values are used as reference, the dispersion ratio of the first quintile using itself as reference is 1.

Another way to measure inequality in food consumption is with elasticities. An income elasticity of demand is used to measure how sensitive the demand for food consumed is with respect to a change in income. The income elasticity of the demand of food could be measured through the responsiveness of dietary energy, food expenditure, or Engel ratio to a variation in income.

Disaggregated by Population Group: Tables 4.1 to 4.5

Table 4.1: Dispersion Ratio of Food Consumption by Income Quintile within Population Groups This table shows dispersion ratios related to food and nonfood consumption. These dispersion ratios measure the inequality between *each* income quintile and the *first* quintile.

While the amount of calories consumed has a limit due to biological factors, expenditures and income do not. Thus, the dispersion ratios of dietary energy consumption are expected to be smaller than those related to monetary values.

Table 4.2: Dispersion Ratios of Share of Food Consumption (in Dietary Energy) by Food Source, Income Quintile, and Population Groups This table shows the dispersion ratios of the percentage of total dietary energy provided by each of the four sources of food acquisition. These dispersion ratios measure the inequality between *each* income quintile and the *first* quintile.

Table 4.3: Dispersion Ratios of Share of Food Consumption (in Monetary Values) by Food Source and Income Quintile within Population Groups This table shows the dispersion ratios of the percentage of total food expenditure that each of the four sources of food acquisition represents. These dispersion ratios measure the inequality between *each* income quintile and the *first* quintile.

It is expected that the dispersion ratio of the food consumed away from home increases with income in general, because rich people spend more on food outside the home than do poor ones.

Table 4.1: Dispersion Ratio of Food Consumption by Income Quintile within Population Groups

	Average household size	Average dietary energy consumption (kcal/person/day)		Average food consumption in monetary value (LCU/person/day)		Average total consumption in monetary value (LCU/person/day)	
		Average	Ratio to the first reference group	Average	Ratio to the first reference group	Average	Ratio to the first reference group
Total							
Quintiles of income							
Lowest quintile	6.6	1596.05	1.00	101.64	1.00	142.49	1.00
2	5.6	2043.27	1.28	166.18	1.64	241.69	1.70
3	5.0	2249.74	1.41	218.23	2.15	333.62	2.34
4	4.2	2604.28	1.63	299.82	2.95	480.80	3.37
Highest quintile	3.4	3051.03	1.91	448.89	4.42	812.53	5.70
Area							
Capital city							
Quintiles of income							
Lowest quintile	5.6	938.17	1.00	119.22	1.00	164.03	1.00
2	6.5	1226.18	1.31	176.55	1.48	262.98	1.60
3	5.8	1433.59	1.53	226.33	1.90	378.08	2.30
4	4.5	1921.70	2.05	342.83	2.88	592.30	3.61
Highest quintile	3.5	2793.36	2.98	597.27	5.01	1160.41	7.07
Other urban areas							
Quintiles of income							
Lowest quintile	6.5	1334.91	1.00	110.75	1.00	152.28	1.00
2	5.7	1634.69	1.22	164.35	1.48	244.85	1.61
3	5.2	1858.39	1.39	221.00	2.00	350.09	2.30
4	4.5	2418.62	1.81	308.50	2.79	517.64	3.40
Highest quintile	3.2	2904.60	2.18	491.51	4.44	894.70	5.88

Table 4.4: Dispersion Ratios of Food Dietary Energy Unit Values, Total Income, and Engel Ratio by Income Quintile within Population Groups This table shows dispersion ratios of dietary energy unit value and income. These dispersion ratios measure the inequality between *each* income quintile and the *first* quintile.

Table 4.5: Income Demand Elasticities by Income Decile within Population Groups This table shows values of the demand elasticity of food consumption with respect to income. The demand for food is analyzed in terms of dietary energy, monetary values, and Engel ratio.

The elasticity values can be 0, negative, or positive. A value of 0 means the demand for food consumption is not sensitive to an income change

Table 4.2: Dispersion Ratios of Share of Food Consumption (in Dietary Energy) by Food Source, Income Quintile, and Population Groups

	Average household size	Share of purchased food in total food consumption (%)		Share of own produced food in total food consumption (%)		Share of food consumed away from home in total food consumption (%)		Share of food from other sources in total food consumption (%)	
		Shares	Ratio to the first reference group	Shares	Ratio to the first reference group	Shares	Ratio to the first reference group	Shares	Ratio to the first reference group
Total									
Quintiles of income									
Lowest quintile	6.6	40.31	1.00	53.34	1.00	1.82	1.00	4.54	1.00
2	5.6	42.01	1.04	51.83	0.97	2.11	1.16	4.06	0.89
3	5.0	51.34	1.27	41.80	0.78	2.62	1.44	4.25	0.94
4	4.2	62.10	1.54	30.64	0.57	3.37	1.86	3.88	0.86
Highest quintile	3.4	67.84	1.68	21.44	0.40	7.19	3.96	3.54	0.78
Area									
Capital city									
Quintiles of income									
Lowest quintile	5.6	87.24	1.00	3.89	1.00	3.53	1.00	5.34	1.00
2	6.5	87.92	1.01	0.98	0.25	7.01	1.98	4.10	0.77
3	5.8	92.12	1.06	0.33	0.08	6.03	1.71	1.51	0.28
4	4.5	87.59	1.00	0.06	0.02	10.61	3.00	1.73	0.32
Highest quintile	3.5	80.00	0.92	0.48	0.12	17.36	4.91	2.17	0.41
Other urban areas									
Quintiles of income									
Lowest quintile	6.5	76.84	1.00	17.09	1.00	1.97	1.00	4.10	1.00
2	5.7	73.27	0.95	19.53	1.14	2.57	1.30	4.63	1.13
3	5.2	78.68	1.02	15.65	0.92	2.32	1.18	3.34	0.82
4	4.5	81.11	1.06	12.29	0.72	4.16	2.11	2.43	0.59
Highest quintile	3.2	81.68	1.06	7.97	0.47	7.68	3.90	2.66	0.65

(i.e., that the demand for food consumption is income inelastic). When the value is negative, it means that the demand for the current food consumed decreases with an increase of income. A positive value could be classified into less than 1 (necessary foods) or more than 1 (luxurious foods) and means that an increase in income would increase the demand for food consumption.

As far as dietary energy is concerned, small values of calorie-income elasticity suggest that an increase in income would not affect much of the calorie intake, but it may improve the quality of the diet consumed by moving from cheap to more expensive food. On the other hand, Engel's law states that given a set of tastes and preferences, an increase in income will

Table 4.3: Dispersion Ratios of Share of Food Consumption (in Monetary Values) by Food Source and Income Quintile within Population Groups

	Average household size	Share of purchased food in total food consumption (%)		Share of own produced food in total food consumption (%)		Share of food consumed away from home in total food consumption (%)		Share of food from other sources in total food consumption (%)	
		Shares	Ratio to the first reference group	Shares	Ratio to the first reference group	Shares	Ratio to the first reference group	Shares	Ratio to the first reference group
Total									
Quintiles of income									
Lowest quintile	6.6	50.15	1.00	42.89	1.00	1.84	1.00	5.12	1.00
2	5.6	53.50	1.07	40.11	0.94	2.19	1.19	4.20	0.82
3	5.0	62.04	1.24	30.88	0.72	2.76	1.50	4.33	0.85
4	4.2	71.56	1.43	20.92	0.49	3.79	2.06	3.73	0.73
Highest quintile	3.4	76.58	1.53	12.06	0.28	7.96	4.32	3.40	0.66
Area									
Capital city									
Quintiles of income									
Lowest quintile	5.6	88.97	1.00	3.10	1.00	3.46	1.00	4.47	1.00
2	6.5	88.32	0.99	1.49	0.48	7.32	2.12	2.88	0.64
3	5.8	91.80	1.03	0.32	0.10	6.09	1.76	1.79	0.40
4	4.5	87.64	0.99	0.12	0.04	10.69	3.09	1.55	0.35
Highest quintile	3.5	80.22	0.90	0.47	0.15	16.22	4.69	3.08	0.69

correspond to an increase in food expenditure, but at a slower rate than that of income. Regarding the Engel ratio, the proportion of income dedicated to acquiring food decreases with an increase in income.

On the whole, the elasticity of food consumption with respect to income is higher for lower income groups of the population than for higher ones. However, the elasticity of food in dietary energy terms with respect to income is lower than its elasticity in monetary terms. In other words, for higher income groups the variation of dietary energy consumption due to a variation in income is lower than the variation of food expenditure with respect to the same income variation.

Availability of Micronutrients

The micronutrients analyzed in the ADePT-Food Security Module are vitamin A, ascorbic acid, thiamine (B1), riboflavin (B2), B6, and cobalamin (B12), as well as the minerals calcium and iron. It is important to remember

Table 4.4: Dispersion Ratios of Food Dietary Energy Unit Values, Total Income, and Engel Ratio by Income Quintile within Population Groups

	Average income (LCU/person/day)		Average dietary energy unit value (LCU/1000 kcals)		Share of food consumption in total income (%) (Engel ratio)
	Mean	Ratio to the first reference group	Shares	Ratio to the first reference group	
Total					
Quintiles of income					
Lowest quintile	152.11	1.00	63.68	1.00	66.8
2	265.79	1.75	81.33	1.28	62.5
3	395.28	2.60	97.00	1.52	55.2
4	614.73	4.04	115.12	1.81	48.8
Highest quintile	1898.29	12.48	147.13	2.31	23.6
Area Capital city					
Quintiles of income					
Lowest quintile	172.46	1.00	127.08	1.00	69.1
2	271.33	1.57	143.99	1.13	65.1
3	396.97	2.30	157.87	1.24	57.0
4	645.43	3.74	178.40	1.40	53.1
Highest quintile	2034.94	11.80	213.82	1.68	29.4
Other urban areas					
Quintiles of income					
Lowest quintile	160.34	1.00	82.97	1.00	69.1
2	268.20	1.67	100.54	1.21	61.3
3	404.36	2.52	118.92	1.43	54.7
4	633.34	3.95	127.55	1.54	48.7
Highest quintile	2208.29	13.77	169.22	2.04	22.3

that the statistics on micronutrients shown in the tables exclude food consumed away from home. Therefore, the statistics of total available vitamins and minerals are underestimated.

In the tables, the available amount of micronutrients (derived from national household survey data) is compared to the estimated average requirement (EAR) and recommended nutrient intake (RNI)[17] through ratios. The available amount is the numerator, and the EAR or RNI are the denominators of the ratios. For instance, if the ratio of vitamin A available to vitamin A required is 100 percent, we could expect (under equal distribution of vitamin A within the population) that half of the healthy individuals in the population meet its required level of vitamin A. As for the ratio of availability to recommend safe intake, if it is greater than 100 percent (under equal distribution of vitamin A within the population) we could expect that almost all apparently healthy individuals meet their requirement.

Table 4.5: Income Demand Elasticities by Income Decile within Population Groups

	Average income (LCU/person/day)	Demand elasticity of food in dietary energy consumption	Demand elasticity of food consumption in monetary value	Demand elasticity of the share of food consumption in monetary value
Total				
Deciles of income				
1	122.00	0.36	2.28	0.91
2	188.26	0.31	1.15	0.91
3	240.31	0.29	0.90	0.90
4	294.60	0.27	0.76	0.90
5	355.73	0.26	0.66	0.90
6	436.89	0.25	0.58	0.90
7	539.38	0.24	0.52	0.90
8	698.55	0.22	0.46	0.89
9	1001.65	0.21	0.39	0.89
10	2927.19	0.17	0.28	0.87
Area				
Capital city				
Deciles of income				
1	127.09	1.20	5.35	0.86
2	185.05	0.83	1.78	0.85
3	243.00	0.68	1.20	0.85
4	300.12	0.59	0.96	0.84
5	357.19	0.54	0.82	0.84
6	439.84	0.48	0.70	0.83
7	540.86	0.44	0.61	0.82
8	720.97	0.39	0.52	0.81
9	1030.48	0.34	0.44	0.80
10	2999.53	0.25	0.30	0.75

If the mean micronutrient intake is equal or exceeds mean micronutrient requirements, it cannot be concluded that group diets (group mean intakes, not individual diets) were adequate and conformed to recognized nutritional standards. The reason is that the prevalence of inadequacy depends on the shape and variation of the usual intake distribution, not on mean intake. If the mean intake equals the EAR, it is likely that a very high proportion of the population will have inadequate usual intake. In fact, roughly half of the population is expected to have intakes less than its requirement (except for energy). (NAS 2000)

Disaggregated by Population Group: Tables 5.1 to 5.7

Table 5.1: Availability of Vitamin A   This table shows the daily per person retinol, beta-carotene, and vitamin A available for human consumption. It also shows the vitamin A estimated average requirement and recommended nutrient intake for a representative individual of the population of analysis.

Table 5.1: Availability of Vitamin A

	Average vitamin A availability (mcg RAE/ person/day)	Vitamin A mean requirement (mcg RAE/ person/day)	Ratio of vitamin A available to required (%)	Vitamin A recommended safe intake (mcg RAE/ person/day)	Ratio of vitamin A available to recommended (%)	Average retinol availability (mcg/person/ day)	Ratio of retinol available to vitamin A available (%)	Average beta-carotene availability (mcg/person/ day)
Total	717	279	257	527	136	22	3.0	8320
Quintiles of income								
Lowest quintile	682	276	247	522	131	12	1.8	8011
2	705	279	252	526	134	18	2.6	8211
3	714	280	255	528	135	21	2.9	8285
4	785	281	279	531	148	28	3.6	9048
Highest quintile	729	282	259	535	136	39	5.3	8247
Area								
Capital city	313	285	110	537	58	22	6.9	3487
Other urban areas	581	283	205	531	109	23	3.9	6660
Rural areas	770	278	277	526	146	22	2.8	8953
Household size								
One person	797	291	274	569	140	36	4.5	9107
Between 2 and 3 people	766	281	272	536	143	27	3.5	8843
Between 4 and 5 people	677	273	248	520	130	22	3.2	7837
Between 6 and 7 people	711	279	255	525	135	19	2.6	8280
More than 7	731	283	258	529	138	21	2.9	8482
Gender of the household head								
Male	694	279	249	528	131	22	3.1	8035
Female	820	282	291	524	156	22	2.7	9556

Vitamin A is an essential nutrient needed in small amounts by humans for the normal functioning of vision, growth and development, maintenance of epithelial cellular integrity, immune system functioning, and reproduction (FAO/WHO 2004). It can be found in food of animal origin or under the form of a precursor of vitamin A in vegetal origin food. Low intake of vitamin A (as carotenoids) tends to reflect low intake of fruits and vegetables (USHHS/USDA 2005). The main consequence of vitamin A deficiency is night blindness, which can develop into irreversible blindness.

Table 5.2: Availability of B Vitamins This table shows daily per person quantities of the vitamins B1 (thiamine), B2 (riboflavin), B6, and B12 (cobalamin) available for human consumption. It also shows their estimated average requirement and the cobalamin recommended nutrient intake for a representative individual of the population of analysis.

Thiamine deficiency occurs when the diet consists mainly of milled white cereals, including polished rice and wheat flour, all of which are very poor sources of thiamine (WHO/UNHCR 1999). A deficiency of thiamine results in the disease beriberi, which provokes damage to the nervous system, heart failure, and gastrointestinal illnesses. A deficiency of riboflavin, which is present in a wide variety of food, results in the condition of hypo- or ariboflavinosis. The major cause of the former is inadequate dietary intake, which is sometimes exacerbated by poor food storage or processing (FAO/WHO 2004).

Vitamin B6 can be found in a wide variety of food, and its deficiency results in an impairment of the immune system. "A deficiency of vitamin B6 alone is uncommon because it usually occurs in association with a deficit in other B-complex vitamins" (FAO/WHO 2004).

A deficiency in cobalamin could cause the autoimmune disease pernicious anemia. "Products from herbivorous animals, such as milk, meat, and eggs, constitute important dietary sources of cobalamin, unless the animal is subsisting in one of the many regions known to be geochemically deficient in cobalt" (FAO/WHO 2004).

Table 5.3: Availability of Vitamin C and Calcium This table shows the daily per person amount of vitamin C (ascorbic acid) and calcium available for human consumption, their recommended intake for a representative individual of the population of analysis, and the ratios between available and recommended quantities.

Table 5.2: Availability of B Vitamins

	Average vitamin B1 availability (mg/person/day)	Vitamin B1 recommended intake (mg/person/day)	Ratio vitamin B1 available to recommended (%)	Average vitamin B2 availability (mg/person/day)	Vitamin B2 recommended intake (mg/person/day)	Ratio vitamin B2 available to recommended (%)	Average vitamin B6 availability (mg/person/day)	Vitamin B6 recommended intake (mg/person/day)	Ratio vitamin B6 available to recommended (%)	Average vitamin B12 availability (mcg/person/day)	Vitamin B12 average requirement (mcg/person/day)	Ratio vitamin B12 available to required (%)	Vitamin B12 recommended intake (mcg/person/day)	Ratio vitamin B12 available to recommended (%)
Total	2.13	0.98	217	1.75	1.01	174	2.31	1.11	207	1.63	1.68	97	2.03	80
Quintiles of income														
Lowest quintile	1.86	0.95	195	1.32	0.97	136	1.90	1.08	177	0.97	1.63	60	1.97	49
2	2.20	0.98	225	2.25	1.00	225	2.22	1.11	200	1.33	1.67	80	2.01	66
3	2.16	0.98	220	1.70	1.01	169	2.37	1.11	213	1.69	1.69	100	2.03	83
4	2.28	1.00	229	1.73	1.02	169	2.59	1.14	228	2.04	1.71	119	2.06	99
Highest quintile	2.29	1.02	224	1.85	1.05	176	2.78	1.16	240	2.77	1.75	158	2.11	132
Area														
Capital city	1.41	1.03	137	1.19	1.05	113	1.49	1.16	128	1.79	1.77	102	2.12	84
Other urban areas	1.80	1.00	180	1.43	1.02	139	2.15	1.13	189	1.76	1.72	102	2.07	85
Rural areas	2.23	0.97	229	1.85	1.00	185	2.39	1.11	216	1.59	1.67	95	2.01	79
Household size														
One person	2.87	1.16	247	2.37	1.22	195	2.77	1.40	198	3.58	2.00	179	2.39	149
Between 2 and 3 people	2.40	1.04	231	1.99	1.07	186	2.62	1.21	215	2.20	1.80	122	2.16	102
Between 4 and 5 people	2.19	0.96	228	2.10	0.99	214	2.30	1.08	212	1.72	1.64	105	1.98	87
Between 6 and 7 people	2.17	0.96	225	1.50	0.98	152	2.31	1.08	213	1.40	1.65	85	1.99	71
More than 7	1.88	0.98	193	1.52	1.00	152	2.15	1.10	195	1.36	1.67	82	2.01	68
Gender of the household head														
Male	2.13	0.98	217	1.74	1.01	172	2.31	1.11	208	1.62	1.68	97	2.02	80
Female	2.11	0.99	215	1.81	1.00	182	2.29	1.13	203	1.66	1.71	97	2.06	80

Table 5.3: Availability of Vitamin C and Calcium

	Average vitamin C availability (mg/person/day)	Vitamin C recommended intake (mg/person/day)	Ratio vitamin C available to recommended (%)	Average calcium availability (mg/person/day)	Calcium recommended intake (mg/person/day)	Ratio calcium available to recommended (%)
Total	92.42	39.57	233.58	295.91	747.00	39.61
Quintiles of income						
Lowest quintile	77.54	38.83	199.69	215.85	739.24	29.20
2	92.20	39.34	234.40	286.70	748.71	38.29
3	94.11	39.60	237.63	301.06	749.28	40.18
4	100.28	40.02	250.58	340.82	752.37	45.30
Highest quintile	109.37	40.75	268.39	403.01	749.18	53.79
Area						
Capital city	50.46	40.70	124.00	279.42	760.71	36.73
Other urban areas	66.81	40.06	166.76	251.53	756.31	33.26
Rural areas	99.83	39.40	253.39	304.71	744.41	40.93
Household size						
One person	109.56	44.92	243.92	514.17	762.83	67.40
Between 2 and 3 people	103.95	41.72	249.18	373.42	749.59	49.82
Between 4 and 5 people	92.29	39.30	234.84	303.94	727.36	41.79
Between 6 and 7 people	93.23	38.92	239.54	270.75	748.61	36.17
More than 7	85.88	39.07	219.81	263.52	760.00	34.67
Gender of the household head						
Male	92.44	39.52	233.89	291.44	742.78	39.24
Female	92.31	39.75	232.23	315.23	765.26	41.19
Age of the household head						
Less than 35	92.49	38.82	238.24	298.52	696.02	42.89
Between 35 and 45	89.91	39.07	230.14	278.70	748.63	37.23
Between 46 and 60	92.93	40.12	231.61	311.90	774.21	40.29
More than 60	96.70	40.87	236.58	297.31	780.73	38.08

Ascorbic acid is an antioxidant, and it is found in many fruits and vegetables. The vitamin C content of food is strongly influenced by many factors, including transport to market, storage, and cooking practices. A common feature of vitamin C deficiency is anemia, because ascorbic acid is a promoter of nonheme iron absorption (FAO/WHO 2004). It is not possible to relate servings of fruits and vegetables to an exact amount of vitamin C, but the WHO dietary goal of 400g of fruits and vegetables consumed per day (five portions of them) is aimed at providing sufficient vitamin C to meet the 1970 FAO/WHO guidelines (FAO/WHO 2004).

Low intake of calcium tends to reflect low intake of milk and milk products (USHHS/USDA 2005). There is a wide variation in calcium intake between countries, generally following the animal protein intake and depending largely on dairy product consumption. Calcium salts provide rigidity to the skeleton, and calcium ions play a role in many, if not most, metabolic processes (FAO/WHO 2004). The populations at risk of calcium deficiency comprise children during the first two years of life, puberty, and adolescence; pregnant, lactating, and postmenopausal women; and, possibly, elderly men (FAO/WHO 2004).

Table 5.4: Availability of Iron   This table shows daily per person iron availability for human consumption according to its source (animal or nonanimal origin) and its status (heme or nonheme). The food commodities considered animal origin are meat (red and white), fish, eggs, milk, and cheese. It also shows the median and the 95th percentile[18] daily requirements of total iron intake for a representative individual of the population.

Table 5.4: Availability of Iron

	Average iron availability from animal sources (mg/person/day)	Average iron availability from nonanimal sources (mg/person/day)	Average heme iron availability (mg/person/day)	Average nonheme iron availability (mg/person/day)	Median of the average absolute iron intake required (mg/person/day)	95th percentile of the average absolute iron intake required (mg/person/day)
Total	0.29	16.14	0.11	16.33	1.09	1.59
Quintiles of income						
Lowest quintile	0.17	13.45	0.07	13.56	1.06	1.52
2	0.24	16.58	0.09	16.73	1.10	1.57
3	0.30	16.44	0.11	16.64	1.10	1.60
4	0.36	17.55	0.13	17.79	1.11	1.62
Highest quintile	0.50	18.47	0.18	18.80	1.12	1.69
Area						
Capital city	0.35	11.13	0.12	11.36	1.17	1.74
Other urban areas	0.30	13.79	0.10	13.99	1.13	1.68
Rural areas	0.29	16.91	0.11	17.09	1.08	1.56
Household size						
One person	0.65	19.81	0.24	20.22	1.11	1.66
Between 2 and 3 people	0.39	18.89	0.14	19.14	1.12	1.73
Between 4 and 5 people	0.32	16.53	0.11	16.74	1.06	1.57
Between 6 and 7 people	0.25	15.47	0.09	15.63	1.09	1.55
More than 7	0.25	14.97	0.09	15.12	1.11	1.58
Gender of the household head						
Male	0.29	16.06	0.11	16.24	1.08	1.57
Female	0.29	16.53	0.10	16.72	1.13	1.68
Age of the household head						
Less than 35	0.33	16.68	0.12	16.89	1.02	1.55
Between 35 and 45	0.29	15.54	0.10	15.73	1.11	1.61
Between 46 and 60	0.28	16.38	0.10	16.56	1.13	1.64
More than 60	0.26	16.05	0.10	16.21	1.10	1.54

Iron has several vital functions in the body, including the transportation of oxygen to the tissues from the lungs by red blood cell hemoglobin (WHO 2004). There are two kinds of iron compounds in the diet with respect to the mechanism of absorption: heme iron (derived from hemoglobin and myoglobin) and nonheme iron (derived mainly from cereals, fruits, and vegetables). Heme iron forms a relatively minor part of iron intake. Even in diets with high meat content it accounts for only 10–15 percent of the total iron intake. Diets in developing countries usually contain negligible amounts of heme iron. Nonheme iron is thus the main source of dietary iron (Hallberg 1981).

Table 5.5: Density of Calcium per 1,000 Kcal This table shows the nutrient density[19] of calcium (mg/1,000 kcal) present in the food consumed by the population, the recommended intake, and the ratio between available and recommended. The first is estimated based on calcium and calorie consumption (using the food consumption data from the survey), and the second is based

Table 5.5: Density of Calcium per 1,000 Kcal

	Average calcium availability (mg/1000 kcal)	Calcium recommended intake (mg/1000 kcal)	Ratio calcium available to recommended (%)	Average dietary energy requirement (kcal/person/day)
Total	139	355	39	2106
Quintiles of income				
Lowest quintile	138	366	38	2018
2	143	360	40	2080
3	137	356	39	2107
4	135	349	39	2155
Highest quintile	142	332	43	2254
Area				
Capital city	156	337	46	2256
Other urban areas	121	349	35	2166
Rural areas	141	357	40	2085
Household size				
One person	171	287	59	2654
Between 2 and 3 people	145	328	44	2285
Between 4 and 5 people	139	351	40	2071
Between 6 and 7 people	133	367	36	2041
More than 7	138	366	38	2078
Gender of the household head				
Male	137	351	39	2117
Female	149	372	40	2059
Age of the household head				
Less than 35	135	344	39	2024
Between 35 and 45	134	361	37	2072
Between 46 and 60	145	354	41	2189
More than 60	146	361	41	2162

on the recommended calcium intake and the average dietary energy require-ment.[20] The ratio compares the available and the recommended amounts and can be used to understand if (and to what extent) the amounts available are above or below the requirements.

The notion of nutrient density is helpful for defining food-based dietary guidelines (FBDG) and evaluating the adequacy of diets. Unlike recommended intakes, FBDG can be used to educate the public through the mass media and provide a practical guide to selecting foods by defining dietary adequacy (WHO 2004).

Table 5.6: Density of Vitamin A and Vitamin C per 1,000 Kcal This table shows the nutrient density[21] of vitamins A and C (mcg retinol activity equivalent [RAE] or mg/1,000 kcal) present in the food consumed by the population, the respective required densities, and the available to recommended ratios.

The nutrient density in the food consumed is estimated based on the nutrient and calorie consumption. The required nutrient density considers the estimated nutrient average requirement,[22] while the recommended one uses the recommended nutrient intake. Both required and recommended nutrient densities are based on the average dietary energy requirement.

The notion of nutrient density is helpful for defining food-based dietary guidelines and evaluating the adequacy of diets. Unlike recommended intakes, FBDG can be used to educate the public through the mass media and provide a practical guide to selecting foods by defining dietary adequacy (WHO 2004).

Table 5.7: Density of B Vitamins per 1,000 Kcal This table shows the nutrient density[23] of vitamins B1, B2, and B6 (in mg/1,000 kcal), and B12 (in mcg/1,000 kcal) present in the food consumed by the population. It also shows the required densities of the vitamins, the recommended one for vitamin B12, and the respective available to recommended ratios.

The nutrient density (grams of nutrient per 1,000 kcal) of the food consumed is estimated based on the nutrient and calorie consumption. Similarly, the required and recommended nutrient densities are calculated using the estimated nutrient average requirement and recommended nutrient intake, respectively. In both cases the 1,000 required calories are based on the average dietary energy requirements for a representative individual of the population.[24] For instance, the protein density of the food consumed refers to how many grams of protein are consumed per 1,000 calories consumed.

Table 5.6: Density of Vitamin A and Vitamin C per 1,000 Kcal

	Average vitamin A availability (mcg RAE/1000 kcal)	Vitamin A mean requirement, mcg RAE/1000 kcal	Ratio of vitamin A available to required (%)	Vitamin A recommended safe intake, mcg RAE/1000 kcal	Ratio of vitamin A available to recommended (%)	Average vitamin C availability (mg/1000 kcal)	Vitamin C recommended safe intake, mg/1000 kcal	Ratio vitamin C available to recommended (%)
Total	338	133	255	250	135	43	19	231
Quintiles of income								
Lowest quintile	435	137	318	259	168	49	19	257
2	352	134	262	253	139	46	19	244
3	326	133	245	250	130	43	19	229
4	312	131	239	246	127	40	19	215
Highest quintile	257	125	206	237	108	39	18	214
Area								
Capital city	175	126	138	238	74	28	18	156
Other urban areas	280	131	214	245	114	32	18	174
Rural areas	357	133	267	252	141	46	19	245
Household size								
One person	264	110	241	214	123	36	17	215
Between 2 and 3 people	298	123	242	234	127	40	18	221
Between 4 and 5 people	310	132	236	251	124	42	19	223
Between 6 and 7 people	349	137	255	257	136	46	19	240
More than 7	384	136	281	255	151	45	19	240
Gender of the household head								
Male	326	132	248	249	131	43	19	233
Female	388	137	284	255	153	44	19	226
Age of the household head								
Less than 35	342	130	263	252	136	42	19	219
Between 35 and 45	326	135	241	254	128	43	19	229
Between 46 and 60	316	132	240	245	129	43	18	236
More than 60	398	134	298	252	158	48	19	252

Table 5.7: Density of B Vitamins per 1,000 Kcal

	Average vitamin B1 availability (mg/1000 kcal)	Vitamin B1 recommended safe intake, mg/1000 kcal	Ratio vitamin B1 available to recommended (%)	Average vitamin B2 availability (mg/1000 kcal)	Vitamin B2 recommended safe intake, mg/1000 kcal	Ratio vitamin B2 available to recommended (%)	Average vitamin B6 availability (mg/1000 kcal)	Vitamin B6 recommended safe intake, mg/1000 kcal	Ratio vitamin B6 available to recommended (%)	Average vitamin B12 availability (mcg/1000 kcal)	Vitamin B12 average requirement, mcg/1000 kcal	Ratio vitamin B12 available to required (%)	Vitamin B12 recommended safe intake (mcg/1000 kcal)	Ratio vitamin B12 available to recommended (%)
Total	1.00	0.47	215	0.82	0.48	172	1.08	0.53	205	0.76	0.80	96	0.96	80
Quintiles of income														
Lowest quintile	1.18	0.47	251	0.84	0.48	175	1.21	0.53	228	0.62	0.81	77	0.97	64
2	1.10	0.47	234	1.13	0.48	234	1.11	0.53	208	0.67	0.80	83	0.97	69
3	0.99	0.47	212	0.78	0.48	163	1.08	0.53	205	0.77	0.80	96	0.96	80
4	0.91	0.46	196	0.69	0.48	145	1.03	0.53	195	0.81	0.80	102	0.96	85
Highest quintile	0.81	0.45	179	0.65	0.47	140	0.98	0.51	191	0.98	0.78	126	0.94	105
Area														
Capital city	0.79	0.45	173	0.67	0.47	142	0.83	0.51	161	1.00	0.78	128	0.94	106
Other urban areas	0.87	0.46	188	0.69	0.47	145	1.03	0.52	198	0.85	0.80	107	0.96	89
Rural areas	1.04	0.47	222	0.86	0.48	179	1.11	0.53	209	0.74	0.80	92	0.96	76
Household size														
One person	0.95	0.44	218	0.79	0.46	171	0.92	0.53	175	1.19	0.75	158	0.90	132
Between 2 and 3 people	0.93	0.46	205	0.77	0.47	165	1.02	0.53	191	0.85	0.79	108	0.95	90
Between 4 and 5 people	1.00	0.46	216	0.96	0.48	203	1.05	0.52	202	0.79	0.79	100	0.96	83
Between 6 and 7 people	1.06	0.47	226	0.74	0.48	153	1.13	0.53	214	0.69	0.81	85	0.97	71
More than 7	0.99	0.47	210	0.80	0.48	166	1.13	0.53	213	0.72	0.81	89	0.97	74
Gender of the household head														
Male	1.00	0.46	216	0.82	0.48	171	1.09	0.52	207	0.76	0.79	96	0.95	80
Female	1.00	0.48	209	0.86	0.48	178	1.08	0.55	198	0.79	0.83	94	1.00	78

Similarly, the nutrient density required/recommended of protein are the grams of protein required/recommended per 1,000 calories required.

The notion of nutrient density is helpful for defining food-based dietary guidelines and evaluating the adequacy of diets. Unlike recommended intakes, FBDG can be used to educate the public through the mass media and provide a practical guide to selecting foods by defining dietary adequacy (WHO 2004).

Disaggregated by Food Commodity Group: Tables 6.1 to 6.6

The micronutrients analyzed in the ADePT-Food Security Module are vitamin A, ascorbic acid, thiamine, riboflavin, B6, cobalamin, and the minerals calcium and iron. It is important to remember that the statistics shown in the tables exclude the food consumed away from home. Therefore, the values of total available vitamins and minerals are underestimated.

Table 6.1: Micronutrient Availability by Food Group   This table shows how much each food commodity group contributes, in quantitative terms, to the total micronutrient availability at the *national level*. Each time N/A replaces a nutrient quantity, it means that the amount of nutrient available from the food commodity group is very low or null, or there was no acquisition of that food group.

Table 6.2: Micronutrient Availability by Food Group and Income Quintile   This table shows how much each food commodity group contributes, in quantitative terms, to the total micronutrient availability in *each income quintile group*. Each time N/A replaces a nutrient quantity, it means that the amount of nutrient available from the food commodity group is very low or null, or there was no acquisition of that food group.

Table 6.3: Micronutrient Availability by Food Group and Area   This table shows how much each food commodity group contributes, in quantitative terms, to the total micronutrient availability in *urban and rural areas*. Each time N/A replaces a nutrient quantity, it means that the amount of nutrient available from the food commodity group is very low or null, or there was no acquisition of that food group.

Table 6.4: Micronutrient Availability by Food Group and Region   This table shows how much each food commodity group contributes, in quantitative terms, to the total micronutrient availability in *each region*. Each time N/A

Table 6.1: Micronutrient Availability by Food Group

Food group	RAE of vitamin A (mcg/person/day)	Retinol (mcg/person/day)	Beta-carotene (mcg/person/day)	Vitamin B1 (mg/person/day)	Vitamin B2 (mg/person/day)	Vitamin B6 (mg/person/day)	Vitamin B12 (mcg/person/day)	Vitamin C (mg/person/day)	Calcium (mg/person/day)	Animal iron (mg/person/day)	Nonanimal iron (mg/person/day)	Heme iron (mg/person/day)	Nonheme iron (mg/person/day)
Cereals	29.23	1.11	312.05	1.26	0.55	1.28	0.01	0.00	44.16	N/A	10.25	N/A	10.25
Roots and tubers	535.47	N/A	6425.59	0.23	0.14	0.51	N/A	52.23	42.72	N/A	1.54	N/A	1.54
Sugars and syrups	0.01	N/A	0.08	N/A	0.14	N/A	N/A	0.02	0.30	N/A	0.03	N/A	0.03
Pulses	1.04	N/A	12.56	0.14	0.06	0.09	N/A	0.37	17.17	N/A	1.75	N/A	1.75
Tree nuts	N/A	N/A	N/A	0.00	0.00	0.00	N/A	0.00	1.20	N/A	0.02	N/A	0.02
Oil crops	0.02	N/A	0.21	0.03	0.01	0.03	N/A	0.22	12.99	N/A	0.62	N/A	0.62
Vegetables	84.39	N/A	1011.89	0.37	0.67	0.11	N/A	14.65	58.88	N/A	1.23	N/A	1.23
Fruits	46.11	N/A	551.57	0.06	0.05	0.12	N/A	24.70	5.62	N/A	0.31	N/A	0.31
Stimulants	0.30	0.30	N/A	0.00	0.00	0.00	0.00	0.01	0.89	N/A	0.04	N/A	0.04
Spices	0.53	N/A	6.01	0.00	0.00	0.05	N/A	0.13	7.51	N/A	0.08	N/A	0.08
Alcoholic beverages	N/A	N/A	N/A	0.00	0.00	0.00	N/A	N/A	2.41	N/A	0.00	N/A	0.00
Meat	1.20	1.20	N/A	0.03	0.04	0.07	0.35	0.00	1.33	0.08	0.27	0.04	0.31
Eggs	1.27	1.27	N/A	0.00	0.00	0.00	0.01	N/A	0.38	0.01	N/A	N/A	0.01
Fish	5.49	5.49	N/A	0.01	0.02	0.04	1.10	0.07	54.76	0.18	N/A	0.06	0.12
Milk and cheese	11.38	11.38	N/A	0.06	0.06	0.00	0.16	0.07	45.41	0.03	N/A	N/A	0.03
Oils and fats (vegetable)	N/A	N/A	N/A	N/A	N/A	N/A	N/A	0.00	N/A	N/A	0.00	N/A	0.00
Oils and fats (animal)	1.03	1.03	N/A	0.00	0.00	N/A	0.00	0.00	0.03	N/A	0.00	N/A	0.00
Nonalcoholic beverages	N/A	N/A	N/A	N/A	N/A	N/A	N/A	N/A	0.15	N/A	N/A	N/A	N/A
Miscellaneous and prepared food													

Average micronutrient availability

Table 6.2: Micronutrient Availability by Food Group and Income Quintile

	Average micronutrient availability												
	RAE of vitamin A (mcg/ person/ day)	Retinol (mcg/ person/ day)	Beta-carotene (mcg/ person/ day)	Vitamin B1 (mg/ person/ day)	Vitamin B2 (mg/ person/ day)	Vitamin B6 (mg/ person/ day)	Vitamin B12 (mcg/ person/ day)	Vitamin C (mg/ person/ day)	Calcium (mg/ person/ day)	Animal iron (mg/ person/ day)	Nonanimal iron (mg/ person/ day)	Heme iron (mg/ person/ day)	Nonheme iron (mg/ person/ day)
Quintiles of income													
Lowest quintile													
Cereals	26.23	0.27	288.14	1.04	0.49	1.05	0.00	0.00	28.30	N/A	8.99	N/A	8.99
Roots and tubers	566.08	N/A	6792.96	0.25	0.13	0.56	N/A	56.86	43.26	N/A	1.52	N/A	1.52
Sugars and syrups	0.00	N/A	0.02	N/A	0.04	N/A	N/A	0.01	0.09	N/A	0.01	N/A	0.01
Pulses	0.73	N/A	8.80	0.10	0.04	0.06	N/A	0.27	12.51	N/A	1.27	N/A	1.27
Tree nuts	N/A	N/A	N/A	0.00	0.00	0.00	N/A	0.00	0.90	N/A	0.01	N/A	0.01
Oil crops	0.02	N/A	0.21	0.02	0.01	0.02	N/A	0.05	8.08	N/A	0.30	N/A	0.30
Vegetables	55.92	N/A	670.31	0.40	0.52	0.08	N/A	9.04	53.36	N/A	1.07	N/A	1.07
Fruits	20.82	N/A	249.41	0.03	0.02	0.05	N/A	11.20	2.17	N/A	0.14	N/A	0.14
Stimulants	0.10	0.10	N/A	0.00	0.00	0.00	0.00	0.00	0.21	N/A	0.01	N/A	0.01
Spices	0.08	N/A	0.95	0.00	0.00	0.00	N/A	0.03	3.83	N/A	0.03	N/A	0.03
Alcoholic beverages	N/A	N/A	N/A	0.00	0.02	0.02	N/A	0.00	1.21	N/A	0.00	N/A	0.00
Meat	0.68	0.68	N/A	0.01	0.02	0.03	0.15	0.00	0.59	0.04	0.11	0.02	0.13
Eggs	0.19	0.19	N/A	0.00	0.00	0.00	0.00	N/A	0.06	0.00	N/A	N/A	0.00
Fish	3.72	3.72	N/A	0.01	0.01	0.03	0.73	0.01	33.48	0.12	N/A	0.04	0.08
Milk and cheese	6.86	6.86	N/A	N/A	0.03	0.00	0.09	0.06	27.77	0.01	N/A	N/A	0.01
Oils and fats (vegetable)	N/A	N/A	N/A	N/A	N/A	N/A	N/A	0.00	N/A	N/A	0.00	N/A	0.00
Oils and fats (animal)	0.56	0.56	N/A	N/A	0.00	N/A	0.00	N/A	0.01	N/A	0.01	N/A	0.00
Nonalcoholic beverages	N/A	N/A	N/A	N/A	N/A	N/A	N/A	N/A	0.01	N/A	N/A	N/A	N/A
Quintile 2													
Cereals	30.37	0.53	334.37	1.23	0.56	1.23	0.00	0.00	37.44	N/A	10.71	N/A	10.71
Roots and tubers	529.41	N/A	6352.88	0.24	0.13	0.52	N/A	53.83	42.79	N/A	1.51	N/A	1.51
Sugars and syrups	0.00	N/A	0.04	N/A	0.08	N/A	N/A	0.01	0.19	N/A	0.02	N/A	0.02
Pulses	0.93	N/A	11.15	0.12	0.05	0.08	N/A	0.32	15.34	N/A	1.55	N/A	1.55

Table 6.3: Micronutrient Availability by Food Group and Area

Area	RAE of vitamin A (mcg/person/day)	Retinol (mcg/person/day)	Beta-carotene (mcg/person/day)	Vitamin B1 (mg/person/day)	Vitamin B2 (mg/person/day)	Vitamin B6 (mg/person/day)	Vitamin B12 (mcg/person/day)	Vitamin C (mg/person/day)	Calcium (mg/person/day)	Animal iron (mg/person/day)	Nonanimal iron (mg/person/day)	Heme iron (mg/person/day)	Nonheme iron (mg/person/day)
Area													
Capital city													
Cereals	18.30	3.55	174.36	1.10	0.36	1.00	0.02	0.00	60.20	N/A	7.42	N/A	7.42
Roots and tubers	140.16	N/A	1681.92	0.03	0.06	0.08	N/A	7.81	9.99	N/A	0.49	N/A	0.49
Sugars and syrups	0.01	N/A	0.13	N/A	0.22	N/A	N/A	0.04	0.65	N/A	0.06	N/A	0.06
Pulses	0.81	N/A	9.74	0.09	0.04	0.06	N/A	0.20	11.79	N/A	1.22	N/A	1.22
Tree nuts	N/A	N/A	N/A	0.00	0.00	0.00	N/A	0.00	0.49	N/A	0.01	N/A	0.01
Oil crops	0.00	N/A	0.02	0.01	0.00	0.03	N/A	0.82	6.42	N/A	0.72	N/A	0.72
Vegetables	111.82	N/A	1341.86	0.07	0.35	0.10	N/A	17.56	20.21	N/A	0.54	N/A	0.54
Fruits	22.22	N/A	256.61	0.05	0.03	0.08	N/A	23.59	11.06	N/A	0.17	N/A	0.17
Stimulants	0.03	0.03	N/A	0.00	0.01	0.00	0.00	0.00	0.68	N/A	0.03	N/A	0.03
Spices	1.96	N/A	22.11	0.00	0.00	0.01	N/A	0.39	10.38	N/A	0.15	N/A	0.15
Alcoholic beverages	N/A	N/A	N/A	0.00	0.00	0.01	N/A	N/A	0.63	N/A	0.00	N/A	0.00
Meat	0.90	0.90	N/A	0.04	0.04	0.07	0.44	0.01	1.51	0.06	0.34	0.03	0.36
Eggs	3.22	3.22	N/A	0.00	0.01	0.00	0.02	N/A	0.95	0.02	N/A	N/A	0.02
Fish	3.79	3.79	N/A	0.01	0.03	0.05	1.24	0.01	123.59	0.25	N/A	0.09	0.16
Milk and cheese	4.98	4.98	N/A	N/A	N/A	0.00	0.07	0.01	20.02	0.02	N/A	N/A	0.02
Oils and fats (vegetable)	N/A	N/A	N/A	N/A	N/A	N/A	N/A	0.00	N/A	N/A	0.00	N/A	0.00
Oils and fats (animal)	5.04	5.04	N/A	N/A	0.00	N/A	0.00	N/A	0.13	N/A	N/A	N/A	N/A
Nonalcoholic beverages	N/A	N/A	N/A	N/A	N/A	N/A	N/A	N/A	0.73	N/A	N/A	N/A	N/A
Other urban areas													
Cereals	27.61	2.46	268.48	1.29	0.52	1.43	0.02	0.00	53.25	N/A	9.27	N/A	9.27
Roots and tubers	400.48	N/A	4805.70	0.12	0.11	0.27	N/A	26.31	25.01	N/A	1.03	N/A	1.03
Sugars and syrups	0.01	N/A	0.13	N/A	0.23	N/A	N/A	0.03	0.48	N/A	0.04	N/A	0.04
Pulses	0.88	N/A	10.63	0.10	0.05	0.06	N/A	0.22	13.14	N/A	1.35	N/A	1.35

Table 6.4: Micronutrient Availability by Food Group and Region

	RAE of vitamin A (mcg/person/day)	Retinol (mcg/person/day)	Beta-carotene (mcg/person/day)	Vitamin B1 (mg/person/day)	Vitamin B2 (mg/person/day)	Vitamin B6 (mg/person/day)	Vitamin B12 (mcg/person/day)	Vitamin C (mg/person/day)	Calcium (mg/person/day)	Animal iron (mg/person/day)	Nonanimal iron (mg/person/day)	Heme iron (mg/person/day)	Nonheme iron (mg/person/day)
Region													
Region 1													
Cereals	40.61	0.91	458.79	1.56	0.73	1.44	0.01	0.00	53.45	N/A	15.65	N/A	15.65
Roots and tubers	238.05	N/A	2856.58	0.04	0.05	0.08	N/A	7.68	9.02	N/A	0.38	N/A	0.38
Sugars and syrups	0.00	N/A	0.05	N/A	0.09	N/A	N/A	0.02	0.24	N/A	0.02	N/A	0.02
Pulses	1.04	N/A	12.49	0.17	0.07	0.12	N/A	0.70	22.12	N/A	2.22	N/A	2.22
Tree nuts	N/A	N/A	N/A	0.00	0.00	0.00	N/A	0.00	0.47	N/A	0.01	N/A	0.01
Oil crops	0.00	N/A	0.03	0.06	0.02	0.06	N/A	0.04	19.44	N/A	0.96	N/A	0.96
Vegetables	95.08	N/A	1137.44	0.49	0.70	0.25	N/A	17.67	190.03	N/A	3.81	N/A	3.81
Fruits	8.78	N/A	104.99	0.02	0.01	0.03	N/A	23.13	4.33	N/A	0.07	N/A	0.07
Stimulants	0.17	0.17	N/A	0.00	0.00	0.00	0.00	0.01	0.50	N/A	0.03	N/A	0.03
Spices	0.74	N/A	8.33	0.00	0.00	0.00	N/A	0.12	6.45	N/A	0.04	N/A	0.04
Alcoholic beverages	N/A	N/A	N/A	0.00	0.00	0.06	N/A	N/A	2.98	N/A	0.00	N/A	0.00
Meat	0.89	0.89	N/A	0.03	0.04	0.06	0.33	0.01	1.16	0.06	0.26	0.03	0.29
Eggs	0.99	0.99	N/A	0.00	0.00	0.00	0.01	N/A	0.29	0.01	N/A	N/A	0.01
Fish	1.70	1.70	N/A	0.00	0.01	0.02	0.56	0.00	33.65	0.08	N/A	0.03	0.05
Milk and cheese	14.84	14.84	N/A	N/A	0.07	0.00	0.21	0.16	62.35	0.02	N/A	N/A	0.02
Oils and fats (vegetable)	N/A	N/A	N/A	N/A	N/A	N/A	N/A	0.00	N/A	N/A	0.00	N/A	0.00
Oils and fats (animal)	0.45	0.45	N/A	0.00	0.00	N/A	0.00	N/A	0.01	N/A	0.00	N/A	0.00
Nonalcoholic beverages	N/A	N/A	N/A	N/A	N/A	N/A	N/A	N/A	0.06	N/A	N/A	N/A	N/A

replaces a nutrient quantity, it means that the amount of nutrient available from the food commodity group is very low or null, or there was no acquisition of that food group.

Table 6.5: Contribution of Food Groups to Micronutrient Availability   This table shows how much each food commodity group contributes, in percentage, to the total micronutrient availability at the *national level*. The total of each column is equal to 100 percent. The disaggregation of these statistics by food commodity groups helps identify the main food commodity group or groups as sources of each micronutrient.

Table 6.6: Contribution of Food Groups to Micronutrient Availability by Area   This table shows how much each food commodity group contributes, in percentage, to the total micronutrient availability in *urban and rural areas*. The total of each column is equal to 100 percent. The disaggregation of these statistics by food commodity groups helps identify differences in urban and rural areas for the main food commodity group or groups as sources of each micronutrient.

Disaggregated by Food Commodity: Tables 6.7 to 6.9

The food commodities analyzed are those collected in the survey excluding those consumed away from home. The food commodity quantities refer to edible portions, which mean they exclude the nonedible parts (peels, bones, etc.).

Table 6.7: Micronutrient Availability by Food Item   This table shows food commodity edible quantities and their contribution to the total micronutrient availability for human consumption at the *national level*. This table is useful to identify which food commodities are the main providers of micronutrients at the national level.

Table 6.8: Micronutrient Availability by Food Item and Area   This table shows food commodity edible quantities and their contribution to the total amount of micronutrients available for human consumption in *urban and rural areas*. This table is useful to identify which food commodities are the main providers of micronutrients within rural and urban areas as well as differences between rural and urban patterns.

Table 6.9: Micronutrient Availability by Food Item and Region   This table shows food commodity edible quantities and their contribution to the total

Table 6.5: Contribution of Food Groups to Micronutrient Availability

Food group	RAE of vitamin A	Retinol	Beta-carotene	Vitamin B1	Vitamin B2	Vitamin B6	Vitamin B12	Vitamin C	Calcium	Animal iron	Nonanimal iron	Heme iron	Nonheme iron
								Average micronutrient availability, % of total availability					
Cereals	4.07	5.09	3.75	59.10	31.32	55.69	0.46	0.00	14.92	0.00	63.46	0.00	62.73
Roots and tubers	74.63	0.00	77.23	11.02	7.77	22.26	0.00	56.51	14.44	0.00	9.54	0.00	9.43
Sugars and syrups	0.00	0.00	0.00	0.00	8.14	0.00	0.00	0.02	0.10	0.00	0.16	0.00	0.16
Pulses	0.15	0.00	0.15	6.38	3.42	3.76	0.00	0.40	5.80	0.00	10.87	0.00	10.74
Tree nuts	0.00	0.00	0.00	0.04	0.21	0.02	0.00	0.00	0.41	0.00	0.11	0.00	0.11
Oil crops	0.00	0.00	0.00	1.39	0.55	1.50	0.00	0.23	4.39	0.00	3.85	0.00	3.80
Vegetables	11.76	0.00	12.16	17.17	38.05	4.74	0.00	15.85	19.90	0.00	7.64	0.00	7.56
Fruits	6.43	0.00	6.63	2.80	2.90	5.11	0.00	26.73	1.90	0.00	1.91	0.00	1.89
Stimulants	0.04	1.37	0.00	0.02	0.26	0.05	0.16	0.01	0.30	0.00	0.25	0.00	0.24
Spices	0.07	0.00	0.07	0.03	0.06	0.12	0.00	0.14	2.54	0.00	0.51	0.00	0.51
Alcoholic beverages	0.00	0.00	0.00	0.00	0.00	2.04	0.00	0.00	0.82	0.00	0.00	0.00	0.00
Meat	0.17	5.51	0.00	1.58	2.30	2.89	21.73	0.00	0.45	26.40	1.68	40.32	1.88
Eggs	0.18	5.82	0.00	0.04	0.21	0.03	0.51	0.00	0.13	3.07	0.00	0.00	0.06
Fish	0.77	25.20	0.00	0.43	1.16	1.79	67.59	0.02	18.51	61.40	0.00	59.68	0.72
Milk and cheese	1.59	52.26	0.00	0.00	3.62	0.00	9.54	0.08	15.35	9.13	0.00	0.00	0.16
Oils and fats (vegetable)	0.00	0.00	0.00	0.00	0.00	0.00	0.00	0.00	0.00	0.00	0.00	0.00	0.00
Oils and fats (animal)	0.14	4.74	0.00	0.00	0.02	0.00	0.02	0.00	0.01	0.00	0.00	0.00	0.00
Nonalcoholic beverages	0.00	0.00	0.00	0.00	0.00	0.00	0.00	0.00	0.05	0.00	0.00	0.00	0.00

Table 6.6: Contribution of Food Groups to Micronutrient Availability by Area

Food group/area	RAE of vitamin A	Retinol	Beta-carotene	Vitamin B1	Vitamin B2	Vitamin B6	Vitamin B12	Vitamin C	Calcium	Animal iron	Nonanimal iron	Heme iron	Nonheme iron
Capital city													
Cereals	5.84	16.50	5.00	77.84	30.13	66.99	1.19	0.00	21.54	0.00	66.63	0.00	65.28
Roots and tubers	44.74	0.00	48.24	2.45	4.95	5.53	0.00	15.49	3.58	0.00	4.40	0.00	4.31
Sugars and syrups	0.00	0.00	0.00	0.00	18.89	0.00	0.00	0.09	0.23	0.00	0.50	0.00	0.49
Pulses	0.26	0.00	0.28	6.65	3.59	3.87	0.00	0.41	4.22	0.00	10.92	0.00	10.70
Tree nuts	0.00	0.00	0.00	0.03	0.13	0.01	0.00	0.00	0.17	0.00	0.07	0.00	0.07
Oil crops	0.00	0.00	0.00	0.58	0.23	2.15	0.00	1.62	2.30	0.00	6.48	0.00	6.35
Vegetables	35.70	0.00	38.48	4.84	29.43	6.56	0.00	34.79	7.23	0.00	4.84	0.00	4.75
Fruits	7.09	0.00	7.36	3.53	2.28	5.24	0.00	46.76	3.96	0.00	1.51	0.00	1.48
Stimulants	0.01	0.15	0.00	0.03	0.45	0.13	0.02	0.00	0.24	0.00	0.26	0.00	0.25
Spices	0.63	0.00	0.63	0.11	0.24	0.39	0.00	0.78	3.72	0.00	1.36	0.00	1.34
Alcoholic beverages	0.00	0.00	0.00	0.00	0.00	0.61	0.00	0.00	0.23	0.00	0.00	0.00	0.00
Meat	0.29	4.18	0.00	2.89	3.48	4.99	24.30	0.03	0.54	17.18	3.03	27.37	3.21
Eggs	1.03	14.96	0.00	0.14	0.80	0.13	1.17	0.00	0.34	6.50	0.00	0.00	0.20
Fish	1.21	17.63	0.00	0.90	2.47	3.39	69.40	0.02	44.23	71.63	0.00	72.63	1.44
Milk and cheese	1.59	23.15	0.00	0.00	2.80	0.00	3.84	0.02	7.17	4.69	0.00	0.00	0.15
Oils and fats (vegetable)	0.00	0.00	0.00	0.00	0.00	0.00	0.00	0.00	0.00	0.00	0.01	0.00	0.01
Oils and fats (animal)	1.61	23.44	0.00	0.00	0.12	0.00	0.08	0.00	0.04	0.00	0.00	0.00	0.00
Nonalcoholic beverages	0.00	0.00	0.00	0.00	0.00	0.00	0.00	0.00	0.26	0.00	0.00	0.00	0.00
Other urban areas													
Cereals	4.75	10.85	4.03	71.65	36.19	66.48	0.90	0.01	21.17	0.00	67.24	0.00	66.30
Roots and tubers	68.97	0.00	72.16	6.53	7.91	12.40	0.00	39.39	9.94	0.00	7.48	0.00	7.37
Sugars and syrups	0.00	0.00	0.00	0.00	16.07	0.00	0.00	0.04	0.19	0.00	0.30	0.00	0.30
Pulses	0.15	0.00	0.16	5.82	3.35	2.98	0.00	0.34	5.22	0.00	9.82	0.00	9.68
Tree nuts	0.00	0.00	0.00	0.03	0.15	0.01	0.00	0.00	0.27	0.00	0.07	0.00	0.07
Oil crops	0.00	0.00	0.00	1.26	0.53	1.51	0.00	0.51	3.68	0.00	4.35	0.00	4.29
Vegetables	16.70	0.00	17.46	9.10	23.36	4.70	0.00	26.12	11.61	0.00	5.09	0.00	5.02
Fruits	5.76	0.00	6.00	2.66	2.68	4.57	0.00	33.12	2.65	0.00	1.68	0.00	1.65

Average micronutrient availability, % of total availability

Table 6.7: Micronutrient Availability by Food Item

Food item	Average edible quantity consumed (g/person/day)	RAE of vitamin A (mcg/person/day)	Retinol (mcg/person/day)	Beta-carotene (mcg/person/day)	Vitamin B1 (mg/person/day)	Vitamin B2 (mg/person/day)	Vitamin B6 (mg/person/day)	Vitamin B12 (mcg/person/day)	Vitamin C (mg/person/day)	Calcium (mg/person/day)	Animal iron (mg/person/day)	Nonanimal iron (mg/person/day)	Heme iron (mg/person/day)	Nonheme iron (mg/person/day)
Rice paddy or rough	6.12	0.00	0.00	0.00	0.00	0.00	0.01	0.00	0.00	0.55	0.00	0.05	0.00	0.05
Rice husked	48.14	0.00	0.00	0.00	0.20	0.02	0.25	0.00	0.00	15.88	0.00	0.87	0.00	0.87
Maize cob fresh	9.29	0.65	0.00	7.80	0.01	0.00	0.00	0.00	0.28	0.09	0.00	0.03	0.00	0.03
Maize grain	72.72	8.00	0.00	70.54	0.28	0.15	0.45	0.00	0.00	5.09	0.00	1.97	0.00	1.97
Maize flour	163.94	18.03	0.00	216.40	0.66	0.33	0.49	0.00	0.00	9.84	0.00	5.74	0.00	5.74
Millet whole grain dried	1.68	0.34	0.00	4.04	0.01	0.00	0.01	0.00	0.00	0.71	0.00	0.13	0.00	0.13
Millet foxtail Italian whole grain	1.17	0.06	0.00	0.70	0.00	0.00	0.00	0.00	0.00	3.22	0.00	0.03	0.00	0.03
Sorghum whole grain brown	7.91	0.47	0.00	5.69	0.02	0.01	0.02	0.00	0.00	1.19	0.00	0.32	0.00	0.32
Sorghum average of all varieties	20.38	1.22	0.00	14.68	0.04	0.02	0.04	0.00	0.00	3.06	0.00	0.84	0.00	0.84
Wheat durum whole grain	0.46	0.00	0.00	0.00	0.00	0.00	0.00	0.00	0.00	0.16	0.00	0.02	0.00	0.02
Wheat meal or flour unspecied wheat	4.41	0.00	0.00	0.00	0.00	0.00	0.00	0.00	0.00	0.66	0.00	0.05	0.00	0.05
Wheat	1.30	0.00	0.00	0.00	0.02	0.01	0.02	0.00	0.00	0.51	0.00	0.08	0.00	0.08
Bread	3.11	0.00	0.00	0.00	0.00	0.00	0.00	0.00	0.00	0.31	0.00	0.02	0.00	0.02
Baby cereals	0.09	0.00	0.00	0.00	0.02	0.00	0.00	0.00	0.00	0.28	0.00	0.00	0.00	0.00
Biscuits wheat from Europe	0.15	0.00	0.00	0.00	0.03	0.00	0.00	0.00	0.00	0.18	0.00	0.00	0.00	0.00
Buns cakes	3.25	1.11	1.11	0.00	0.00	0.00	0.00	0.01	0.00	1.24	0.00	0.01	0.00	0.01
Macaroni spaghetti	0.27	0.00	0.00	0.00	0.00	0.00	0.00	0.00	0.00	0.04	0.00	0.00	0.00	0.00
Oats	2.31	0.00	0.00	0.00	0.02	0.00	0.00	0.00	0.00	1.24	0.00	0.11	0.00	0.11
Cassava sweet roots raw	28.98	0.29	0.00	3.48	0.03	0.00	0.03	0.00	5.97	4.64	0.00	0.09	0.00	0.09
Cassava sweet roots dried	14.31	2.00	0.00	24.04	0.04	0.01	0.10	0.00	10.30	6.58	0.00	0.27	0.00	0.27
Cassava flour	35.67	4.99	0.00	59.93	0.11	0.04	0.25	0.00	25.68	16.41	0.00	0.68	0.00	0.68
Sweet potato	50.00	527.96	0.00	6335.53	0.05	0.05	0.10	0.00	9.00	10.00	0.00	0.20	0.00	0.20
Coco yam tuber	5.45	0.22	0.00	2.62	0.01	0.00	0.02	0.00	0.25	2.35	0.00	0.01	0.00	0.01

Average micronutrient availability

Table 6.8: Micronutrient Availability by Food Item and Area

Food item/area	Average edible quantity consumed (g/person/day)	RAE of vitamin A (mcg/person/day)	Retinol (mcg/person/day)	Beta-carotene (mcg/person/day)	Vitamin B1 (mg/person/day)	Vitamin B2 (mg/person/day)	Vitamin B6 (mg/person/day)	Vitamin B12 (mcg/person/day)	Vitamin C (mg/person/day)	Calcium (mg/person/day)	Animal iron (mg/person/day)	Nonanimal iron (mg/person/day)	Heme iron (mg/person/day)	Nonheme iron (mg/person/day)
Capital city														
Rice paddy or rough	0.60	0.00	0.00	0.00	0.00	0.00	0.00	0.00	0.00	0.05	0.00	0.00	0.00	0.00
Rice husked	108.34	0.00	0.00	0.00	0.45	0.05	0.55	0.00	0.00	35.75	0.00	1.95	0.00	1.95
Maize cob fresh	0.68	0.05	0.00	0.57	0.00	0.00	0.00	0.00	0.02	0.01	0.00	0.00	0.00	0.00
Maize grain	7.68	0.84	0.00	7.45	0.03	0.02	0.05	0.00	0.00	0.54	0.00	0.21	0.00	0.21
Maize flour	125.27	13.78	0.00	165.36	0.50	0.25	0.38	0.00	0.00	7.52	0.00	4.38	0.00	4.38
Millet whole grain dried	0.42	0.08	0.00	1.00	0.00	0.00	0.00	0.00	0.00	0.17	0.00	0.03	0.00	0.03
Millet foxtail Italian whole grain	0.71	0.04	0.00	0.42	0.00	0.00	0.00	0.00	0.00	1.94	0.00	0.02	0.00	0.02
Sorghum whole grain brown	0.13	0.01	0.00	0.09	0.00	0.00	0.00	0.00	0.00	0.02	0.00	0.01	0.00	0.01
Sorghum average of all varieties	0.04	0.00	0.00	0.03	0.00	0.00	0.00	0.00	0.00	0.01	0.00	0.00	0.00	0.00
Wheat durum whole grain	0.24	0.00	0.00	0.00	0.00	0.00	0.00	0.00	0.00	0.08	0.00	0.01	0.00	0.01
Wheat meal or flour unspecified wheat	10.40	0.00	0.00	0.00	0.01	0.00	0.00	0.00	0.00	1.56	0.00	0.12	0.00	0.12
Wheat	0.21	0.00	0.00	0.00	0.00	0.00	0.00	0.00	0.00	0.08	0.00	0.01	0.00	0.01
Bread	16.83	0.00	0.00	0.00	0.02	0.02	0.00	0.00	0.00	1.68	0.00	0.08	0.00	0.08
Baby cereals	0.04	0.00	0.00	0.00	0.00	0.00	0.00	0.00	0.00	0.12	0.00	0.00	0.00	0.00
Biscuits wheat from Europe	0.50	0.13	0.00	1.57	0.01	0.00	0.00	0.00	0.00	0.60	0.00	0.01	0.00	0.01
Buns cakes	10.44	3.55	3.55	0.00	0.00	0.01	0.00	0.02	0.00	3.97	0.00	0.04	0.00	0.04
Macaroni spaghetti	2.18	0.00	0.00	0.00	0.00	0.00	0.00	0.00	0.00	0.33	0.00	0.03	0.00	0.03
Oats	10.69	0.00	0.00	0.00	0.08	0.01	0.01	0.00	0.00	5.77	0.00	0.50	0.00	0.50
Cassava sweet roots raw	13.06	0.13	0.00	1.57	0.01	0.00	0.01	0.00	2.69	2.09	0.00	0.04	0.00	0.04
Cassava sweet roots dried	1.09	0.15	0.00	1.83	0.00	0.00	0.01	0.00	0.78	0.50	0.00	0.02	0.00	0.02
Cassava flour	0.83	0.12	0.00	1.40	0.00	0.00	0.01	0.00	0.60	0.38	0.00	0.02	0.00	0.02
Sweet potato	13.23	139.66	0.00	1675.95	0.01	0.01	0.03	0.00	2.38	2.65	0.00	0.05	0.00	0.05
Coco yam tuber	2.45	0.10	0.00	1.18	0.00	0.00	0.01	0.00	0.11	1.06	0.00	0.00	0.00	0.00

Average micronutrient availability

Table 6.9: Micronutrient Availability by Food Item and Region

Food item/region	Average edible quantity consumed (g/person/ day)	RAE of vitamin A (mcg/ person/ day)	Retinol (mcg/ person/ day)	Beta-carotene (mcg/ person/ day)	Vitamin B1 (mg/ person/ day)	Vitamin B2 (mg/ person/ day)	Vitamin B6 (mg/ person/ day)	Vitamin B12 (mcg/ person/ day)	Vitamin C (mg/ person/ day)	Calcium (mg/ person/ day)	Animal iron (mg/ person/ day)	Nonanimal iron (mg/ person/ day)	Heme iron (mg/ person/ day)	Nonheme iron (mg/ person/ day)
Region 1														
Rice paddy or rough	0.29	0.00	0.00	0.00	0.00	0.00	0.00	0.00	0.00	0.03	0.00	0.00	0.00	0.00
Rice husked	26.25	0.00	0.00	0.00	0.11	0.01	0.13	0.00	0.00	8.66	0.00	0.47	0.00	0.47
Maize cob fresh	11.73	0.82	0.00	9.85	0.01	0.00	0.00	0.00	0.35	0.12	0.00	0.04	0.00	0.04
Maize grain	50.15	5.52	0.00	48.64	0.19	0.10	0.31	0.00	0.00	3.51	0.00	1.36	0.00	1.36
Maize flour	240.10	26.41	0.00	316.93	0.96	0.48	0.72	0.00	0.00	14.41	0.00	8.40	0.00	8.40
Millet whole grain dried	1.68	0.34	0.00	4.03	0.01	0.00	0.01	0.00	0.00	0.71	0.00	0.13	0.00	0.13
Millet foxtail Italian whole grain	1.67	0.08	0.00	1.00	0.01	0.00	0.00	0.00	0.00	4.59	0.00	0.05	0.00	0.05
Sorghum whole grain brown	20.07	1.20	0.00	14.45	0.04	0.02	0.04	0.00	0.00	3.01	0.00	0.82	0.00	0.82
Sorghum average of all varieties	102.41	6.14	0.00	73.74	0.20	0.10	0.20	0.00	0.00	15.36	0.00	4.20	0.00	4.20
Wheat durum whole grain	0.05	0.00	0.00	0.00	0.00	0.00	0.00	0.00	0.00	0.02	0.00	0.00	0.00	0.00
Wheat meal or flour unspecified wheat	3.35	0.00	0.00	0.00	0.00	0.00	0.00	0.00	0.00	0.50	0.00	0.04	0.00	0.04
Wheat	1.40	0.00	0.00	0.00	0.03	0.01	0.02	0.00	0.00	0.55	0.00	0.09	0.00	0.09
Bread	1.07	0.00	0.00	0.00	0.00	0.00	0.00	0.00	0.00	0.11	0.00	0.01	0.00	0.01
Baby cereals	0.04	0.00	0.00	0.00	0.00	0.00	0.00	0.00	0.00	0.11	0.00	0.00	0.00	0.00
Biscuits wheat from Europe	0.09	0.00	0.00	0.00	0.01	0.00	0.00	0.00	0.00	0.11	0.00	0.00	0.00	0.00
Buns cakes	2.69	0.91	0.91	0.00	0.00	0.00	0.00	0.01	0.00	1.02	0.00	0.01	0.00	0.01
Macaroni spaghetti	0.12	0.00	0.00	0.00	0.00	0.00	0.00	0.00	0.00	0.02	0.00	0.00	0.00	0.00
Oats	1.38	0.00	0.00	0.00	0.01	0.00	0.00	0.00	0.00	0.74	0.00	0.00	0.00	0.00
Cassava sweet roots raw	11.73	0.12	0.00	1.41	0.01	0.00	0.01	0.00	2.42	1.88	0.00	0.04	0.00	0.04
Cassava sweet roots dried	0.16	0.02	0.00	0.27	0.00	0.00	0.00	0.00	0.11	0.07	0.00	0.00	0.00	0.00
Cassava flour	0.29	0.04	0.00	0.48	0.00	0.00	0.00	0.00	0.21	0.13	0.00	0.01	0.00	0.01
Sweet potato	22.52	237.86	0.00	2854.31	0.02	0.02	0.05	0.00	4.05	4.50	0.00	0.09	0.00	0.09
Coco yam tuber	0.24	0.01	0.00	0.11	0.00	0.00	0.00	0.00	0.01	0.10	0.00	0.00	0.00	0.00

micronutrient availability for human consumption at the *regional level*. This table is useful to identify which food commodities are the main providers of micronutrients within each region and to detect differences across regions.

Availability of Amino Acids

Amino acids are the building blocks of proteins and have an important role in human bodies. Some of their functions include building cells, protecting the body from viruses or bacteria, repairing damaged tissue, providing nitrogen, and carrying oxygen throughout the body. They can be classified as dispensable or indispensable. The latter are also called essential amino acids and cannot be synthesized by the human body. Therefore, the indispensable amino acids should be supplied to the body through the consumption of proteins in food.

Please note that the statistics on amino acids shown in the tables exclude the food consumed away from home. Therefore, the total available amino acids are underestimated.

Disaggregated by Population Group: Tables 7.1 to 7.2

Table 7.1: Protein Consumption and Amino Acid Availability This table shows the availability of indispensable amino acids in terms of grams per person per day.

Table 7.2: Amino Acid Availability per Gram of Protein This table shows the availability of indispensable amino acids in terms of milligrams per gram of protein.

Disaggregated by Population Group: Tables 8.1 to 8.7

It is important to know that the statistics shown exclude the food consumed away from home. Therefore, the total available amino acids are underestimated.

Table 8.1: Availability of Amino Acids by Food Group This table shows the available grams of amino acids provided by each food commodity group at the *national level*. Each time N/A replaces a nutrient quantity, it means that the amount of nutrient available from the food commodity group is very low or null, or there was no acquisition of that food group.

Table 7.1: Protein Consumption and Amino Acid Availability

	Average food consumption in monetary value (LCU/person/day)	Average protein consumption (g/person/day)	Average amino acid availability (g/person/day)								
			Lysine	Valine	Isoleucine	Leucine	Methionine and cystine	Threonine	Histidine	Phenylalanine and tyrosine	Tryptophan
Total	211.61	46.64	1.83	1.73	1.39	2.88	1.20	1.28	0.95	2.67	0.61
Quintiles of income											
Lowest quintile	99.77	34.03	1.17	1.16	0.91	1.99	0.82	0.85	0.62	1.78	0.47
2	162.53	44.18	1.59	1.55	1.24	2.60	1.07	1.14	0.84	2.39	0.56
3	212.21	47.62	1.85	1.76	1.41	2.95	1.22	1.31	0.97	2.73	0.62
4	288.45	54.36	2.24	2.10	1.70	3.47	1.46	1.56	1.17	3.26	0.71
Highest quintile	413.21	64.14	2.94	2.63	2.16	4.22	1.83	1.97	1.46	4.05	0.82
Area											
Capital city	343.33	40.96	1.89	1.70	1.39	2.61	1.17	1.26	0.92	2.61	0.43
Other urban areas	277.28	45.48	1.94	1.85	1.49	3.12	1.29	1.38	1.04	2.90	0.53
Rural areas	190.86	47.25	1.80	1.71	1.37	2.85	1.19	1.27	0.93	2.64	0.64
Household size											
One person	421.07	67.97	3.20	2.69	2.24	4.28	1.86	2.05	1.50	4.13	0.83
Between 2 and 3 people	295.05	56.93	2.33	2.13	1.73	3.46	1.46	1.59	1.17	3.28	0.72
Between 4 and 5 people	228.21	48.36	1.90	1.79	1.44	2.96	1.24	1.33	0.99	2.77	0.61
Between 6 and 7 people	191.95	43.41	1.65	1.59	1.27	2.71	1.12	1.18	0.88	2.48	0.59
More than 7	165.59	42.15	1.61	1.56	1.24	2.61	1.09	1.15	0.84	2.41	0.57
Gender of the household head											
Male	209.51	46.58	1.83	1.73	1.39	2.89	1.20	1.28	0.95	2.68	0.61
Female	220.73	46.90	1.81	1.71	1.37	2.84	1.18	1.27	0.93	2.64	0.60
Age of the household head											
Less than 35	225.51	48.67	1.92	1.80	1.45	3.00	1.25	1.34	0.99	2.78	0.63
Between 35 and 45	213.95	45.43	1.80	1.70	1.36	2.83	1.18	1.26	0.93	2.63	0.60
Between 46 and 60	206.17	47.06	1.81	1.75	1.39	2.89	1.20	1.28	0.94	2.70	0.61
More than 60	192.61	44.84	1.76	1.65	1.32	2.72	1.15	1.22	0.89	2.53	0.61

Table 7.2: Amino Acid Availability per Gram of Protein

	Lysine	Valine	Isoleucine	Leucine	Methionine and cystine	Threonine	Histidine	Phenylalanine and tyrosine	Tryptophan
					Mg amino acid/g protein				
Total	39.2	37.1	29.7	61.7	25.7	27.5	20.3	57.3	13.1
Quintiles of income									
Lowest quintile	34.4	34.0	26.6	58.4	24.0	25.0	18.1	52.3	13.7
2	36.1	35.2	28.0	58.8	24.1	25.8	18.9	54.2	12.7
3	38.9	37.0	29.6	61.9	25.6	27.4	20.3	57.3	13.1
4	41.2	38.7	31.2	63.8	26.8	28.8	21.5	60.1	13.0
Highest quintile	45.8	40.9	33.6	65.8	28.5	30.7	22.8	63.1	12.8
Area									
Capital city	46.2	41.6	34.1	63.7	28.5	30.7	22.5	63.6	10.5
Other urban areas	42.6	40.7	32.8	68.6	28.3	30.4	22.8	63.8	11.6
Rural areas	38.2	36.2	29.0	60.4	25.1	26.8	19.7	55.9	13.5
Household size									
One person	47.1	39.6	32.9	63.0	27.3	30.2	22.1	60.7	12.2
Between 2 and 3 people	40.9	37.4	30.4	60.7	25.6	27.9	20.5	57.6	12.6
Between 4 and 5 people	39.4	37.1	29.9	61.2	25.6	27.5	20.4	57.3	12.7
Between 6 and 7 people	38.0	36.7	29.2	62.5	25.7	27.3	20.3	57.1	13.5
More than 7	38.3	37.0	29.4	61.9	25.8	27.2	19.9	57.1	13.4
Gender of the household head									
Male	39.3	37.2	29.8	61.9	25.9	27.6	20.4	57.5	13.1
Female	38.5	36.5	29.3	60.5	25.2	27.1	19.9	56.4	12.8
Age of the household head									
Less than 35	39.5	36.9	29.7	61.7	25.7	27.6	20.4	57.1	12.9
Between 35 and 45	39.6	37.4	30.0	62.2	26.0	27.8	20.6	57.9	13.1
Between 46 and 60	38.5	37.1	29.6	61.5	25.5	27.3	20.1	57.3	12.9
More than 60	39.3	36.9	29.4	60.7	25.6	27.2	19.9	56.5	13.6

Table 8.1: Availability of Amino Acids by Food Group

Food group	Lysine	Valine	Isoleucine	Leucine	Methionine and cystine	Threonine	Histidine	Phenylalanine and tyrosine	Tryptophan
					Average amino acid availability (g/person/day)				
Cereals	499.01	778.65	559.99	1419.81	526.21	526.08	384.94	1237.03	140.35
Roots and tubers	13.25	13.08	9.50	15.53	57.50	10.90	7.50	20.14	209.93
Sugars and syrups	N/A	N/A	N/A	N/A	N/A	N/A	N/A	N/A	N/A
Pulses	215.13	152.61	131.89	248.01	78.85	121.70	96.17	281.47	37.57
Tree nuts	2.55	3.94	3.32	5.95	2.24	2.83	2.14	6.97	1.37
Oil crops	64.65	96.02	77.37	138.92	54.21	66.87	49.60	161.46	30.55
Vegetables	65.02	71.99	62.47	112.38	34.24	54.66	31.35	84.27	13.13
Fruits	8.26	5.17	3.31	5.40	14.16	3.28	27.98	6.14	43.48
Stimulants	2.76	2.19	1.93	2.75	1.13	1.79	0.88	3.21	0.47
Spices	2.09	2.53	1.87	2.71	1.26	1.57	0.97	2.73	0.62
Alcoholic beverages	N/A	N/A	N/A	N/A	N/A	N/A	N/A	N/A	N/A
Meat	419.64	245.40	230.07	392.42	187.63	217.53	168.80	363.80	55.49
Eggs	6.58	5.58	4.99	7.82	4.98	4.39	2.17	8.59	1.11
Fish	406.45	227.96	204.13	359.87	178.61	194.01	130.10	322.51	49.72
Milk and cheese	122.12	125.31	95.94	164.42	59.56	76.30	43.52	174.94	25.52
Oils and fats (vegetable)	N/A	N/A	N/A	N/A	N/A	N/A	N/A	N/A	N/A
Oils and fats (animal)	N/A	N/A	N/A	N/A	N/A	N/A	N/A	N/A	N/A
Nonalcoholic beverages	N/A	N/A	N/A	N/A	N/A	N/A	N/A	N/A	N/A

Table 8.2: Availability of Amino Acids by Food Group and Income Quintile This table shows the available grams of amino acids provided by each food commodity group at the *income quintile level*. Each time N/A replaces a nutrient quantity, it means that the amount of nutrient available from the food commodity group is very low or null, or there was no acquisition of that food group.

Table 8.3: Availability of Amino Acids by Food Group and Area This table shows the available grams of amino acids provided by each food commodity group at the *urban/rural level*. Each time N/A replaces a nutrient quantity, it means that the amount of nutrient available from the food commodity group is very low or null, or there was no acquisition of that food group.

Table 8.4: Availability of Amino Acids by Food Group and Region This table shows the available grams of amino acids provided by each food commodity group at the *regional level*. Each time N/A replaces a nutrient quantity, it means that the amount of nutrient available from the food commodity group is very low or null, or there was no acquisition of that food group.

Table 8.5: Contribution of Food Groups to Amino Acid Availability This table shows how much each food commodity group contributes, in percentage, to the total micronutrient availability at the *national level*. The total of each column is equal to 100 percent. This information is useful to identify the main food commodity groups that provide the available indispensable amino acids in the diet.

Table 8.6: Contribution of Food Groups to Amino Acid Availability by Area This table shows how much each food commodity group contributes, in percentage, to the total micronutrient availability at the *urban/rural level*. The total of each column is equal to 100 percent. This information is useful to identify the main food commodity groups that provide the available indispensable amino acids in the diet, and to highlight differences by area.

Table 8.2: Availability of Amino Acids by Food Group and Income Quintile

	Average amino acid availability (g/person/day)									
	Lysine	Valine	Isoleucine	Leucine	Methionine and cystine	Threonine	Histidine	Phenylalanine and tyrosine	Tryptophan
Quintiles of income									
Lowest quintile									
Cereals	0.37	0.58	0.41	1.10	0.39	0.40	0.29	0.91	0.10
Roots and tubers	0.01	0.01	0.00	0.01	0.06	0.01	0.00	0.01	0.23
Sugars and syrups	N/A	N/A	N/A	N/A	N/A	N/A	N/A	N/A	N/A
Pulses	0.15	0.11	0.09	0.18	0.06	0.09	0.07	0.20	0.03
Tree nuts	0.00	0.00	0.00	0.00	0.00	0.00	0.00	0.01	0.00
Oil crops	0.03	0.05	0.04	0.07	0.03	0.03	0.02	0.08	0.02
Vegetables	0.05	0.06	0.05	0.10	0.03	0.05	0.03	0.07	0.01
Fruits	0.00	0.00	0.00	0.00	0.01	0.00	0.01	0.00	0.02
Stimulants	0.00	0.00	0.00	0.00	0.00	0.00	0.00	0.00	0.00
Spices	0.00	0.00	0.00	0.00	0.00	0.00	0.00	0.00	0.00
Alcoholic beverages	N/A	N/A	N/A	N/A	N/A	N/A	N/A	N/A	N/A
Meat	0.18	0.11	0.10	0.17	0.08	0.10	0.07	0.16	0.02
Eggs	0.00	0.00	0.00	0.00	0.00	0.00	0.00	0.00	0.00
Fish	0.26	0.15	0.13	0.23	0.12	0.13	0.08	0.21	0.03
Milk and cheese	0.09	0.09	0.07	0.12	0.04	0.05	0.03	0.12	0.02
Oils and fats (vegetable)	N/A	N/A	N/A	N/A	N/A	N/A	N/A	N/A	N/A
Oils and fats (animal)	N/A	N/A	N/A	N/A	N/A	N/A	N/A	N/A	N/A
Nonalcoholic beverages	N/A	N/A	N/A	N/A	N/A	N/A	N/A	N/A	N/A
Quintile 2									
Cereals	0.45	0.70	0.50	1.29	0.47	0.47	0.35	1.11	0.12
Roots and tubers	0.01	0.01	0.01	0.01	0.06	0.01	0.01	0.02	0.22
Sugars and syrups	N/A	N/A	N/A	N/A	N/A	N/A	N/A	N/A	N/A
Pulses	0.19	0.14	0.12	0.22	0.07	0.11	0.09	0.25	0.03

Table 8.3: Availability of Amino Acids by Food Group and Area

Area/food group	Average amino acid availability (g/person/day)								
	Lysine	Valine	Isoleucine	Leucine	Methionine and cystine	Threonine	Histidine	Phenylalanine and tyrosine	Tryptophan
Capital city									
Cereals	0.54	0.82	0.61	1.25	0.54	0.53	0.37	1.28	0.18
Roots and tubers	0.01	0.01	0.01	0.01	0.01	0.01	0.01	0.02	0.03
Sugars and syrups	N/A	N/A	N/A	N/A	N/A	N/A	N/A	N/A	N/A
Pulses	0.16	0.11	0.10	0.19	0.06	0.09	0.07	0.21	0.03
Tree nuts	0.00	0.00	0.00	0.00	0.00	0.00	0.00	0.00	0.00
Oil crops	0.04	0.07	0.05	0.08	0.04	0.04	0.03	0.10	0.02
Vegetables	0.04	0.04	0.04	0.05	0.02	0.03	0.02	0.05	0.01
Fruits	0.02	0.01	0.01	0.01	0.01	0.01	0.03	0.01	0.02
Stimulants	0.00	0.00	0.00	0.00	0.00	0.00	0.00	0.00	0.00
Spices	0.01	0.01	0.00	0.01	0.00	0.00	0.00	0.01	0.00
Alcoholic beverages	N/A	N/A	N/A	N/A	N/A	N/A	N/A	N/A	N/A
Meat	0.48	0.28	0.26	0.45	0.22	0.25	0.20	0.42	0.06
Eggs	0.02	0.01	0.01	0.02	0.01	0.01	0.01	0.02	0.00
Fish	0.54	0.30	0.27	0.48	0.24	0.26	0.17	0.43	0.07
Milk and cheese	0.03	0.04	0.03	0.05	0.02	0.03	0.01	0.05	0.01
Oils and fats (vegetable)	N/A	N/A	N/A	N/A	N/A	N/A	N/A	N/A	N/A
Oils and fats (animal)	N/A	N/A	N/A	N/A	N/A	N/A	N/A	N/A	N/A
Non alcoholic beverages	N/A	N/A	N/A	N/A	N/A	N/A	N/A	N/A	N/A
Other urban areas									
Cereals	0.59	0.93	0.67	1.70	0.63	0.63	0.47	1.50	0.18
Roots and tubers	0.02	0.02	0.01	0.02	0.03	0.01	0.01	0.02	0.11
Sugars and syrups	N/A	N/A	N/A	N/A	N/A	N/A	N/A	N/A	N/A
Pulses	0.18	0.13	0.11	0.21	0.07	0.10	0.08	0.24	0.03

Table 8.4: Availability of Amino Acids by Food Group and Region

	Average amino acid availability (g/person/day)								
	Lysine	Valine	Isoleucine	Leucine	Methionine and cystine	Threonine	Histidine	Phenylalanine and tyrosine	Tryptophan
Region									
Region 1									
Cereals	0.59	0.92	0.65	1.56	0.62	0.60	0.42	1.40	0.16
Roots and tubers	0.01	0.01	0.01	0.01	0.01	0.01	0.00	0.01	0.03
Sugars and syrups	N/A	N/A	N/A	N/A	N/A	N/A	N/A	N/A	N/A
Pulses	0.21	0.15	0.13	0.25	0.08	0.12	0.09	0.27	0.04
Tree nuts	0.00	0.00	0.00	0.00	0.00	0.00	0.00	0.00	0.00
Oil crops	0.12	0.18	0.15	0.27	0.10	0.13	0.10	0.32	0.06
Vegetables	0.10	0.12	0.10	0.18	0.06	0.09	0.05	0.15	0.03
Fruits	0.01	0.00	0.00	0.00	0.00	0.00	0.02	0.01	0.00
Stimulants	0.00	0.00	0.00	0.00	0.00	0.00	0.00	0.00	0.00
Spices	0.00	0.00	0.00	0.00	0.00	0.00	0.00	0.00	0.00
Alcoholic beverages	N/A	N/A	N/A	N/A	N/A	N/A	N/A	N/A	N/A
Meat	0.39	0.23	0.21	0.36	0.17	0.20	0.16	0.33	0.05
Eggs	0.01	0.00	0.00	0.01	0.00	0.00	0.00	0.01	0.00
Fish	0.18	0.10	0.09	0.16	0.08	0.09	0.06	0.14	0.02
Milk and cheese	0.23	0.22	0.16	0.29	0.11	0.13	0.07	0.30	0.03
Oils and fats (vegetable)	N/A	N/A	N/A	N/A	N/A	N/A	N/A	N/A	N/A
Oils and fats (animal)	N/A	N/A	N/A	N/A	N/A	N/A	N/A	N/A	N/A
Nonalcoholic beverages	N/A	N/A	N/A	N/A	N/A	N/A	N/A	N/A	N/A
Region 2									
Cereals	0.58	0.97	0.70	2.08	0.71	0.69	0.54	1.65	0.16
Roots and tubers	0.02	0.02	0.01	0.02	0.01	0.01	0.01	0.02	0.03
Sugars and syrups	N/A	N/A	N/A	N/A	N/A	N/A	N/A	N/A	N/A
Pulses	0.21	0.15	0.13	0.24	0.08	0.12	0.10	0.28	0.04
Tree nuts	0.00	0.00	0.00	0.00	0.00	0.00	0.00	0.00	0.00
Oil crops	0.01	0.01	0.01	0.02	0.01	0.01	0.01	0.02	0.00

Table 8.5: Contribution of Food Groups to Amino Acid Availability

Food group	Lysine	Valine	Isoleucine	Leucine	Methionine and cystine	Threonine	Histidine	Phenylalanine and tyrosine	Tryptophan
Cereals	27.31	45.00	40.38	49.37	43.83	41.04	40.69	46.27	23.03
Roots and tubers	0.73	0.76	0.69	0.54	4.79	0.85	0.79	0.75	34.45
Sugars and syrups	0.00	0.00	0.00	0.00	0.00	0.00	0.00	0.00	0.00
Pulses	11.77	8.82	9.51	8.62	6.57	9.49	10.17	10.53	6.17
Tree nuts	0.14	0.23	0.24	0.21	0.19	0.22	0.23	0.26	0.23
Oil crops	3.54	5.55	5.58	4.83	4.52	5.22	5.24	6.04	5.01
Vegetables	3.56	4.16	4.50	3.91	2.85	4.26	3.31	3.15	2.15
Fruits	0.45	0.30	0.24	0.19	1.18	0.26	2.96	0.23	7.14
Stimulants	0.15	0.13	0.14	0.10	0.09	0.14	0.09	0.12	0.08
Spices	0.11	0.15	0.14	0.09	0.11	0.12	0.10	0.10	0.10
Alcoholic beverages	0.00	0.00	0.00	0.00	0.00	0.00	0.00	0.00	0.00
Meat	22.96	14.18	16.59	13.64	15.63	16.97	17.84	13.61	9.11
Eggs	0.36	0.32	0.36	0.27	0.41	0.34	0.23	0.32	0.18
Fish	22.24	13.17	14.72	12.51	14.88	15.13	13.75	12.06	8.16
Milk and cheese	6.68	7.24	6.92	5.72	4.96	5.95	4.60	6.54	4.19
Oils and fats (vegetable)	0.00	0.00	0.00	0.00	0.00	0.00	0.00	0.00	0.00
Oils and fats (animal)	0.00	0.00	0.00	0.00	0.00	0.00	0.00	0.00	0.00
Nonalcoholic beverages	0.00	0.00	0.00	0.00	0.00	0.00	0.00	0.00	0.00

Average amino acid availability, % of total availability

Table 8.6: Contribution of Food Groups to Amino Acid Availability by Area

	Average amino acid availability, % of total availability									
Area	Lysine	Valine	Isoleucine	Leucine	Methionine and cystine	Threonine	Histidine	Phenylalanine and tyrosine	Tryptophan
Capital city									
Cereals	28.71	48.03	43.76	48.10	46.26	41.94	40.60	49.23	42.14
Roots and tubers	0.70	0.75	0.66	0.55	1.19	0.70	0.60	0.73	7.62
Sugars and syrups	0.00	0.00	0.00	0.00	0.00	0.00	0.00	0.00	0.00
Pulses	8.53	6.73	7.07	7.11	5.10	7.26	7.92	8.19	6.66
Tree nuts	0.05	0.09	0.10	0.09	0.08	0.09	0.09	0.11	0.13
Oil crops	2.37	3.84	3.28	3.24	3.33	3.27	3.08	3.66	3.65
Vegetables	2.15	2.24	2.93	1.90	1.53	2.47	1.72	1.82	1.79
Fruits	0.88	0.68	0.53	0.39	0.95	0.48	3.65	0.53	3.84
Stimulants	0.06	0.06	0.06	0.04	0.04	0.06	0.04	0.06	0.05
Spices	0.29	0.39	0.35	0.27	0.29	0.33	0.27	0.27	0.38
Alcoholic beverages	0.00	0.00	0.00	0.00	0.00	0.00	0.00	0.00	0.00
Meat	25.50	16.55	18.88	17.43	18.47	20.08	21.27	16.13	15.05
Eggs	0.88	0.83	0.91	0.76	1.08	0.89	0.60	0.84	0.66
Fish	28.34	17.68	19.32	18.22	20.20	20.41	18.68	16.34	15.25
Milk and cheese	1.55	2.13	2.16	1.89	1.49	2.03	1.49	2.10	2.79
Oils and fats (vegetable)	0.00	0.00	0.00	0.00	0.00	0.00	0.00	0.00	0.00
Oils and fats (animal)	0.00	0.00	0.00	0.00	0.00	0.00	0.00	0.00	0.00
Nonalcoholic beverages	0.00	0.00	0.00	0.00	0.00	0.00	0.00	0.00	0.00
Other urban areas									
Cereals	30.23	49.97	45.06	54.42	49.14	45.33	44.86	51.66	33.30
Roots and tubers	0.87	0.87	0.79	0.58	2.57	0.85	0.74	0.83	20.01
Sugars and syrups	0.00	0.00	0.00	0.00	0.00	0.00	0.00	0.00	0.00
Pulses	9.36	6.94	7.40	6.67	5.19	7.39	7.88	8.25	6.09

Table 8.7: Contribution of Food Groups to Amino Acid Availability by Region This table shows how much each food commodity group contributes, in percentage, to the total micronutrient availability at the *regional level*. The total of each column is equal to 100 percent. This information is useful to identify the main food commodity groups that provide the available indispensable amino acids in the diet, and to highlight regional differences.

Disaggregated by Food Commodity: Tables 8.8 to 8.10

The food commodities analyzed are those collected in the survey excluding those consumed away from home. The food commodity quantities refer to edible portions, which mean they exclude the nonedible parts (peels, bones, etc.)

Table 8.8: Availability of Amino Acid by Food Item This table shows food commodity edible quantities and the available grams of amino acids provided by them at the *national level*. This table is useful to identify the main food commodities that provide indispensable amino acids at national level.

Table 8.9: Availability of Amino Acid by Food Item and Area This table shows food commodity edible quantities and the available grams of amino acids provided by them at the *urban/rural level*. This table is useful to identify the main food commodities that provide indispensable amino acids within rural and urban areas as well as to highlight differences between rural and urban patterns.

Table 8.10: Availability of Amino Acid by Food Item and Region This table shows food commodity edible quantities and the available grams of amino acids provided by them at the *regional level*. This table is useful to identify the main food commodity groups that provide the available of indispensable amino acids at the national level, and to highlight regional differences.

Table 8.7: Contribution of Food Groups to Amino Acid Availability by Region

	Lysine	Valine	Isoleucine	Leucine	Methionine and cystine	Threonine	Histidine	Phenylalanine and tyrosine	Tryptophan
	Average amino acid availability, % of total availability								
Region									
Region 1									
Cereals	31.89	47.31	43.04	50.26	50.11	43.73	42.95	47.38	37.70
Roots and tubers	0.45	0.40	0.38	0.27	0.91	0.39	0.37	0.39	7.40
Sugars and syrups	0.00	0.00	0.00	0.00	0.00	0.00	0.00	0.00	0.00
Pulses	11.48	7.79	8.71	8.02	6.19	8.81	9.36	9.15	8.23
Tree nuts	0.05	0.08	0.08	0.07	0.07	0.08	0.08	0.09	0.12
Oil crops	6.42	9.42	10.06	8.84	8.41	9.54	10.03	10.88	14.62
Vegetables	5.60	6.05	6.42	5.94	4.67	6.63	5.12	5.17	6.03
Fruits	0.34	0.22	0.19	0.14	0.23	0.20	2.45	0.17	0.79
Stimulants	0.21	0.16	0.18	0.13	0.13	0.18	0.13	0.15	0.15
Spices	0.08	0.09	0.08	0.06	0.07	0.08	0.07	0.06	0.10
Alcoholic beverages	0.00	0.00	0.00	0.00	0.00	0.00	0.00	0.00	0.00
Meat	20.87	11.62	13.87	11.67	13.95	14.62	15.85	11.34	11.86
Eggs	0.28	0.22	0.26	0.20	0.31	0.25	0.17	0.23	0.20
Fish	9.76	5.22	5.96	5.15	6.43	6.29	5.88	4.85	5.12
Milk and cheese	12.56	11.43	10.77	9.25	8.53	9.21	7.55	10.14	7.68
Oils and fats (vegetable)	0.00	0.00	0.00	0.00	0.00	0.00	0.00	0.00	0.00
Oils and fats (animal)	0.00	0.00	0.00	0.00	0.00	0.00	0.00	0.00	0.00
Nonalcoholic beverages	0.00	0.00	0.00	0.00	0.00	0.00	0.00	0.00	0.00
Region 2									
Cereals	32.94	52.72	47.93	61.11	55.97	49.94	51.90	55.59	37.04
Roots and tubers	1.03	0.90	0.83	0.53	1.13	0.80	0.68	0.82	6.57
Sugars and syrups	0.00	0.00	0.00	0.00	0.00	0.00	0.00	0.00	0.00
Pulses	11.90	7.97	8.61	6.98	6.15	8.48	9.18	9.38	8.66

Table 8.8: Availability of Amino Acid by Food Item

Food item	Average edible quantity consumed (g/person/day)	Average amino acid availability (g/person/day)								
		Lysine	Valine	Isoleucine	Leucine	Methionine and cystine	Threonine	Histidine	Phenylalanine and tyrosine	Tryptophan
Rice paddy or rough	6.12	0.01	0.02	0.02	0.03	0.02	0.01	0.01	0.03	0.00
Rice husked	48.14	0.13	0.19	0.14	0.27	0.11	0.12	0.08	0.29	0.04
Maize cob fresh	9.29	0.02	0.03	0.02	0.05	0.01	0.02	0.01	0.02	0.00
Maize grain	72.72	0.13	0.24	0.17	0.59	0.19	0.18	0.15	0.43	0.03
Maize flour	163.94	0.11	0.14	0.10	0.27	0.07	0.10	0.07	0.21	0.02
Millet whole grain dried	1.68	0.00	0.01	0.00	0.01	0.00	0.00	0.00	0.01	0.00
Millet foxtail Italian whole grain	1.17	0.00	0.01	0.00	0.01	0.00	0.00	0.00	0.01	0.00
Sorghum whole grain brown	7.91	0.01	0.02	0.02	0.03	0.02	0.01	0.01	0.03	0.00
Sorghum average of all varieties	20.38	0.04	0.06	0.04	0.08	0.04	0.04	0.02	0.09	0.01
Wheat durum whole grain	0.46	0.00	0.00	0.00	0.00	0.00	0.00	0.00	0.00	0.00
Wheat meal or flour unspecified wheat	4.41	0.02	0.03	0.02	0.04	0.02	0.02	0.01	0.04	0.01
Wheat	1.30	0.01	0.01	0.01	0.02	0.01	0.01	0.01	0.02	0.00
Bread	3.11	0.01	0.01	0.01	0.02	0.01	0.01	0.01	0.02	0.00
Baby cereals	0.09	0.00	0.00	0.00	0.00	0.00	0.00	0.00	0.00	0.00
Biscuits wheat from Europe	0.15	0.00	0.00	0.00	0.00	0.00	0.00	0.00	0.00	0.00
Buns cakes	3.25	0.01	0.01	0.01	0.01	0.01	0.00	0.00	0.01	0.00
Macaroni spaghetti	0.27	0.00	0.00	0.00	0.00	0.00	0.00	0.00	0.00	0.00
Oats	2.31	0.01	0.02	0.01	0.02	0.01	0.01	0.01	0.03	0.00
Cassava sweet roots raw	28.98	0.00	0.00	0.00	0.00	0.01	0.00	0.00	0.00	0.03
Cassava sweet roots dried	14.31	0.00	0.00	0.00	0.00	0.01	0.00	0.00	0.00	0.04
Cassava flour	35.67	0.00	0.00	0.00	0.00	0.02	0.00	0.00	0.00	0.10
Sweet potato	50.00	0.00	0.00	0.00	0.00	0.01	0.00	0.00	0.00	0.03
Coco yam tuber	5.45	0.00	0.00	0.00	0.01	0.00	0.00	0.00	0.00	0.00
Potatoes tubers raw	9.00	0.01	0.01	0.00	0.01	0.01	0.01	0.00	0.01	0.00
Banana cooking	42.28	0.00	0.00	0.00	0.00	0.01	0.00	0.00	0.00	0.04
Starch	2.17	0.00	0.00	0.00	0.00	0.00	0.00	0.00	0.00	0.00

Table 8.9: Availability of Amino Acid by Food Item and Area

Area/food item	Average edible quantity consumed (g/person/day)	Average amino acid availability (g/person/day)								
		Lysine	Valine	Isoleucine	Leucine	Methionine and cystine	Threonine	Histidine	Phenylalanine and tyrosine	Tryptophan
Capital city										
Rice paddy or rough	0.60	0.00	0.00	0.00	0.00	0.00	0.00	0.00	0.00	0.00
Rice husked	108.34	0.28	0.43	0.31	0.61	0.26	0.27	0.19	0.66	0.09
Maize cob fresh	0.68	0.00	0.00	0.00	0.00	0.00	0.00	0.00	0.00	0.00
Maize grain	7.68	0.01	0.03	0.02	0.06	0.02	0.02	0.02	0.05	0.00
Maize flour	125.27	0.08	0.11	0.08	0.21	0.06	0.08	0.05	0.16	0.01
Millet whole grain dried	0.42	0.00	0.00	0.00	0.00	0.00	0.00	0.00	0.00	0.00
Millet foxtail Italian whole grain	0.71	0.00	0.00	0.00	0.01	0.00	0.00	0.00	0.01	0.00
Sorghum whole grain brown	0.13	0.00	0.00	0.00	0.00	0.00	0.00	0.00	0.00	0.00
Sorghum average of all varieties	0.04	0.00	0.00	0.00	0.00	0.00	0.00	0.00	0.00	0.00
Wheat durum whole grain	0.24	0.00	0.00	0.00	0.00	0.00	0.00	0.00	0.00	0.00
Wheat meal or flour unspecified wheat	10.40	0.04	0.06	0.05	0.09	0.05	0.04	0.03	0.11	0.02
Wheat	0.21	0.00	0.00	0.00	0.00	0.00	0.00	0.00	0.00	0.00
Bread	16.83	0.03	0.06	0.05	0.10	0.06	0.04	0.03	0.11	0.02
Baby cereals	0.04	0.00	0.00	0.00	0.00	0.00	0.00	0.00	0.00	0.00
Biscuits wheat from Europe	0.50	0.00	0.00	0.00	0.00	0.00	0.00	0.00	0.00	0.00
Buns cakes	10.44	0.02	0.02	0.02	0.03	0.02	0.01	0.01	0.04	0.01
Macaroni spaghetti	2.18	0.00	0.01	0.01	0.01	0.01	0.01	0.00	0.02	0.00
Oats	10.69	0.06	0.08	0.06	0.11	0.06	0.05	0.04	0.13	0.02
Cassava sweet roots raw	13.06	0.00	0.00	0.00	0.00	0.00	0.00	0.00	0.00	0.02
Cassava sweet roots dried	1.09	0.00	0.00	0.00	0.00	0.00	0.00	0.00	0.00	0.00
Cassava flour	0.83	0.00	0.00	0.00	0.00	0.00	0.00	0.00	0.00	0.00
Sweet potato	13.23	0.00	0.00	0.00	0.00	0.00	0.00	0.00	0.00	0.01
Coco yam tuber	2.45	0.00	0.00	0.00	0.00	0.00	0.00	0.00	0.00	0.00
Potatoes tubers raw	10.96	0.01	0.01	0.01	0.01	0.01	0.01	0.00	0.02	0.00

Table 8.10: Availability of Amino Acid by Food Item and Region

Region/food item	Average edible quantity consumed (g/person/day)	Average amino acid availability (g/person/day)								
		Lysine	Valine	Isoleucine	Leucine	Methionine and cystine	Threonine	Histidine	Phenylalanine and tyrosine	Tryptophan
Region 1										
Rice paddy or rough	0.29	0.00	0.00	0.00	0.00	0.00	0.00	0.00	0.00	0.00
Rice husked	26.25	0.07	0.11	0.08	0.15	0.06	0.07	0.05	0.16	0.02
Maize cob fresh	11.73	0.03	0.04	0.02	0.07	0.02	0.02	0.02	0.03	0.00
Maize grain	50.15	0.09	0.17	0.12	0.41	0.13	0.12	0.10	0.30	0.02
Maize flour	240.10	0.16	0.21	0.15	0.40	0.11	0.15	0.10	0.31	0.03
Millet whole grain dried	1.68	0.00	0.01	0.00	0.01	0.00	0.00	0.00	0.01	0.00
Millet foxtail Italian whole grain	1.67	0.00	0.01	0.01	0.02	0.01	0.01	0.00	0.01	0.00
Sorghum whole grain brown	20.07	0.04	0.06	0.04	0.08	0.04	0.03	0.02	0.08	0.01
Sorghum average of all varieties	102.41	0.18	0.30	0.22	0.41	0.22	0.18	0.12	0.43	0.06
Wheat durum whole grain	0.05	0.00	0.00	0.00	0.00	0.00	0.00	0.00	0.00	0.00
Wheat meal or flour unspecified wheat	3.35	0.01	0.02	0.02	0.03	0.02	0.01	0.01	0.03	0.01
Wheat	1.40	0.02	0.02	0.01	0.02	0.01	0.01	0.01	0.02	0.00
Bread	1.07	0.00	0.00	0.00	0.01	0.00	0.00	0.00	0.01	0.00
Baby cereals	0.04	0.00	0.00	0.00	0.00	0.00	0.00	0.00	0.00	0.00
Biscuits wheat from Europe	0.09	0.00	0.00	0.00	0.00	0.00	0.00	0.00	0.00	0.00
Buns cakes	2.69	0.00	0.01	0.00	0.01	0.00	0.00	0.00	0.01	0.00
Macaroni spaghetti	0.12	0.00	0.00	0.00	0.00	0.00	0.00	0.00	0.00	0.00
Oats	1.38	0.01	0.01	0.01	0.01	0.01	0.01	0.00	0.02	0.00
Cassava sweet roots raw	11.73	0.00	0.00	0.00	0.00	0.00	0.00	0.00	0.02	0.01
Cassava sweet roots dried	0.16	0.00	0.00	0.00	0.00	0.00	0.00	0.00	0.00	0.00
Cassava flour	0.29	0.00	0.00	0.00	0.00	0.00	0.00	0.00	0.00	0.00
Sweet potato	22.52	0.00	0.00	0.00	0.00	0.00	0.00	0.00	0.00	0.01
Coco yam tuber	0.24	0.00	0.00	0.00	0.00	0.00	0.00	0.00	0.00	0.00
Potatoes tubers raw	7.74	0.01	0.01	0.01	0.01	0.00	0.00	0.00	0.01	0.00

Glossary of Indicators

Overall Food Consumption Indicators

average carbohydrates consumption (g/person/day)

Average quantity of available carbohydrates (excluding fiber) consumed by the household. See tables 1.9, 1.14, 2.1, 2.3, 2.4, 2.6, and 2.7.

average carbohydrates unit value (LCU/100 g)

Measures the cost of 100 grams of carbohydrates by food groups. From this cost it is possible to identify among the food groups that provide carbohydrates those that provide low-cost carbohydrates. See table 2.8.

average dietary energy consumption (kcal/person/day)

Measures the amount of calories consumed by the household. It is expressed in kilocalories per person per day. The dietary energy consumption is estimated from the food quantities collected in the survey. Food quantities that are collected "as purchased" (including bones, peels, etc.) first are transformed into edible quantities by taking into consideration the respective food item refuse factor and then are expressed in grams. Once all edible quantities are transformed into grams of nutrients, the nutrient densities (grams of nutrient per gram of food product) of each food item are used to estimate the amount of calories consumed. The dietary energy consumption should be within reasonable ranges from 800 to 4,000 kcal (whichever decile), and it tends to increase as income increases (although it is also possible that better-off households purchase more expensive and less energetic food). See tables 1.1, 1.3, 1.4, 1.9, 1.10, 1.11, 1.12, 2.1, 2.3, 2.4, 2.6, 2.7, 3.1, 3.3, 3.5, and 4.1.

average dietary energy requirement (kcal/person/day)

Proper normative reference for adequate nutrition in the population. While it would be mistaken to take the average dietary energy requirement value as the cutoff point to determine the prevalence of undernourishment, its value is used to calculate

	the depth of the food deficit (FD), which is the amount of dietary energy needed to ensure that, if properly distributed, hunger would be eliminated. It is also used to estimate the nutrient recommended intake expressed in mg per 1000 kcal. See tables 1.1, 1.2, and 5.5.
average dietary energy unit value (LCU/1,000 kcals)	Measures the average cost of 1,000 kcal (in local currency). It usually increases as income increases because better-off households are more likely to buy food that is less caloric but more expensive (for instance meat instead of pulses) or to have meals in restaurants. Note that for all the tables presenting statistics by food commodity group or food commodity, the average dietary energy unit value refers to the median of the dietary energy value. See tables 1.3, 1.4, 2.8, 3.1, 3.3, 3.5, and 4.4.
average edible quantity consumed (g/person/day)	For each food item, provides the quantity of food consumed in grams per person per day after the nonedible portion has been removed. See tables 3.1, 3.2, 3.3, 3.4, 3.5, 3.6, 6.6, 6.8, 6.9, 8.8, 8.9, and 8.10.
average fat consumption (g/person/day)	Average quantity of fat consumed by the household (expressed in grams per person per day). See tables 1.9, 1.14, 2.1, 2.3, 2.4, 2.6, and 2.7.
average fat unit value (LCU/100 g)	Measures the cost of 100 grams of fat by food groups. From this cost it is possible to identify among the food groups that provide fat those that provide low-cost fat (for instance, to obtain 100 grams of fats from milk and cheese may cost more than to get 100 grams of fat from vegetable oil). See table 2.8.
average food consumption in monetary value (LCU/person/day)	Usually increases as income increases. It should be lower than the total consumption expenditure (which includes nonfood consumption expenditures such as education, health, transport, durable goods, etc.). See tables 1.3, 1.4, 1.9, 2.1, 2.3, 2.4, 2.6, 2.7, 3.1, 3.2, 3.3, 3.4, 3.5, 3.6, 4.1, and 7.1.

average household size   Corresponds to the total number of household members, and usually wealthier households have fewer members than poor households. See tables 1.3, 1.4, 4.1, 4.2, and 4.3.

average income (LCU/person/day)   Average per person per day income, expressed in local unit of measurement. When the survey does not collect information on income or this information is not reliable, total expenditures corresponding to the sum of total consumption and nonconsumption is used as a proxy of income. See tables 1.4, 1.6, 1.8, 4.4, and 4.5.

average protein consumption (g/person/day)   Average quantity of proteins consumed. See tables 1.9, 1.14, 2.1, 2.3, 2.4, 2.6, 2.7, 3.2, 3.4, 3.6, and 7.1.

average protein unit value (LCU/100 g)   Measures the cost of 100 grams of proteins by food groups. From this cost it is possible to identify among the food groups that provide proteins those that provide low-cost proteins (for instance proteins from cereals may be less expensive than proteins coming from animal sources). See tables 2.8, 3.2, 3.4, and 3.6.

average total consumption in monetary value (LCU/person/day)   Usually increases as income increases and should be lower than total expenditures and income. See tables 1.3, 1.4, and 4.1.

coefficient of variation of dietary energy consumption (%)   Indicator of the dispersion of the dietary energy consumption within the general population. It should not be higher than 35 percent (maximum acceptable). A high CV should be corrected for excess variability. The CV should not be lower than 20 percent to account for at least the variability of dietary energy consumption due to factors other than income/household characteristics. See tables 1.1 and 1.2.

contribution of food groups to total nutrient consumption: share of total carbohydrates consumption (%)	Measures the contribution of each food group to the consumption of carbohydrates in percent (e.g., a share of 55 percent from cereal indicates that the group of cereals contributes 55 percent to the total carbohydrates consumption). See tables 2.2 and 2.5.
contribution of food groups to total nutrient consumption: share of total dietary energy consumption (%)	Measures the contribution of each food group to the total dietary energy consumption in percent (e.g., a share of 55 percent from cereals indicates that the group of cereals contributes 55 percent to the total dietary energy consumption). See tables 2.2, 2.5, and 2.9.
contribution of food groups to total nutrient consumption: share of total fat consumption (%)	Measures the contribution of each food group to the consumption of fats in percent (e.g., a share of 17 percent from vegetable oils indicates that the group of vegetable oils contributes 17 percent to the total fats consumption). See tables 2.2 and 2.5.
contribution of food groups to total nutrient consumption: share of total protein consumption (%)	Measures the contribution of each food group to the total consumption of proteins in percent (e.g., a share of 20 percent from the group meat and meat products indicates that the group of meat and products contributes 20 percent to the total protein consumption). See tables 2.2 and 2.5.
density—average carbohydrates consumption (g/1,000 kcal)	Measures the amount in grams of carbohydrates included in 1,000 kcal. See table 1.12.
density—average fat consumption (g/1,000 kcal)	Measures the amount in grams of fats contributing to 1,000 kcal. See table 1.12.
density—average protein consumption (g/1,000 kcal)	Measures the amount in grams of proteins contributing to 1,000 kcal. See table 1.12.

depth of food deficit (kcal/person/day)

Indicates how many calories would be needed to lift the undernourished from its status, everything else being constant and considering food is equally distributed. The average intensity of food deprivation of the undernourished, estimated as the difference between the average dietary energy requirement and the average dietary energy consumption of the undernourished population (food-deprived), is multiplied by the number of undernourished to provide an estimate of the total food deficit in the country, and is then normalized by the total population. This usually is within the range of 100–400 kilocalories per day. When it is lower than 200 kcal, it is considered low; between 200 and 300, moderate; and above 300 kcal, high. See tables 1.1 and 1.2.

dietary energy supply adjusted for losses (kcal/person/day)

Corresponds to the dietary energy supply as derived from the food balance sheets reduced by losses that occur at the retail level. It is expressed in kilocalories per person per day. It is used in the calculation of the prevalence of undernourishment indicator 1.9 of the MDG. See table 1.2.

estimated population

Corresponds to the total number of people within a population group. It is calculated from the survey data as the sum of the product between household weight and number of household members. See table 1.4.

minimum dietary energy requirement (MDER) (kcal/person/day)

Amount of energy needed for light activity and minimum acceptable body mass index (weight for attained height). MDER is the cutoff point, or threshold, used to estimate the prevalence (percentage) of the undernourished population in a country. Dietary energy requirements differ by gender and age, and for different levels of physical activity. As a result, minimum dietary energy requirements vary by country, and from year to year, depending on the sex and age structure of the population.

In countries with a high prevalence of undernourishment, a large proportion of the population typically consumes dietary energy levels close to the cutoff point, making the MDER a highly sensitive parameter. It is computed as a weighted average of the minimum energy requirements of different age/sex groups in the population.[25] See tables 1.1, 1.2, and 1.3.

The MDER shown at the national level in table 1.3 is calculated using the structure of the population as from the survey. Note that this MDER value is different from the MDER shown in the first row of tables 1.1 and 1.2. The MDER at the national level in tables 1.1 and 1.2 is based on the country population as published by the United Nations, biennially, and it is used to estimate the MDG 1.9 indicators. The difference in the values of these two MDERs at the national level can be due to differences in (1) the structure of the population by age and sex groups; (2) the heights used by age and sex groups; and (3) the birthrate used.

number of sampled households

Total should be equal to the size of the survey sample: to obtain reliable estimates (at income decile levels) it is suggested to have more than 500 sampled households by category of analysis: region, household head's characteristics, etc. A statistic obtained with fewer than 30 households is considered not reliable. See tables 1.3, 1.4, 1.5, 1.6, 1.7, and 1.8.

other sources— proportion of households in total households (%)

Measures the percentage of households whose consumption of a food item is coming from other sources (e.g., at national level, 5 percent associated to maize in grain means that 5 percent of households of this country have received maize in grain as a gift). See tables 3.7, 3.8, and 3.9.

own consumption— proportion of households in total households (%)	Measures the percentage of households whose consumption of a food item is coming from their own production (e.g., at the national level 55 percent associated to wheat flour means that 55 percent of households of this country have consumed wheat flour coming from their own production). See tables 3.7, 3.8, and 3.9.
population ('000s)	Corresponds to the total number of people (expressed in thousands) within a population group. It is calculated from the survey data as the sum of the product between household weight and number of household members. At the national level, the population estimates should be close to those published by the UN for the same year. See tables 1.1 and 1.2.
prevalence of undernourishment (%)	Proportion of the population estimated to be at risk of caloric inadequacy. A value less than 5 percent is considered low, a value between 5 and 19 percent is considered moderate, and a value higher than 20 percent is considered high. For computing the official MDG 1.9 indicator FAO uses, as mean of the distribution, the dietary energy supply from food balance sheets minus waste of calories at the retail level. When the average dietary energy consumption from the national household surveys is used as the estimate of the mean of the distribution, the corresponding indicator should not be considered the official MDG 1.9. However, the two indicators should be compared and critically evaluated. See tables 1.1 and 1.2.
purchase—proportion of households in total households (%)	Measures the percentage of households whose consumption of a food item is coming from purchases (e.g., at the national level, 55 percent associated to wheat flour means that 55 percent of households of this country have consumed wheat flour coming from purchases).

	Note that the sum of the proportion of households (HHs) that acquire the product through purchase, or received in kind, or from own consumption does not necessarily equal 100 percent because not all HH might have consumed the food. See tables 3.7, 3.8, and 3.9.
quantity as "produced" (g/person/day)	Measures the quantity of food product consumed coming from own production. It is expressed in grams per person per day. See tables 3.7, 3.8, and 3.9.
quantity as "purchased" (g/person/day)	Measures the quantity of food product consumed coming from purchases. It is expressed in grams per person per day. See tables 3.7, 3.8, and 3.9.
quantity as "received" from other sources (g/person/day)	Measures the quantity of food product consumed from other sources. It is expressed in grams per person per day. See tables 3.7, 3.8, and 3.9.
ratio to the first reference group of average dietary energy consumption	Measures the inequality in the average dietary energy consumption between the first quintile (used as the reference group) and the other quintiles. For instance, if the value of the ratio associated to quintile 4 is equal to 5, this means that the average dietary energy consumption in quintile 4 is five times higher than in quintile 1. It's a measure of inequality easier to interpret than the Gini coefficient or the coefficient of variation. This ratio is computed for the average dietary energy value, average food consumption in monetary value, average total consumption in monetary value, average income, and share of food source in dietary and monetary value. See table 4.1.
share of animal protein in total protein consumption (%)	Proportion of protein consumed from food of animal origin (meat [red and white], fish, eggs, milk, and cheese). See table 1.13.

share of dietary energy consumption from fats (%)	Proportion of total calories from fats. The experts from WHO/FAO/UNU recommend a consumption of calories from fats between 15 and 30 percent of total calories consumed. See tables 1.10 and 1.11.
share of dietary energy consumption from protein (%)	Proportion of total calories from proteins. The experts from WHO/FAO/UNU recommend a consumption of calories from proteins between 10 and 15 percent of total calories consumed. See tables 1.10 and 1.11.
share of dietary energy consumption from total carbohydrates and alcohol (%)	Proportion of total calories from available carbohydrates and alcohol. The experts from WHO/FAO/UNU recommend a consumption of calories from available carbohydrates and alcohol between 55 and 75 percent of total calories consumed. See tables 1.10 and 1.11.
share of food consumed away from home in total food consumption (%) in dietary energy	Share of dietary energy coming from the food eaten away from home (canteen at work, restaurants, bars, street food, etc.). Usually is greater for better-off households. Yet this rule widely depends on the eating habits of the country. Indeed, street food (sometimes cheap and highly caloric) may contribute significantly to the diet of poor people; whereby restaurants may provide expensive but not highly caloric food. See tables 1.5, 1.6, and 4.2.
share of food consumed away from home in total food consumption (%) in monetary value	Contribution (expressed in monetary value) of food consumed away from home in total food monetary value. Usually is higher in urban areas and for higher income groups. Yet the rule widely depends on the eating habits of the country. See tables 1.7, 1.8, and 4.3.
share of food consumption in total income (%) (Engel ratio)	According to Engel's law, the higher the income, the lower the proportion of income is spent on food. This ratio reflects the living standard of a population group and its vulnerability

to food price increases. It can get close to 80 percent for low-income groups and 20 percent for high-income groups. See tables 1.7, 1.8, and 4.4.

share of food from other sources in total food consumption (%) in dietary energy

Share of dietary energy coming from food received from other sources (e.g., received as payment, gift, aid, etc.). Usually is higher for low-income groups as they are more likely to receive food aid, gifts, etc. See tables 1.5, 1.6, and 4.2.

share of food from other sources in total food consumption (%) in monetary value

Contribution (expressed in monetary value) of food received in kind to the total food monetary value. Usually it is higher for lower income deciles, which are mainly those receiving food in kind. See tables 1.7, 1.8, and 4.3.

share of own produced food in total food consumption (%) in dietary energy

Share of dietary energy coming from own produced food. Should be higher in rural areas than urban areas, and it is usually higher for lower income groups. The greater the share is, the higher is the vulnerability to natural shocks affecting agricultural production. See tables 1.5, 1.6, and 4.2.

share of own produced food in total food consumption (%) in monetary value

Contribution (expressed in monetary value) of food taken from own production to the total food monetary value. Should be higher in rural areas than urban areas and it is usually higher for lower income groups. The greater the share is, the higher is the vulnerability to natural shocks affecting agricultural production. Indeed, farming households will need to buy from the market the same amount of food they would have taken from their own production. See tables 1.7, 1.8, and 4.3.

share of purchased food in total food consumption (%) in dietary energy

Share of dietary energy coming from food purchased from the market. Usually higher in urban areas. The greater the share is, the higher is the vulnerability to price increase. This share can

	be high for households living in urban areas and nonagricultural households. See tables 1.5, 1.6, and 4.2.
share of purchased food in total food consumption (%) in monetary value	Contribution (expressed in monetary value) of purchased food to the total food monetary value. Usually higher in urban areas where most people get food from the market. The greater the share is, the higher is the vulnerability to price increase. See tables 1.7, 1.8, and 4.3.
skewness of dietary energy consumption	Skewness is a measure of the asymmetry of the probability distribution of a real-valued random variable. It measures the length of the tail of the distribution. In a lognormal distribution, the skewness is a function of the coefficient of variation: skewness = $CV * (3 + CV2)$. In a skew(log) normal distribution, the skewness is independent from the CV's values. For this reason, the adoption of a skew(log)normal model allows for greater flexibility and for a truer representation of the consumption distribution. See tables 1.1 and 1.2.
within range of population fat intake goal: 15%–30%	Indicates whether the proportion of total calories available from fats is within the range of 15–30 percent. See table 1.11.
within range of population protein intake goal: 10%–15%	Indicates whether the proportion of total calories available from protein is within the range of 10–15 percent. See table 1.11.
within range of population total carbohydrates and alcohol intake goal: 55%–75%	Indicates whether the proportion of total calories available from carbohydrates is within the range of 55–75 percent. See table 1.11.

Indicators on Micronutrients

95th percentile of the average absolute iron intakes required (mg/person/day)

Total absolute iron requirements depend on sex, age, and lactating and menopausal status (the latter two for women only). Values are those reported in FAO/WHO (2004, 196). See table 5.4.

average animal iron availability (mg/person/day)

Average amount of iron from animal sources available for consumption. Iron has several vital functions in the body. It serves as a carrier of oxygen to the tissues from the lungs by red blood cell hemoglobin. Iron deficiency (sideropenia or hypoferremia) is one of the most common nutritional deficiencies. Symptoms of iron deficiency include fatigue, dizziness, pallor, hair loss, twitches, irritability, weakness, pica, brittle or grooved nails, Plummer-Vinson syndrome, impaired immune function, pagophagia, and restless legs syndrome. See tables 5.4, 6.1, 6.2, 6.3, 6.4, 6.7, 6.8, and 6.9.

average availability of animal iron provided by each food group, out of total availability (%)

Relative contribution (percent) of each food group to total animal iron. Table 6.5 provides national values. Table 6.6 provides values disaggregated by area of residence.

average availability of beta-carotene provided by each food group, out of total availability (%)

Relative contribution (percent) of each food group to total beta-carotene availability. Table 6.5 provides national values. Table 6.6 provides values disaggregated by area of residence.

average availability of calcium provided by each food group, out of total availability (%)

Relative contribution (percent) of each food group to total calcium availability. Table 6.5 provides national values. Table 6.6 provides values disaggregated by area of residence.

average availability of heme iron provided by each food group, out of total availability (%)

Relative contribution (percent) of each food group to total heme iron. Table 6.5 provides national values. Table 6.6 provides values disaggregated by area of residence.

average availability of nonanimal iron provided by each food group, out of total availability (%)	Relative contribution (percent) of each food group to total nonanimal iron. Table 6.5 provides national values. Table 6.6 provides values disaggregated by area of residence.
average availability of nonheme iron provided by each food group, out of total availability (%)	Relative contribution (percent) of each food group to total nonheme iron. Table 6.5 provides national values. Table 6.6 provides values disaggregated by area of residence.
average availability of retinol provided by each food group, out of total availability (%)	Relative contribution (percent) of each food group to total retinol availability. Table 6.5 provides national values. Table 6.6 provides values disaggregated by area of residence.
average availability of vitamin B1 provided by each food group, out of total availability (%)	Relative contribution (percent) of each food group to total vitamin B1 availability. Table 6.5 provides national values. Table 6.6 provides values disaggregated by area of residence.
average availability of vitamin B12 provided by each food group, out of total availability (%)	Relative contribution (percent) of each food group to total vitamin B12 availability. Table 6.5 provides national values. Table 6.6 provides values disaggregated by area of residence.
average availability of vitamin B2 provided by each food group, out of total availability (%)	Relative contribution (percent) of each food group to total vitamin B2 availability. Table 6.5 provides national values. Table 6.6 provides values disaggregated by area of residence.
average availability of vitamin B6 provided by each food group, out of total availability (%)	Relative contribution (percent) of each food group to total vitamin B6 availability. Table 6.5 provides national level values. Table 6.6 provides values disaggregated by area of residence.

163

average availability of vitamin C provided by each food group, out of total availability (%)

Relative contribution (percent) of each food group to total vitamin C availability. Table 6.5 provides national level values. Table 6.6 provides values disaggregated by area of residence.

average beta-carotene availability (mcg/person/day)

Average amount of beta-carotene available, expressed in micrograms per person per day. Beta-carotene (β-Carotene) is a strongly colored red-orange pigment abundant in plants and fruits. Its absorption is enhanced if eaten with fats, as carotenes are fat-soluble. See tables 5.1, 6.1, 6.2, 6.3, 6.4, 6.7, 6.8, and 6.9.

average calcium availability (mg/person/day)

Average amount of calcium available for consumption. Calcium salts provide rigidity to the skeleton, and calcium ions play a role in many if not most metabolic processes. A positive calcium balance (i.e., net calcium retention) is required throughout growth, particularly during the first two years of life and during puberty and adolescence. See tables 5.3, 6.1, 6.2, 6.3, 6.4, 6.7, 6.8, and 6.9.

average calcium availability per 1,000 kcal

Average amount of calcium (expressed in milligrams) available in 1,000 kilocalories. Being a relative measure, we can talk about density of calcium per 1,000 kcal. See table 5.5.

average heme iron availability (mg/person/day)

Average amount of heme iron available for consumption. With respect to the mechanism of absorption, there are two kinds of dietary iron: heme iron and nonheme iron. Primary sources of heme iron are the hemoglobin and myoglobin from consumption of meat, poultry, and fish. Heme iron can be degraded and converted to nonheme iron if foods are cooked at a high temperature for a long time. See tables 5.4, 6.1, 6.2, 6.3, 6.4, 6.7, 6.8, and 6.9.

average nonanimal iron availability (mg/person/day)

Average amount of iron from nonanimal sources available for consumption. Iron has several vital functions in the body. It serves as a carrier of oxygen to the tissues from the lungs by red blood cell hemoglobin. Iron deficiency (sideropenia or hypoferremia) is one of the most common nutritional deficiencies. Symptoms of iron deficiency include fatigue, dizziness, pallor, hair loss, twitches, irritability, weakness, pica, brittle or grooved nails, Plummer-Vinson syndrome, impaired immune function, pagophagia, and restless legs syndrome. See tables 5.4, 6.1, 6.2, 6.3, 6.4, 6.7, 6.8, and 6.9.

average nonheme iron availability (mg/person/day)

Average amount of nonheme iron available for consumption. With respect to the mechanism of absorption, there are two kinds of dietary iron: heme iron and nonheme iron. Primary sources of nonheme iron are cereals, pulses, legumes, fruits, and vegetables. The absorption of nonheme iron is influenced by the individual's iron status and the presence of some food components such as ascorbic acid, polyphenols, and phytates. See tables 5.4, 6.1, 6.2, 6.3, 6.4, 6.7, 6.8, and 6.9.

average retinol activity equivalent of vitamin A availability (mcg/person/day)

Average amount of retinol activity equivalent of vitamin A available for consumption. There are two sources of vitamin A: one is food from animal origin, which includes retinol, and the second one is food from plant origin, which includes beta-carotene. One unit of retinol is equivalent to one unit of vitamin A; however, in the case of carotenoids, the body converts them to vitamin A as shown in this formula:

Vitamin A = mcg of retinol
+ (mcg of beta-carotene/12)
+ (mcg of other carotenoids)/24

Vitamin A is an essential nutrient needed for the normal functioning of the visual system, growth and development, maintenance of epithelial cellular integrity, immune system functioning, and reproduction. The main consequence of vitamin A deficiencies is night blindness, which could develop into irreversible blindness. See tables 5.1, 5.6, 6.1, 6.2, 6.3, 6.4, 6.7, 6.8, and 6.9.

average retinol availability (mcg/person/day)

Average amount of retinol available for consumption. See tables 5.1, 6.1, 6.2, 6.3, 6.4, 6.7, 6.8, and 6.9

average vitamin A availability in 1,000 kcal

Average amount of vitamin A (expressed in micrograms of retinol activity equivalents) available in 1,000 kcal. Being a relative measure, we can talk about density of calcium per 1,000 kcal. See table 5.6.

average vitamin B1 availability in 1,000 kcal

Average amount of vitamin B1 (expressed in milligrams) available in 1,000 kcal. Being a relative measure, we can talk about density of vitamin B1 per 1,000 kcal. See table 5.7.

average vitamin B1 availability (mg/person/day)

Average amount of vitamin B1 available for consumption. B1 (otherwise called thiamin) deficiency results in the disease called beriberi. Beriberi occurs in breastfed infants whose nursing mothers are deficient. It also occurs in adults with high carbohydrate intake mainly from milled rice and with intake of antithiamin factors. See tables 5.2, 6.1, 6.2, 6.3, 6.4, 6.7, 6.8, and 6.9.

average vitamin B12 availability in 1,000 kcal

Average amount of vitamin B12 (expressed in micrograms) available in 1,000 kcal. Being a relative measure, we can talk about density of vitamin B12 per 1,000 kcal. See table 5.7.

average vitamin B12 availability (mcg/person/day)

Average amount of vitamin B12 available for consumption. Vitamin B12 (otherwise called cobalamin) enters the human food chain through food of animal origin. Products from herbivorous animals, such as milk, meat, and eggs, constitute important dietary sources of vitamin B12. Vitamin B12 deficiency can cause permanent damage to nervous tissue if left untreated longer than six months. See tables 5.2, 6.1, 6.2, 6.3, 6.4, 6.7, 6.8, and 6.9.

average vitamin B2 availability in 1,000 kcal

Average amount of vitamin B2 (expressed in milligrams) available in 1,000 kcal. Being a relative measure, we can talk about density of vitamin B2 per 1,000 kcal. See table 5.7.

average vitamin B2 availability (mg/person/day)

Average amount of vitamin B2 available for consumption. B2 (otherwise called riboflavin) deficiency results into hypo- or ariboflavinosis, with sore throat, hyperemia, oedema of the pharyngeal and oral mucous membranes, cheilosis, angular stomatitis, glossitis, seborrheic dermatitis, and normochromic, normocytic bone marrow. The major cause of hyporiboflavinosis is inadequate dietary intake as a result of limited food supply, which is sometimes exacerbated by poor food storage or processing. See tables 5.2, 6.1, 6.2, 6.3, 6.4, 6.7, 6.8, and 6.9.

average vitamin B6 availability in 1,000 kcal

Average amount of vitamin B6 (expressed in milligrams) available in 1,000 kcal. Being a relative measure, we can talk about density of vitamin B6 per 1,000 kcal. See table 5.7.

average vitamin B6 availability (mg/person/day)

Average amount of vitamin B6 available for consumption. Vitamin B6 deficiency usually occurs in association with a deficit in other B-complex vitamins. Infants are especially susceptible to insufficient intakes, which can lead to epileptiform convulsions. Skin changes include dermatitis with cheilosis and glossitis. A decrease in the metabolism of glutamate in the brain, which is found in vitamin B6 insufficiency, reflects a nervous system dysfunction. As is the case with other micronutrient deficiencies, vitamin B6 deficiency results in an impairment of the immune system. See tables 5.2, 6.1, 6.2, 6.3, 6.4, 6.7, 6.8, and 6.9.

average vitamin C availability in 1,000 kcal

Average amount of vitamin C (expressed in milligrams) available in 1,000 kcal. Being a relative measure, we can talk about density of vitamin C per 1,000 kcal. See table 5.6.

average vitamin C availability (mg/person/day)

Average amount of vitamin C available for consumption. Vitamin C mainly works as an antioxidant. Therefore chronic lack of vitamin C in the diet can lead to a condition called scurvy (i.e., easy bruising, spontaneous bleeding, and the joint and muscle pains). The populations at risk of vitamin C deficiency are those for whom the fruit and vegetable supply is minimal. Epidemics of scurvy are associated with famine and war, when people are forced to become refugees and the food supply is small and irregular. In many developing countries, limitations in the supply of vitamin C are often determined by seasonal factors. See tables 5.3, 6.1, 6.2, 6.3, 6.4, 6.7, 6.8, and 6.9.

calcium recommended intake in 1,000 kcal

Amount of recommended calcium intake per 1,000 kcal. See table 5.5.

calcium recommended intake (mg/person/day)

Amount of recommended calcium intake to meet the average daily nutrient intake needed by almost all apparently healthy individuals in the population group. Values are those reported in FAO/WHO (2004, 162). See table 5.3.

median of the average absolute iron intake required (mg/person/day)

Total absolute iron requirements depend on sex, age, and lactating and menopausal status (the latter two for women only). Values are those reported in FAO/WHO (2004, 196). See table 5.4.

ratio of calcium available to recommended (%)

Indicates whether the amount of calcium available to the households is sufficient to meet the average daily nutrient intake needed by almost all apparently healthy individuals in the population group. When the amount of available calcium exceeds the recommended amount, the ratio is above 1. However, we cannot talk about population out of risk of calcium deficiency because we do not have information of the actual intake. See tables 5.3 and 5.5.

ratio of retinol available to vitamin A available (%)	Ratio between retinol and vitamin A available for consumption, or the percentage of vitamin A that is due to the presence of retinol. See table 5.1.
ratio of vitamin A available to recommended (%)	Indicates whether the amount of vitamin A available to the households is sufficient to meet the average daily nutrient intake needed by almost all apparently healthy individuals in the population group. When the amount of available vitamin A exceeds the recommended amount, the ratio is above 1. However, we cannot talk about population out of risk of vitamin A deficiency because we do not have information of the actual intake. See tables 5.1 and 5.6.
ratio of vitamin A available to required (%)	Indicates whether the amount of vitamin A available to the households is sufficient to meet the average daily nutrient intake needed by 50 percent of the "healthy" individuals in the population group. When the amount of available vitamin A exceeds the required amount, the ratio is above 1. However, we cannot talk about population out of risk of vitamin A deficiency because we do not have information of the actual intake. See tables 5.1 and 5.6.
ratio of vitamin B1 available to recommended (%)	Indicates whether the amount of vitamin B1 available to the households is sufficient to meet the average daily nutrient intake needed by almost all apparently healthy individuals in the population group. When the amount of available

vitamin B1 exceeds the recommended amount, the ratio is above 1. However, we cannot talk about population out of risk of vitamin B1 deficiency because we do not have information of the actual intake. See tables 5.2 and 5.7.

ratio vitamin B12 available to recommended (%)

Indicates whether the amount of vitamin B12 available to the households is sufficient to meet the average daily nutrient intake needed by almost all apparently healthy individuals in the population group. When the amount of available vitamin B12 exceeds the recommended amount, the ratio is above 1. However, we cannot talk about population out of risk of vitamin B12 deficiency because we do not have information of the actual intake. See tables 5.2 and 5.7.

ratio vitamin B12 available to required (%)

Indicates whether the amount of vitamin B12 available to the households is sufficient to meet the average daily nutrient intake needs by 50 percent of the "healthy" individuals in the population group. When the amount of available vitamin B12 exceeds the required amount, the ratio is above 1. However, we cannot talk about population out of risk of vitamin B12 deficiency because we do not have information of the actual intake. See tables 5.2 and 5.7.

ratio vitamin B2 available to recommended (%)

Indicates whether the amount of vitamin B2 available to the households is sufficient to meet the average daily nutrient intake needed by almost all apparently healthy individuals in the population group. When the amount of available vitamin B2 exceeds the recommended amount, the ratio is above 1. However, we cannot talk about population out of risk of vitamin B2 deficiency because we do not have information of the actual intake. See tables 5.2 and 5.7.

ratio vitamin B6 available to recommended (%)	Indicates whether the amount of vitamin B6 available to the households is sufficient to meet the average daily nutrient intake needed by almost all apparently healthy individuals in the population group. When the amount of available vitamin B6 exceeds the recommended amount, the ratio is above 1. However, we cannot talk about population out of risk of vitamin B6 deficiency because we do not have information of the actual intake. See tables 5.2 and 5.7.
ratio vitamin C available to recommended (%)	Indicates whether the amount of vitamin C available to the households is sufficient to meet the average daily nutrient intake needed by almost all apparently healthy individuals in the population group. When the amount of available vitamin C exceeds the recommended amount, the ratio is above 1. However, we cannot talk about population out of risk of vitamin C deficiency because we do not have information of the actual intake. See tables 5.3 and 5.6.
vitamin A mean requirement in 1,000 kcal	Required amount of vitamin A (expressed in micrograms of retinol activity equivalent) per 1,000 kcalories. See table 5.6.
vitamin A mean requirement (mcg retinol activity equivalent/person/day)	Amount of required vitamin A intake to meet the average daily nutrient intake needed by 50 percent of the healthy individuals in the population group. Values are those reported in FAO/WHO (2004, 100). See table 5.1.
vitamin A recommended safe intake in 1,000 kcal	Recommended amount of vitamin A (expressed in micrograms of retino activity equivalent) per 1,000 kcal. The difference between vitamin A requirements and vitamin A recommended safe intake is reported in FAO/WHO (2004). See table 5.6.

vitamin A recommended safe intake (mcg retinol activity equivalent/ person/day)	Amount of recommended vitamin A intake to meet the average daily nutrient intake needed by almost all apparently healthy individuals in the population group. Values are those reported in FAO/WHO (2004, 100). See table 5.1.
vitamin B1 recommended intake (mg/person/day)	Amount of recommended vitamin B1 intake to meet the average daily nutrient intake needed by almost all apparently healthy individuals in the population group. Values are those reported in FAO/WHO (2004, 30). See table 5.2.
vitamin B1 recommended safe intake in 1,000 kcal	Recommended amount of vitamin B1 (expressed in milligrams) per 1,000 kcal. See table 5.7.
vitamin B12 average requirement in 1,000 kcal	Recommended amount of vitamin B12 (expressed in micrograms) per 1,000 kcal. See table 5.7.
vitamin B12 average requirement (mcg/person/day)	Amount of required vitamin B12 intake to meet the average daily nutrient intake needed by 50 percent of the healthy individuals in the population group. Values are those reported in FAO/WHO (2004, 69). See table 5.2.
vitamin B12 recommended intake (mcg/person/day)	Amount of recommended vitamin B12 intake to meet the average daily nutrient intake needed by almost all apparently healthy individuals in the population group. Values are those reported in FAO/WHO (2004, 69). See table 5.2.
vitamin B12 recommended safe intake in 1,000 kcal	Recommended amount of vitamin B12 (expressed in micrograms) per 1,000 kcal. See table 5.7.
vitamin B2 recommended intake (mg/person/day)	Amount of recommended vitamin B2 intake to meet the average daily nutrient intake needed by almost all apparently healthy individuals in the population group. Values are those reported in FAO/WHO (2004, 33). See table 5.2.

vitamin B2 recommended safe intake in 1,000 kcal	Recommended amount of vitamin B2 (expressed in milligrams) per 1,000 kcal. See table 5.7.
vitamin B6 recommended intake (mg/person/day)	Amount of recommended vitamin B6 intake to meet the average daily nutrient intake needed by almost all apparently healthy individuals in the population group. Values are those reported in FAO/WHO (2004, 38). See table 5.2.
vitamin B6 recommended safe intake in 1,000 kcal	Recommended amount of vitamin B6 (expressed in milligrams) per 1,000 kcal. See table 5.7.
vitamin C recommended intake (mg/person/day)	Amount of recommended vitamin C intake to meet the average daily nutrient intake needed by almost all apparently healthy individuals in the population group. Values are those reported in FAO/WHO (2004, 79). See table 5.3.
vitamin C recommended safe intake in 1,000 kcal	Recommended amount of vitamin C (expressed in milligrams) per 1,000 kcal. See table 5.6.

Indicators on Amino Acids

amino acid availability as percentage of total availability (%)	Proportion of the essential amino acids (provided by a group of food items) in total availability of the same amino acid, after correcting for protein digestibility. See tables 8.5, 8.6, and 8.7.
amino acid availability per gram of protein (mg)	Amount of the essential amino acids available for consumption per gram of protein after correcting for protein digestibility. See table 7.2.
histidine—average amino acid availability (g/person/day)	Average amount of the essential amino acid histidine available for consumption after correcting for protein digestibility. Statistics shown by population group are expressed in daily milligrams per person. Statistics shown at food group or food item level are expressed in daily grams per person. Histidine belongs to the aromatic amino acids and was accepted as an

indispensable amino acid in human adults, despite controversy regarding its essentiality (WHO 2002). See tables 7.1, 8.1, 8.2, 8.3, 8.4, 8.8, 8.9, and 8.10.

isoleucine—average amino acid availability (g/person/day)

Average amount of the essential amino acid isoleucine available for consumption after correcting for protein digestibility. Statistics shown by population group are expressed in daily milligrams per person. Statistics shown at food group or food item level are expressed in daily grams per person. See tables 7.1, 8.1, 8.2, 8.3, 8.4, 8.8, 8.9, and 8.10.

leucine—average amino acid availability (g/person/day)

Average amount of the essential amino acid leucine available for consumption after correcting for protein digestibility. Statistics shown by population group are expressed in daily milligrams per person. Statistics shown at food group or food item level are expressed in daily grams per person. Leucine is the most abundant amino acid in tissue and food proteins (WHO 2002). See tables 7.1, 8.1, 8.2, 8.3, 8.4, 8.8, 8.9, and 8.10.

lysine—average amino acid availability (g/person/day)

Average amount of the essential amino acid lysine available for consumption after correcting for protein digestibility. Statistics shown by population group are expressed in daily milligrams per person. Statistics shown at food group or food item level are expressed in daily grams per person. Lysine is the likely limiting amino acid in cereals, especially wheat (WHO 2002). See tables 7.1, 8.1, 8.2, 8.3, 8.4, 8.8, 8.9, and 8.10.

methionine and cystine—average amino acid availability (g/person/day)

Average amount of the essential amino acids methionine and cystine available for consumption after correcting for protein digestibility. Statistics shown by population group are expressed in daily milligrams per person. Statistics shown at food group or food item level are expressed in daily grams per person. Methionine and cystine are also called sulfur amino acids. The former is nutritionally indispensable while the latter, as a metabolic product of methionine catabolism, is dependent on there being sufficient methionine to supply the needs for both amino acids. Their concentrations are marginal in legume proteins, although they are equally abundant in cereal and animal proteins (WHO 2002). See tables 7.1, 8.1, 8.2, 8.3, 8.4, 8.8, 8.9, and 8.10.

phenylalanine and tyrosine—average amino acid availability (g/person/day)

Average amount of the essential amino acids phenylalanine and tyrosine available for consumption after correcting for protein digestibility. Statistics shown by population group are expressed in daily milligrams per person. Statistics shown at food group or food item level are expressed in daily grams per person. These two amino acids belong to the aromatic amino acids. Phenylalanine is nutritionally indispensable while tyrosine, as a metabolic product of phenylalanine catabolism, is dependent on there being sufficient phenylalanine to supply the needs for both amino acids (WHO 2002). See tables 7.1, 8.1, 8.2, 8.3, 8.4, 8.8, 8.9, and 8.10.

threonine—average amino acid availability (g/person/day)

Average amount of the essential amino acid threonine available for consumption after correcting for protein digestibility. Statistics shown by population group are expressed in daily milligrams per person. Statistics shown at food group or food item level are expressed in daily grams per person. Threonine is present at low concentrations in cereal proteins (WHO 2002). See tables 7.1, 8.1, 8.2, 8.3, 8.4, 8.8, 8.9, and 8.10.

tryptophan—average amino acid availability (g/person/day)

Average amount of the essential amino acid tryptophan available for consumption after correcting for protein digestibility. Statistics shown by population group are expressed in daily milligrams per person. Statistics shown at food group or food item level are expressed in daily grams per person. Tryptophan belongs to the aromatic amino acids. The occurrence of tryptophan in proteins is generally less than many other amino acids because its content is low in cereals, especially maize (WHO 2002). See tables 7.1, 8.1, 8.2, 8.3, 8.4, 8.8, 8.9, and 8.10.

valine—average amino acid availability (g/person/day)

Average amount of the essential amino acid valine available for consumption after correcting for protein digestibility. Statistics shown by population group are expressed in daily milligrams per person. Statistics shown at food group or food item level are expressed in daily grams per person. See tables 7.1, 8.1, 8.2, 8.3, 8.4, 8.8, 8.9, and 8.10.

Notes

1. Before executing ADePT-FSM, the user classifies the food commodities in different food groups. Further details can be found in chapter 2.
2. Further details can be found in chapter 2.
3. For the methodology applied at the subnational level, further details can be found in chapter 2.
4. Further details can be found in chapter 2.
5. See the following link: http://www.fao.org/economic/ess/ess-fs/fs -methods/adept-fsn/en/.
6. Further details can be found in chapter 2.
7. Further details can be found in chapter 2.
8. Available carbohydrates = total carbohydrates − fibers.

9. Available carbohydrates = total carbohydrates – fibers.
10. Available carbohydrates = total carbohydrates – fibers.
11. Available carbohydrates = total carbohydrates – fibers.
12. Available carbohydrates = total carbohydrates – fibers.
13. The food commodity quantities cannot be used for this comparison unless refuse factors and technical conversion factors for agricultural commodities (the same used in FBS) are applied to the food quantities consumed.
14. All food quantities include both the edible and the nonedible parts (i.e., peels, bones, spines, etc.).
15. All food quantities include both the edible and the nonedible parts (i.e., peels, bones, spines, etc.).
16. All food quantities include both the edible and the nonedible parts (i.e., peels, bones, spines, etc.).
17. EAR is the average daily nutrient intake level that meets the needs of 50 percent of the "healthy" individuals in a particular age and gender group. The RNI is the daily intake, set at the EAR plus 2 standard deviations, which meets the nutrient requirements of almost all apparently healthy individuals in an age- and sex-specific population group (FAO/WHO 2004). To express nutrient requirements and recommended intakes for population groups, the requirements by sex and age are applied to individuals and then summed for each population group of analysis. The individual requirements were defined for gender-age population groups by a FAO/WHO group of experts in 1998 (WHO 2004).
18. Iron deficiency is defined as a hemoglobin concentration below the optimum value in an *individual*, whereas iron deficiency anemia implies that the hemoglobin concentration is below the 95th percentile of the distribution of hemoglobin concentration in a *population* (disregarding effects of altitude, age, sex, etc., on hemoglobin concentration) (WHO 2004).
19. Further details can be found in chapter 2.
20. Further details can be found in chapter 2.
21. Further details can be found in chapter 2.
22. Further details can be found in chapter 2.
23. Further details can be found in chapter 2.
24. Further details can be found in chapter 2.
25. Further details can be found in chapter 2.

References

FAO, WHO (World Health Organization). 2004. *Vitamin and Mineral Requirements in Human Nutrition*, 2nd ed. Rome: FAO.

Fiedler, J. L. 2009. "Strengthening Household Income and Expenditure Surveys as a Tool for Designing and Assessing Food Fortification Programs." IHSN (International Household Survey Network) Working Paper 001. IHSN, United Nations, New York.

Hallberg, L. 1981. "Bioavailability of Dietary Iron in Man." *Annual Review of Nutrition* (1): 123–47.

NAS (National Academy of Sciences). 2000. *Dietary Reference Intakes: Applications in Dietary Assessment*. Washington, DC: National Academy Press. http://www.nap.edu/catalog/9956.html.

Schmidhuber, J. 2003. "Measurement and Assessment of Food Deprivation and Undernutrition: Household Expenditure Surveys." Discussion Group Report, International Scientific Symposium, Rome, June 26–28.

Smith, R. M. 1987. "Cobalt." In *Trace Elements in Human and Animal Nutrition*, 5th ed., edited by W. Mertz, 143–84, San Diego: Academic Press.

USHHS (United States Department of Health and Human Services), and USDA (United States Department of Agriculture). 2005. *Dietary Guidelines for Americans 2005*, 6th ed. Washington, DC: U.S. Government Printing Office.

WHO. 2002. *Protein and Amino Acid Requirements in Human Nutrition*. Geneva: WHO.

———. 2003. *Diet, Nutrition and the Prevention of Chronic Diseases*. WHO Technical Report Series 961, Geneva: WHO.

———. 2004. *Vitamin and Mineral Requirements in Human Nutrition*. 2nd ed. Joint FAO/WHO Expert Consultation on Human Vitamin and Mineral Requirements. Bangkok: WHO.

———. 2007. *Protein and Amino Acid Requirements in Human Nutrition*. WHO Technical Report Series 935, Geneva: WHO.

Bibliography

Aromolaran, A. 2004. "Intra-Household Redistribution of Income and Calorie Consumption in South-Western Nigeria." Discussion Paper 890. Yale University Economic Growth Center, New Haven, CT.

Cafiero, C. 2011. "Measuring Food Insecurity: Meaningful Concepts and Indicators for Evidence-Based Policy Making." Paper presented at the Food and Agriculture Organization conference "Round Table on Monitoring Food Security," Rome, September 12–13.

FAO (Food and Agriculture Organization). 1996. *The Sixth World Food Survey*. Rome: FAO.

———. 1999–2013. *The State of Food Insecurity in the World*. Rome: FAO.

McCormick, D. B. 1988. "Vitamin B6." In *Modern Nutrition in Health and Disease*, 6th ed., edited by M. E. Shils and V. R. Young, 376–82. Philadelphia: Lea and Febiger.

WHO, and UNHCR (United Nations High Commissioner for Refugees). 1999. *Thiamine Deficiency and Its Prevention and Control in Major Emergencies*. Geneva: WHO.

Chapter 4

Datasets

Ana Moltedo, Andrea Borlizzi, Chiara Brunelli, Yassin Firas,
Seevalingum Ramasawmy, Zurab Sajaia

Introduction

ADePT-FSM requires four datasets (loaded either in STATA or SPSS format). Three datasets contain data extracted mainly from the original national household surveys (NHS) files:

- Dataset 1 (HOUSEHOLD), including mainly household characteristics.
- Dataset 2 (INDIVIDUAL), with household member characteristics.
- Dataset 3 (FOOD), ideally with quantities and monetary values of food commodities habitually consumed by households. However, just a few surveys, such as yearly panel surveys' collecting information on food partakers, are designed to capture the household habitual food consumption. For this reason, in this book we refer to actual food consumed or acquired by households.

These three datasets include a household identification code that allows for matching information among them.

The fourth dataset contains data extracted from national and/or regional food composition tables (FCTs):

- Dataset 4 (COUNTRY_NCT [nutrition conversion table]), with calorie and nutrient values for the food commodities collected in the survey.

Datasets Description

Dataset 1 (HOUSEHOLD)

Dataset 1 has one record for each household and provides information on household characteristics (household size, region and area of residence, total consumption expenditure, income, etc.), and price indexes (i.e., the consumer price index [CPI] and the food price index [FPI]). While household characteristics are extracted from national household survey (NHS) data, the FPI and CPI are provided by national or international organizations, such as the International Labour Organization (ILO). The household characteristics are mainly used to create groupings and produce subnational estimates. The FPI and CPI are instrumental for deflating the food expenditures and income/expenditure values, respectively, in the presence of one-year surveys.

Table 4.1 shows the main characteristics of the variables included in dataset 1, the values they can assume, and the associated checks to be performed.

Variable names depicted in the table are not mandatory; however comparison of results intra- and intercountries is greatly facilitated if a common set of variable names is adopted. Each variable, and each value of categorical variables, has to be described by an appropriate label. Finally, none of the variables are allowed to have missing values.

An important distinction has to be made between *Household member* and *Food partaker*. While only household members share the household income, the food acquired by the household can be distributed to nonhousehold members (such as guests and employees). Therefore, the number of food partakers corresponds to the number of people who actually consumed the food during the reference period.

Example of a reference period for food consumption data for one month:

- A household reported four members
- One member was absent
- One guest and one housekeeper with a child also consumed the food acquired by the household

In this case, the number of partakers for the reference period will be six instead of four: four household members minus the absent member plus the guest, the housekeeper, and the child.

Table 4.1: Dataset 1 (HOUSEHOLD)

Variable name and format	Rationale and values	Remarks and checks
Household number (hh_no) Format: Numeric or string	Identification code of the surveyed household. Sequential numbers or a combination of geographical codes (district, area, village, region, etc.). Necessary to link dataset 1 with datasets 2 and 3.	Each household has to be identified by a unique code. Only households declaring food consumption should be included.
Location of the household (region) Format: Numeric	Identification code of the district, province, or region of residence of the surveyed household. This variable has to *include the labels* corresponding to the geographical groups.	It is recommended that each location is represented by about 500 households to have reliable estimates also at the income deciles level (a statistic obtained with fewer than 30 households is considered not reliable). Thus it may be necessary to group some locations into a new one.
Area of residence of the household (urb_rur) Format: Numeric	Identification code of the area (urban, rural, semiurban, etc.) of residence of the surveyed household. This variable has to *include the labels* corresponding to the areas. Examples: • Code = 1, Label: *Urban* • Code = 2, Label: *Rural*	It is recommended that each area is represented by about 500 households to have reliable estimates also at the income deciles level (a statistic obtained with fewer than 30 households is considered not reliable). Thus it may be necessary to group some areas into a new one (for instance, urban with semiurban).
Household size (hh_size) Format: Numeric	Number of people who usually live together and share the household income.	Excludes • Domestic workers, friends, or relatives who neither live in the house nor share the income • Domestic workers, friends, or relatives who live in the house but don't share the household income
Category of household size (hhsizec) Format: Numeric	Identification code of category of household size. This variable has to *include the labels*. Examples: • Code = 1, Label: *Less than three* • Code = 2, Label: *Three or four* • Code = 3, Label: *Five or six* • Code = 4, Label: *More than six*	It is recommended that each category of household size is represented by about 500 households to have reliable estimates also at the income deciles level (a statistic obtained with fewer than 30 households is considered not reliable).
Number of food partakers (partakers) Format: Numeric	Average number of people who shared the food during the period of food data collection (reference period).	Partakers are individuals who shared the household food during the reference period. Includes housekeepers, friends, and relatives who may not live in the house but shared the food. Excludes household members who were absent during the food data reference period and therefore did not consume the food.
Household weight (hh_wgt) Format: Decimal	The value of the household weight depends on the sampling frame and is equal to the expansion factor divided by the probability of the household to be sampled. *Household weight* should be *adjusted* for nonresponding households.	The sum of the product *number of household members * household weight* has to be close to the total country population at the year of the survey. Only households declaring food consumption should be included in this dataset. Therefore, after deleting households that did not declare food consumption, household weight should be amended accordingly. Details are provided at the bottom of the table.

(continued)

Table 4.1: Dataset 1 (HOUSEHOLD) (continued)

Variable name and format	Rationale and values	Remarks and checks
Total household consumption expenditure (thh_cexp) Format: Decimal	Sum of household food and nonfood consumption expenditures. Excludes all expenditures not related to household *consumption*, such as investments, life insurance premiums, food for pets or given away, etc.	Monetary values should be expressed in *daily basis*. Each household should have a *positive* value of total consumption expenditure. This value has to be greater than or at least equal to the respective household total food expenditure.
Total household income (thh_inc) Format: Decimal	Sum of the income received by each household member; includes all the possible sources (wages, profit from self-employment, sales of self-produced goods and services, income in kind, transfers, rent received, etc.).[a]	Monetary values should be expressed in *daily basis*. If income data are either not available or not reliable, *total expenditure* can be used as a proxy of income. Total expenditure includes consumption and nonconsumption expenditures such as direct taxes, insurance premiums, food given away or animal feed, etc. Each household should have a *positive* value of total income. Also, this value has to be greater than or at least equal to the respective household total consumption expenditure.
Primary sampling unit (psu) Format: Numeric	Identification code of the smallest sampling geographic unit from which households are selected.	
Month of food data collection (month) Format: Numeric	Identification code of the month during which the food consumption/acquisition data were collected. This variable has to include labels, e.g., values of *1, 2, 3 . . . 12* corresponding to the months January, February, March . . . December.	
Year of the food data collection (year) Format: Numeric	Identification code of the year during which the food consumption/acquisition data were collected. Examples: Values of *1998, 1999, 2000, 2003 . . .* etc.	
Consumer price index (cpi) Format: Decimal	Measures the changes in the purchasing power of a currency and the rate of inflation. The consumer price index expresses the current prices of a basket of goods and services in terms of the prices during the same period in a previous year, which shows the effect of inflation on purchasing power. It is one of the best-known lagging indicators. It is used to correct total consumption expenditure and total income for inflation or deflation. All the consumer price indexes should refer to the same base period.[b]	Use the value corresponding to the month and year in which the household food consumption data were collected. If the monetary values are already deflated (or the survey was conducted only over a period of a few months), this variable is not needed.

(continued)

Table 4.1: Dataset 1 (HOUSEHOLD) (continued)

Variable name and format	Rationale and values	Remarks and checks
Food price index (fpi) Format: Decimal	Measures the changes in the purchasing power of a currency and the rate of inflation. The food price index expresses the current prices of a food basket in terms of the prices during the same period in a previous year, which shows the effect of inflation on purchasing power. It is used to correct food monetary values for inflation or deflation. All the food price indexes should refer to the same base period.[c]	Use the value corresponding to the month and year in which the household food consumption data was collected. If the monetary values are already deflated (or the survey was conducted only over a period of a few months), this variable is not needed.

a. For detailed information refer to the *Canberra Handbook on Household Income Statistics* (2nd ed., 2011) at http://www.unece.org/index.php?id=28894.
b. Sources of data: National or international institutions such as ILO. This information can also be found in FAOSTAT: http://faostat.fao.org/site/683/Default.aspx#ancor.
c. Sources of data: National or international institutions such as ILO. This information can also be found in FAOSTAT: http://faostat.fao.org/site/683/Default.aspx#ancor.

The number of partakers is not always collected in household surveys. However, it is highly recommended to check if this information is available. If so, the variable *Number of partakers* has to be included in dataset 1.

When deriving the statistics related to a variable of analysis such as the location or area of residence, ADePT-FSM excludes all records with missing values in that variable. The consequence of this could be to produce unreliable statistics for that group of analysis. Therefore, it is important to avoid the presence of missing values as much as possible.

Another crucial note regards the variable *Location of the household*. The analyst should always select the geographical domain(s) of which the survey data is representative.[1] For instance, if the original NHS datasets include both the variable *Province* and the variable *Region*, and the survey was designed to be representative at the province level, then the analyst should select the province.

Finally, only the households that declared food consumption should be in dataset 1; the other ones should be deleted. After the deletion, the household weights should be amended, as follows:

1. Sum by enumeration area: (*hh_size* * *hh_wgt*); note that at the national level (*hh_size* * *hh_wgt*) = *population_original* (≈ total country population at the survey year).
2. Delete the households that did not declare food from dataset 1.
3. Sum by enumeration area: (*hh_size* * *hh_wgt*) = *population_new*.
4. Compute: *hh_wgt_adj* = *hh_wgt* * (*population_original* / *population_new*).

Screenshot 4.1: Example of Dataset 1 in SPSS Format (L: Data View, R: Variable View)

Dataset 2 (INDIVIDUAL)

Dataset 2 has one record for each member of the household and provides information on members' characteristics such as gender, age, height, occupation, and education.

Age, gender, and height are necessary to estimate the dietary energy requirements of the population. Even though some NHS collect data on height, this is usually done only for children under five years of age and/or for women of reproductive age. Therefore, the distribution of height across the gender/age groups is usually derived from other sources such as demographic and health surveys, country reference tables, or specific publications (for example, James and Schofield 1990).[2]

Characteristics of the household members, particularly of the household head, can be used to disaggregate food consumption statistics by population groups (i.e., derive subnational estimates).

In addition, the analyst can also define up to five "spare" variables to further disaggregate the food consumption statistics (hm_var1, hm_var2, ..., hm_var5). The spare variables can correspond to household/household head characteristics or can be a combination of them.

When deriving statistics related to a variable such as education or occupation, ADePT-FSM excludes all records with missing values in that variable. The consequence of this could be to produce unreliable statistics for that group of analysis. Therefore, it is important to avoid the presence of missing values as much as possible.

Gender Disaggregated Analysis

Combining two variables into one is particularly useful in the context of gender analysis. ADePT automatically disaggregates all the statistics by gender of the household head. However, a more in-depth analysis can be carried out by combining the gender of the household head with other demographic and economic characteristics to produce a household typology. For instance, combining gender with the region/area of residence provides useful information for targeting aid and development programs. The following interaction effects are worth consideration:

- *Gender of the household head and area/region:* Gender-based gaps might be very different in urban and rural areas.
- *Gender of the household head and household size:* It is particularly interesting to assess gender disparities controlling for the household size. It is especially relevant to look at large and single-headed households that might be more exposed to poverty and food insecurity.
- *Gender of the household head and household composition:* Similarly, it is important to interpret gender-based disparities in view of the household demographic profile. This might include comparisons between male/female single parents, male/female-headed households with and without children under five years of age, etc.
- *Gender of the household head and presence of dependents in the household*
- *Gender and age of the household head*
- *Gender of the household head and household income group:* It is particularly interesting to see if gender-based differences exist by controlling for the household income status.
- *Gender and education of the household head*
- *Gender and marital status of the household head*
- *Gender and economic sector/occupation of the household head*

In many countries, female-headed households are a small percentage of the entire sample. Therefore, the combination of two variables may result in a very low number of observations. This is particularly true when the survey sample is not very large. The analyst should take this issue into consideration and avoid creating categories with very few observations.

A preliminary cross-tabulation helps to detect the combinations with a low number of cases. In screenshot 4.2, the cross-tabulation of gender and education of the household head clearly suggests one should merge the educational status into broader categories to build a combined variable whose categories have an acceptable number (a minimum of 500) of elements.

It is not always possible to reach the suggested minimum number (a minimum of 500) of observations. For instance, in screenshot 4.2, the merging of no education and primary education gives 550 observations to the category *female heads–no education or primary*. But the merging of secondary and more than secondary gives only 250 observations to the category *female–secondary or more*. Even though 250 is enough to obtain reliable estimates at the national level, it might not be sufficient to obtain reliable estimates across the income deciles. In fact, with only 250 cases, it is very likely to have fewer than 30 heads of households in one or more of the income decile groups (table 4.2).

In such cases, it is important to keep in mind that the food consumption statistics with fewer than 30 heads of households have poor reliability. Table 4.3 shows the main characteristics of the variables included in dataset 2, the values they can assume, and the associated checks to be performed. Like dataset 1, variable names depicted in the table are not mandatory.

Screenshot 4.2: Cross-Tabulation of Gender and Education of the Household Head

		no edu	primary	secondary	more than secondary			Number of households
Gender HH head	Male	726	762	761	776		female-no education or primary	550
	Female	350	200	150	100		female-secondary or more	250
							male-no education or primary	1488
							female-secondary or more	1537

Table 4.2: Review of the Number of Observations within the Population Groups

	Number of households	DEC (kcal/person/day)
Female—secondary or more	250	1650
Lowest	37	1400
2	30	1400
3	25	1450
4	25	1500
5	25	1670
6	28	1640
7	30	1800
8	25	1940
9	10	1800
Highest	15	1900

Table 4.3: Dataset 2 (INDIVIDUAL)

Variable name and format	Rationale and values	Remarks and checks
Household number (hh_no) Format: Numeric or string	Identification code of the household. Sequential numbers or a combination of geographical codes (district, area, village, region, etc.). Necessary for linking dataset 2 with datasets 1 and 3.	Each household has to be identified by a unique code. Only the households declaring food consumption should be included in this dataset.
Relationship between the household member and the head of the household (hm_rel) Format: Numeric	Identification code of the relationship between the household member and the head of the household. This variable has to *include labels*. The *compulsory value code* for the head of the household is 1. *Exclude* all individuals who do not share the household income, such as housekeeper, guests, and relatives who do not live in the house or live in the household but do not share the household income.	*All households* must have a household head. There has to be only *one head* per household.
Gender of the household member (gender) Format: Numeric	Identification code of the gender of the household member. This variable has to *include labels* corresponding to both sexes. Compulsory value codes: • Code = 1, Label: *Male* • Code = 2, Label: *Female*	Missing data on gender are not valid; each household member has to have a value of 1 or 2.
Age of the household member (hm_age) Format: Numeric	Values are to be expressed in years. For children less than one year of age, assign the value 0.	Missing data on age are not valid; each household member has to have an age value.
Household member age category (hmagec) Format: Numeric	Identification code of the group to which the household member belongs according to age. This variable has to *include the labels*. Example: • Code = 1, Label: *Less than 30* • Code = 2, Label: *Between 30 and 44* • Code = 3, Label: *Between 45 and 59* • Code = 4, Label: *More than 59*	Records with missing values are deleted by the program, and this may cause unreliable estimates for the variable. To have reliable estimates of the age of the household head, it is recommended that about 500 *household heads* are represented in each age category. The reason for this is to also have reliable estimates by income deciles (a statistic obtained with fewer than 30 households is considered unreliable).
Height of the household member (height) Format: Decimal	Values are to be expressed in cm.	Missing data on height are not valid; each household member must have a value greater than 0 in this variable. When height data are not collected in the survey, the median height by age/sex groups obtained from national reference tables, specific publications, or household demographic surveys should be used.
Marital status of the household member (hm_mar) Format: Numeric	Identification code of the group to which the household member belongs according to marital status. This variable has to *include the labels*. Examples: • Code = 1, Label: *Single* • Code = 2, Label: *Married or living together* • Code = 3, Label: *Widower* • Code = 4, Label: *Divorced or separated*	Missing values are not allowed for the household heads (*hm_rel = 1*). To have reliable estimates, of the marital status of the household head, it is recommended that about 500 *household heads* are represented in each category of marital status. The reason for this is to also have reliable estimates by income deciles (a statistic obtained with fewer than 30 households is considered unreliable).

(continued)

189

Table 4.3: Dataset 2 (INDIVIDUAL) (continued)

Variable name and format	Rationale and values	Remarks and checks
Economic activity (hm_eact) Format: Numeric	Identification code of the group to which the household member belongs according to economic activity. Recode the economic activities collected in the survey into major economic activity groups defined by the first digit of national or international classifications such as ISIC (Rev. 4).[a] This variable has to *include labels*. Examples: • Code = 1, Label: *Primary (agriculture, fishing, hunting, and mining)* • Code = 2, Label: *Secondary (manufacturing)* • Code = 3, Label: *Services* • Code = 4, Label: *Without an activity*	Records with missing values are deleted by the program and this may cause unreliable estimates for the variable. To have reliable estimates, of by the economic activity of the household head, it is recommended that about 500 *household heads* are represented in each major activity. The reason for this is to also have reliable estimates by income deciles (a statistic obtained with fewer than 30 households is considered unreliable).
Occupation (hm_occ) Format: Numeric	Identification code of the group to which the household member belongs according to occupation. It is highly recommended to recode the occupations collected in the survey into major occupation groups defined by the first digit of national/international classifications such as ISCO.[b] This variable has to *include labels*. Examples: • Code = 1, Label: *Managers and professionals* • Code = 2, Label: *Technicians and clerical support* • Code = 3, Label: *Service and sales workers* • Code = 4, Label: *Agricultural, forest, fishery workers* • Code = 5, Label: *Without occupation*	Records with missing values are deleted by the program and this may cause unreliable estimates for the variable. To have reliable estimates, of by the occupation of the household head, it is recommended that about 500 *household heads* are represented in each major occupation. The reason for this is to also have reliable estimates by income deciles (a statistic obtained with fewer than 30 households is considered unreliable).
Highest level of education (hm_edu) Format: Numeric	Identification code of the group to which the household member belongs according to the highest level of education attended by them. This variable has to *include labels*. Examples: • Code = 1, Label: *No education* • Code = 2, Label: *Primary school* • Code = 3, Label: *Secondary school* • Code = 4, Label: *Tertiary education*	Records with missing values are deleted by the program and this may cause unreliable estimates for the variable. To have reliable estimates, of by the highest level of education the household head attended, it is recommended that about 500 *household heads* are represented in each level of education. The reason for this is to also have reliable estimates by income deciles (a statistic obtained with fewer than 30 households is considered unreliable).
Additional variables with household/household member characteristics (hm_var1, . . ., hm_var5) Format: Numeric	Identification code of the group to which the household member belongs according to additional variables. Some examples are *Religion, Ethnic group, Household with or without children under 5, Source of drinkable water*, etc. These variables should *include the labels*.	Records with missing values are deleted by the program and this may cause unreliable estimates for the variable. To have reliable estimates, of the characteristic of the household head, it is recommended that about 500 *household heads* are represented in each category of the group. The reason for this is to also have reliable estimates by income deciles (a statistic obtained with fewer than 30 households is considered unreliable).

Note: ISCO - International Standard Classification of Occupations.

a. For more information, see http://unstats.un.org/unsd/cr/registry/isic-4.asp.

b. For more information, see http://www.ilo.org/public/english/bureau/stat/isco/index.htm.

Screenshot 4.3: Example of Dataset 2 in SPSS Format (L: Data View, R: Variable View)

hh_no	hm_rel	gender	hm_age	hmagec	height	hm_mar	hm_eact	hm_occ	hm_edu	hm_var1	hm_var2	hm_var3	hm_var4	hm_var5
100101	3	1	1	2	76.5	1	3	2	1	3	1	2	1	
100101	1	1	38	2	166.7	1	3	2	1	3	1	2	1	
100101	2	2	34	2	153.1	1	3	2	1	3	1	2	1	
100101	3	2	13	2	138.3	1	3	2	1	3	1	2	1	
100101	3	2	8	2	115.0	1	3	2	1	3	1	2	1	
100102	3	1	10	2	131.1	1	1	1	1	2	1	1	1	
100102	1	1	39	2	166.7	1	1	1	1	2	1	1	1	
100102	2	2	34	2	153.1	1	1	1	1	2	1	1	1	
100102	3	2	13	2	138.3	1	1	1	1	2	1	1	1	
100103	3	1	23	3	164.8	1	1	1	1	3	1	1	1	
100103	1	1	46	3	163.4	1	1	1	1	3	1	1	1	
100103	3	2	13	3	138.3	1	1	1	1	3	1	1	1	
100103	3	2	11	3	129.0	1	1	1	1	3	1	1	1	
100103	3	2	5	3	101.1	1	1	1	1	3	1	1	1	
100103	2	2	46	3	151.2	1	1	1	1	3	1	1	1	

Name	Type	Width	Decimals	Label	Values
hh_no	Numeric	7	0	Household number	None
hm_rel	Numeric	11	0	Relationship	{1, Head}...
gender	Numeric	1	0	Sex	{1, Male}...
hm_age	Numeric	3	0	Age in whole years	None
hmagec	Numeric	1	0	Age group	{1, Less than 35 years old}...
height	Numeric	8	1	Height in cm	None
hm_mar	Numeric	8	0	Marital status	{1, Married}...
hm_eact	Numeric	8	0	Economic activity	{1, Agriculture}...
hm_occ	Numeric	8	0	Occupation	{1, Agriculture}...
hm_edu	Numeric	8	0	Education	{1, Primary school}...
hm_var1	Numeric	8	0	Number of children under 18 years old	{1, One child}...
hm_var2	Numeric	8	0	Type of access to potable water	{1, Public fountain}...
hm_var3	Numeric	6	0	Gender - Economic Activity	{1, Male - Agriculture}...
hm_var4	Numeric	8	0	Gender-Education	{1, Male - Primary School}...
hm_var5	Numeric	8	0	Gender - Area	{1, Male - Urban}...

Each variable/variable's value has to be described by an appropriate label explaining its content of information. None of the variables are allowed to have missing values for the household head.[3]

Finally, for each household, the number of records in dataset 2 should be equal to the corresponding value of the variable *hh_size* (size of the household) in dataset 1. This means only information about household members is required in this dataset. Therefore, records related to food partakers, such as housekeepers, friends, and relatives who are not household members, should be excluded from dataset 2.

Dataset 3 (FOOD)

Dataset 3 contains information on the household food consumption both in quantity and monetary terms, disaggregated by four main food sources. Each record corresponds to a food item consumed/acquired by the household through a specific source; the dataset may therefore have one or more entries of a given food item per household, depending on the number of sources from which the food item is obtained.[4]

Data in the food dataset should fulfill the following requirements:

- All the food item quantities (including beverages) should be expressed in only one standard unit of measurement to be chosen among kilogram, gram, or pound. For this reason, the analyst has to transform all the food quantities into one unit.

191

- Food quantities and monetary values should be expressed on a daily basis. It is important to identify the actual reference period for which the households declared food consumption. The recall period is usually clearly stated at the beginning of the food module in the questionnaire, and the enumerators should have had the responsibility to convey the message as clearly as possible. This check is particularly relevant when food data are collected with a diary. In a consumption survey, if a diary is given to the households for a week, households may skip some days. In these cases, the reference period is the actual number of days the diary was filled in. However, in an acquisition survey, the same situation may require a different treatment. If a household is asked to report the food acquired in a week, and the diary is filled in for three days with considerable daily quantities, then it is likely that the food acquired in the three days also covers the four days with missing data. In this case, the most accurate reference period is still seven.

- Food quantities must be related with the variable *Number of food partakers* or *Household size*. Food quantities should be expressed at the household level, not in "per person" amounts. ADePT-FSM automatically calculates the per person values by using the variable *Number of food partakers*, if available; otherwise, it uses the variable *Household size*. Also, food monetary values have to be expressed at the household level so that ADePT automatically calculates the per person values by using the variable *Household size* (note that the variable *Food partakers* is not taken into consideration when deriving food monetary values at the individual level).

The preparation of the food dataset may require some computational steps to accurately estimate missing quantities of food consumed or monetary values.

Estimate Accurate Quantities of Food Consumption

Since the analysis is focused on the food consumed by the household (HH), the food given away, processed for resale, given to pets/livestock, and wasted has to be excluded. Such detailed data are rarely collected in the NHS, but if they are collected they should be subtracted from the total amount of food acquired. Details are provided in table 4.4.

Table 4.4: Treatment of Food Acquired but Not Consumed by the Household

• Food given away (e.g., to other households, neighbors)	⟹	Subtract from the household food consumption the food given away
• Food processed for resale (e.g., flour, sugar, eggs used for a cake to be sold)	⟹	Subtract from the household food consumption the food acquired for resale
• Food given to pets or for feeding livestock	⟹	Subtract from the household food consumption the food given to pets or used for feeding livestock
• Food thrown away (e.g., rotten, wasted, etc.)	⟹	Subtract from the household food consumption the food thrown away

Table 4.5: Dataset 3 (FOOD)

Variable name and format	Rationale and values	Remarks and checks
Household number (hh_no) Format: Numeric or string	Identification code of the household. Sequential numbers or a combination of geographical codes (district, area, village, region, etc.). Necessary to link dataset 3 with datasets 1 and 2.	Each household has to be identified by a unique code. Only the households declaring food consumption should be included in the dataset.
Food item code (item_cod) Format: Numeric	Identification code of the food items listed in the survey. This variable should *include labels*. COICOP[a] or national classification codes can be used.	Include alcoholic beverages and food consumed away from home (canteens, bars, restaurants, etc.). Exclude nonfood items, such as cigars, cigarettes, tobacco, and drugs.
Food item quantity (fd_qty) Format: Decimal	Food quantities should reflect the *food consumption or acquisition* of the household. All food quantities should be expressed on a *daily basis*. All food quantities, *including beverages*, should be expressed in the *same unit of measurement*. The unit of measurement can only be *grams, kilograms, or pounds*. Keep track (by using labels or adding an extra variable) of the unit of measurement used.	ADePT estimates the calories and nutrients of missing food quantities *only* for the food consumed away from home. If a household *declared* expenditure for a food item with a food source different from 4 (consumed away), the quantity cannot be missing or 0. *The analyst has to estimate* the missing/0 quantities based on the unit values. The estimation has to be carried out *before* loading the dataset in ADePT.
Food item monetary value in local currency (fd_mv) Format: Decimal	Amount paid or estimated for the reported quantity. All food monetary values should be expressed on a *daily basis*.	If a household declared a quantity for a food item, the expenditure/monetary value cannot be missing or 0. *The analyst has to estimate* the missing/0 expenditure/monetary values based on the food item unit values. The estimation has to be carried out *before* loading the dataset in ADePT.
Source of food item (f_source) Format: Numeric	Identification code of the food source. This variable should *include labels*. Compulsory value codes. Examples: • Code = 1, Label: *Purchased and consumed at home* • Code = 2, Label: *Own production* • Code = 3, Label: *Received in kind* • Code = 4, Label: *Consumed away from home*	ADePT analyzes *four food sources*. If there are *fewer than four food sources, keep this coding structure.* Food sources such as received free or as a gift, from food aid, income in kind, gathering, or fishing should be labeled as *Received in kind* with code 3. No missing values are allowed in this variable.

Note: COICOP = Classification of Individual Consumption According to Purpose.
a. For further information see http://unstats.un.org/unsd/cr/registry/regcst.asp?Cl=5.

Screenshot 4.4: Example of Dataset 3 in SPSS Format (L: Data View, R: Variable View)

hh_no	item_cod	fd_qty	fd_mv	f_source
100101	1061	581.25	2386.67	1
100101	1080	275.00	1000.00	1
100101	1090	7000.00	83000.0	1
100101	1091	1625.35	17496.4	1
100101	1100	880.56	10582.5	1
100101	1130	2500.00	34000.0	1
100101	1130	1291.67	12857.1	3
100101	1170	250.00	6000.00	1
100102	1010	30000.0	85800.0	2
100102	1050	4000.00	4800.00	1
100102	1051	400.00	2000.00	1
100102	1052	710.00	3100.00	1
100102	1090	6900.00	82700.0	1
100102	1130	5000.00	63000.0	1

Name	Type	Width	Decimals	Label	Values	
hh_no	Numeric	7	0	Household Number	None	N
item_cod	Numeric	8	0	Food item code	{1010, Rice}...	N
fd_qty	Numeric	8	2	Food quantity	None	N
fd_mv	Numeric	8	2	Food monetary value	None	N
f_source	Numeric	8	0	Food source	None	N

It is also important to check if information on the *starting and ending levels of food stock* are available, especially when the survey collects food acquisition data. If data on stocks are collected, they should be used as follows to derive the household food consumption:

$$\text{HH food consumption} = \text{HH food acquired} + \text{HH starting food stock} - \text{HH ending food stock}$$

Estimate Missing Quantities and Expenditures

For a food item reported by the household, a food quantity with a missing or 0 value is allowed *only* if the food item was consumed away from home ($f\_source = 4$). For food expenditure, missing or 0 values are not accepted. Therefore, before loading the data in ADePT, the analyst must estimate the missing/0 values based on median food item unit values. See chapter 2 for a detailed account of such procedures.

Table 4.5 illustrates the main characteristics of the variables included in dataset 3, the values they can assume, and the associated checks to be performed.

Variable names depicted in the table are not mandatory. Each variable has to be described by an appropriate *label* explaining its content.

Dataset 4 (COUNTRY_NCT)

Dataset 4 contains information on the composition of each food item listed in the survey, in terms of energy and nutrients per 100 grams *edible*[5] portion (nutrient values). This information is found in national or regional food composition tables (FCT) available either online (e.g., USDA FCT) or in hard copy (e.g., ASEAN FCT). To build dataset 4, the analyst has to match each food item listed in the survey with a food item described in the selected FCT.

This section is divided into two parts. The first one describes the variables to be included in the dataset; the second provides detailed guidelines on how to build it.

Variables in Dataset 4

Dataset 4 includes three distinct groups of variables.

- The first group includes calorie and macronutrient values, and it represents the minimum information required to execute the ADePT-Food Security Module.
- The second group includes nutrient values for some vitamins and minerals, necessary to conduct a micronutrient analysis.
- The third group includes nutrient values for essential amino acids, necessary to conduct an analysis of amino acids.

The following tables show the main characteristics of the variables included in dataset 4 and the associated checks to be performed.

Table 4.6 describes the minimum information required:

Table 4.7 focuses on the micronutrient analysis.

Finally, Table 4.8 regards the information needed for the amino acids analysis. Not all the food composition tables have information on amino acids. Information on amino acids can be found in the following sources:

- U.S. Department of Agriculture: http://www.nal.usda.gov/fnic /foodcomp/search/index.html
- FAO website for Amino-Acid Content of Foods and Biological Data on Proteins: http://www.fao.org/docrep/005/AC854T/AC854T00 .HTM
- Tanzania Food Composition Table: http://www.fao.org/infoods /infoods/tables-and-databases/africa/en/
- Danish Food Composition Databank (Rev 5.0): http://www.fao.org /infoods/infoods/tables-and-databases/europe/en/

Table 4.6: Dataset 4 (COUNTRY_NCT): Minimum Information Required

Variable name and format	Rationale and values	Remarks and checks
Food item code (item_cod) Format: Numeric	Identification code of the food item in the survey (e.g., COICOP or national classification codes). This variable has to *include labels* corresponding to the food items.	Includes alcoholic beverages and food consumed away from home (canteens, bars, restaurants, etc.). Excludes cigars, cigarettes, tobacco, and drugs. There has to be one record for each food item collected in the survey. No missing values are allowed for this variable.
Food commodity group (item_grp) Format: Numeric	Identification code of the food commodity group to which the food item belongs. The file FOOD_GROUPS.xls suggests a classification of food items into food item groups.[a] This variable has to *include labels.*	No missing values are allowed in this variable.
Refuse factor (refuse) Format: Numeric	Proportion of the nonedible portion of the food item.[b]	The refuse factor has to be expressed in *percentage*: • 0% if the food item is 100% edible (e.g., rice, milk, fillet of fish without spines, meat without bones, and peanuts without shell). • In the case of tea (in leaves) and coffee (in powder) it is suggested to assign 95%. This estimation is based on the assumption that only 1/20 of nutrients is going to the liquid tea/coffee. • Between 1% and 95% for food items having nonedible portions (e.g., meat with bones, whole fish, peanuts in shell, bananas).
Nutrient value for water (water) Format: Decimal	Grams of water per 100 grams *edible portion* of the food item. Values are compiled from food composition tables.	Missing data are accepted *only* for food items for which it is not possible to define their food composition, such as meals at school or restaurant, lunch, and dinner (food consumed away from home).
Nutrient value for ash (ash) Format: Decimal	Grams of ash per 100 grams *edible portion* of the food item. Values are compiled from food composition tables.	Missing data are accepted *only* for food items for which it is not possible to define their food composition, such as meals at school or restaurant, lunch, and dinner (food consumed away from home).
Nutrient value for protein (fd_pro) Format: Decimal	Grams of protein per 100 grams *edible portion* of the food item. Values are compiled from food composition tables.	Missing data are accepted *only* for food items for which it is not possible to define their food composition, such as meals at school or restaurant, lunch, and dinner (food consumed away from home).
Nutrient value for fats (fd_fat) Format: Decimal	Grams of fats per 100 grams *edible portion* of the food item. Values are compiled from food composition tables.	Missing data are accepted *only* for food items for which it is not possible to define their food composition, such as meals at school or restaurant, lunch, and dinner (food consumed away from home).
Nutrient value for fiber (fd_fib) Format: Decimal	Grams of *total fiber* per 100 grams *edible portion* of the food item. Values are compiled from food composition tables.	Missing data are accepted *only* for food items for which it is not possible to define their food composition, such as meals at school or restaurant, lunch, and dinner (food consumed away from home).
Nutrient value for alcohol (fd_alc) Format: Decimal	Grams of alcohol per 100 grams *edible portion* of the food item. Values are compiled from food composition tables.	Missing data are accepted *only* for food items for which it is not possible to define their food composition, such as meals at school or restaurant, lunch, and dinner (food consumed away from home).

(continued)

196

Table 4.6: Dataset 4 (COUNTRY_NCT): Minimum Information Required (continued)

Variable name and format	Rationale and values	Remarks and checks
Nutrient value for available carbohydrates (fd_car) Format: Decimal	Grams of available carbohydrates per 100 grams *edible portion* of the food item. Values are *not compiled* from food composition tables. They are estimated with the formula: *Available carbohydrates = 100 – grams of water – grams of ash – grams of protein – grams of fats – grams of alcohol – grams of total fiber.*	Missing data are accepted *only* for food items for which it is not possible to define their food composition, such as meals at school or restaurant, lunch, and dinner (food consumed away from home). *Total* carbohydrates are the sum of *available* carbohydrates and total fibers. Before applying the formula: • Check that none of the nutrient values involved in the formula are missing. After applying the formula: • Ensure that the values of carbohydrates equal to 100 do not come from having missing data on all the nutrient values involved in the formula. Since food items have at least one macronutrient, it is impossible to have all missing values. For instance, mineral water has 100 grams of water, and salt has about 99.8 grams of ash. • Check for negative values (only nonnegative values are allowed).
Dietary energy value (fd_kcal) Format: Decimal	Expressed in kilocalories per 100 grams *edible portion* of the food item. Values *are not* compiled from food composition tables. They are calculated using the Atwater system coefficients with the formula: *kilocalories = grams of protein * 4 + grams of fats * 9 + grams of available carbohydrates * 4 + grams of alcohol * 7 + grams of fiber * 2.* If the food item is classified as food consumed away from home and it is not possible to have the nutrient values, the nutrient value of the dietary energy has to be *missing (not 0).*	Missing data are accepted *only* for food items for which it is not possible to define their food composition, such as meals at school or restaurant (food consumed away from home). Nutrient values are available for some food products classified as consumed away from home such as beer, carbonated beverage, roasted maize on the cob, and roasted chicken. Therefore, for these food products consumed away from home, it is possible to obtain the conversion factor for dietary energy using the Atwater system coefficients. Only very few food items have a calorie nutrient value equal 0 (e.g., salt, water, and ice). *To detect errors:* • Check for big differences between the dietary energy values calculated with the formula and those reported in food composition tables (note that there will always be differences between the two variables). • Check for big differences in calories among food items belonging to the same food group.

Note: COICOP - Classification of Individual Consumption According to Purpose.
a. It can be downloaded from the FAO webpage of ADePT-FSM: http://www.fao.org/fileadmin/templates/ess/documents/food_security_statistics/Adept.zip.
b. If no country specific data is available, refer to the file refuse factors.xls on the FAO webpage of ADePT-FSM.

How to Build Dataset 4

Below are some guidelines to build the COUNTRY_NCT input dataset. Steps 7 and 8 can be skipped if micronutrients and amino acids analyses, respectively, are not conducted.

Step 1   Open the template file COUNTRY_NCT_template.xlsx and save it on your computer. See also http://www.fao.org/fileadmin/templates/ess/documents/food_security_statistics/Adept.zip.

Table 4.7: Dataset 4 (COUNTRY_NCT): Micronutrient Analysis

Variable name and format	Rationale and values	Remarks and checks
Nutrient value for retinol (retinol) Format: Decimal	Micrograms of retinol per 100 grams *edible portion* of the food item. Values are compiled from food composition tables.	Missing data are accepted *only* for food items for which it is not possible to define their food composition, such as meals at school or restaurant, lunch, and dinner (food consumed away from home).
Nutrient value for beta-carotene (betacar) Format: Decimal	Micrograms of beta-carotene per 100 grams *edible portion* of the food item. Values are compiled from food composition tables.	Missing data are accepted *only* for food items for which it is not possible to define their food composition, such as meals at school or restaurant, lunch, and dinner (food consumed away from home).
Nutrient value for total vitamin A (rae_vita) Format: Decimal	Micrograms of vitamin A per 100 grams *edible portion* of the food item. The micrograms are expressed in *retinol activity equivalent (RAE) NOT in retinol equivalent (RE)*. The difference between RAE and RE is the formula used to estimate the total amount of vitamin A: *Vitamin A (RAE) = mcg of retinol + (mcg of beta-carotene/12) + (mcg of other carotenoids)/24* *Vitamin A (RE) = mcg of retinol + (mcg of beta-carotene/6) + (mcg of other carotenoids)/12* Values are compiled from food composition tables.	If the values are compiled from more than one food composition table (FCT) it is necessary to do a careful analysis of the units in which the unit values of vitamin A are expressed in each food composition table (FCT). Vitamin A can be expressed in retinol equivalent, retinol activity equivalent, or international units (IU). Missing data are accepted *only* for food items for which it is not possible to define their food composition, such as meals at school or restaurant, lunch, and dinner (food consumed away from home).
Nutrient value for vitamin C (vit_c) Format: Decimal	Milligrams of vitamin C per 100 grams *edible portion* of the food item. Values are compiled from food composition tables.	Missing data are accepted *only* for food items for which it is not possible to define their food composition, such as meals at school or restaurant (food consumed away from home).
Nutrient value for vitamin B1 (thiamine) (vit_b1) Format: Decimal	Milligrams of vitamin B1 per 100 grams *edible portion* of the food item. Values are compiled from food composition tables.	Missing data are accepted *only* for food items for which it is not possible to define their food composition, such as meals at school or restaurant (food consumed away from home).
Nutrient value for vitamin B2 (riboflavin) (vit_b2) Format: Decimal	Milligrams of vitamin B2 per 100 grams *edible portion* of the food item. Values are compiled from food composition tables.	Missing data are accepted *only* for food items for which it is not possible to define their food composition, such as meals at school or restaurant (food consumed away from home).
Nutrient value for total vitamin B6 (vit_b6) Format: Decimal	Milligrams of total vitamin B6 per 100 grams *edible portion* of the food item. Values are compiled from food composition tables.	Missing data are accepted *only* for food items for which it is not possible to define their food composition, such as meals at school or restaurant (food consumed away from home).
Nutrient value for vitamin B12 (cobalamin) (vit_b12) Format: Decimal	Micrograms of vitamin B12 per 100 grams *edible portion* of the food item. Values are compiled from food composition tables.	Missing data are accepted *only* for food items for which it is not possible to define their food composition, such as meals at school or restaurant (food consumed away from home).
Nutrient value for iron of animal origin (fe_anim) Format: Decimal	Milligrams of iron from animal origin per 100 grams *edible portion* of the food item. Values of iron are compiled from food composition tables. Then the user classifies the iron as from animal origin if the food item is red or white meat, milk, eggs, or their respective products.	Missing data are accepted *only* for food items for which it is not possible to define their food composition, such as meals at school or restaurant (food consumed away from home).

(continued)

Table 4.7: Dataset 4 (COUNTRY_NCT): Micronutrient Analysis (continued)

Variable name and format	Rationale and values	Remarks and checks
Nutrient value for iron of nonanimal origin (fe_nanim) Format: Decimal	Milligrams of iron from nonanimal origin per 100 grams *edible portion* of the food item. Values of iron are compiled from food composition tables. Then the analyst classifies the iron as from nonanimal origin if the food item is *different* from red or white meat, milk, eggs, or their respective products.	Missing data are accepted *only* for food items for which it is not possible to define their food composition, such as meals at school or restaurant (food consumed away from home).
Nutrient value for calcium (calcium) Format: Decimal	Milligrams of calcium per 100 grams *edible portion* of the food item. Values are compiled from food composition tables.	Missing data are accepted *only* for food items for which it is not possible to define their food composition, such as meals at school or restaurant (food consumed away from home).

Table 4.8: Dataset 4 (COUNTRY_NCT): Amino Acids Analysis

Variable name and format	Rationale and values	Remarks and checks
Nutrient value for ilsoleucine (isoleuc) Format: Decimal	Grams of isoleucine per 100 grams *edible portion* of the food item. Values are compiled from food composition tables.	Missing data are accepted *only* for food items for which it is not possible to define their food composition, such as meals at school or restaurant (food consumed away from home).
Nutrient value for leucine (leucine) Format: Decimal	Grams of leucine per 100 grams *edible portion* of the food item. Values are compiled from food composition tables.	Missing data are accepted *only* for food items for which it is not possible to define their food composition, such as meals at school or restaurant (food consumed away from home).
Nutrient value for lysine (lysine) Format: Decimal	Grams of lysine per 100 grams *edible portion* of the food item. Values are compiled from food composition tables.	Missing data are accepted *only* for food items for which it is not possible to define their food composition, such as meals at school or restaurant (food consumed away from home).
Nutrient value for methionine (methion) Format: Decimal	Grams of methionine per 100 grams *edible portion* of the food item. Values are compiled from food composition tables.	Missing data are accepted *only* for food items for which it is not possible to define their food composition, such as meals at school or restaurant (food consumed away from home).
Nutrient value for phenylalanine (phenyl) Format: Decimal	Grams of phenylalanine per 100 grams *edible portion* of the food item. Values are compiled from food composition tables.	Missing data are accepted *only* for food items for which it is not possible to define their food composition, such as meals at school or restaurant (food consumed away from home).
Nutrient value for threonine (threon) Format: Decimal	Grams of threonine per 100 grams *edible portion* of the food item. Values are compiled from food composition tables.	Missing data are accepted *only* for food items for which it is not possible to define their food composition, such as meals at school or restaurant (food consumed away from home).
Nutrient value for tryptophan (trypto) Format: Decimal	Grams of tryptophan per 100 grams *edible portion* of the food item. Values are compiled from food composition tables.	Missing data are accepted *only* for food items for which it is not possible to define their food composition, such as meals at school or restaurant (food consumed away from home).
Nutrient value for valine (valine) Format: Decimal	Grams of valine per 100 grams *edible portion* of the food item. Values are compiled from food composition tables.	Missing data are accepted *only* for food items for which it is not possible to define their food composition, such as meals at school or restaurant (food consumed away from home).

(continued)

Table 4.8: Dataset 4 (COUNTRY_NCT): Amino Acids Analysis (continued)

Variable name and format	Rationale and values	Remarks and checks
Nutrient value for histidine (histid) Format: Decimal	Grams of histidine per 100 grams *edible portion* of the food item. Values are compiled from food composition tables.	Missing data are accepted *only* for food items for which it is not possible to define their food composition, such as meals at school or restaurant (food consumed away from home).
Nutrient value for cystine (cistyne) Format: Decimal	Grams of cystine per 100 grams *edible portion* of the food item. Values are compiled from food composition tables.	Missing data are accepted *only* for food items for which it is not possible to define their food composition, such as meals at school or restaurant (food consumed away from home).
Nutrient value for tyrosine (tyrosine) Format: Decimal	Grams of tyrosine per 100 grams *edible portion* of the food item. Values are compiled from food composition tables.	Missing data are accepted *only* for food items for which it is not possible to define their food composition, such as meals at school or restaurant (food consumed away from home).
Protein digestibility (pro_dig) Format: Numeric	Values are expressed as a percentage.[a]	Missing data are accepted *only* for food items for which it is not possible to define their food composition, such as meals at school or restaurant (food consumed away from home).

a. For protein digestibility values refer to the file Protein Digestibility Values.xls available on the FAO web page of ADePT-FSM at the link: http://www.fao.org/fileadmin/templates/ess/documents/food_security_statistics/Adept.zip.

The template file is composed of different worksheets; one of these is named Archival. Go to Archival and list here all the food items collected in the NHS, inserting their survey code and description in columns A, *Food item code in household survey (item_cod)*, and B, *Food item description in household survey (desc)*. All the food items collected during the survey should be included in the list, including the food items consumed away from home.

Step 2: 2a. Selecting the Food Composition Table   Identify the most suitable national or regional food composition table or database (reference file) for matching the food items in the survey with those described in the selected FCT. Some criteria that should be taken into consideration in the selection of a FCT are the year of publication, the completeness of information (especially for macronutrients), geographic/cultural proximity between the country under study, and those countries/regions for which the food composition table is written.

Some FCT are available on the web at the following addresses:

- U.S. Department of Agriculture FCT: http://www.nal.usda.gov/fnic /foodcomp/search/index.html
- European FCT: http://www.eurofir.net/eurofir_knowledge/european _databases
- Latin Foods: http://www.inta.cl/latinfoods/

- INFOODS databases: http://www.fao.org/infoods/infoods/tables-and -databases/en/
- LANGUAL: http://www.langual.org/langual_linkcategory.asp?Category ID=4&Category=Food+Composition

2b. Food Matching   Once the FCT is identified, insert its name in column C, *Reference food composition table (FCT)*.

After matching a food item listed in the Archival worksheet with a food item in the FCT, insert the reference food item's code and description in columns D, *Food code in FCT*, and E, *Food description in FCT*, respectively.[6]

It may happen that a food product listed in the NHS cannot be matched directly with any of the foods in the reference table. Reasons could be: (1) the food item does not exist in the FCT or (2) the food product listed in the NHS includes more than one food item of the FCT or is broadly described. In the first case, the food matching (step 2b) for that specific item is done using another FCT (selected using the criteria mentioned in step 2a) to find out the appropriate food product of reference. In the second case, a weighted average of the nutritional values of all the relevant (i.e., similar, corresponding) food products should be performed. By default, all food items involved have equal weight factor, unless their respective proportion of consumption in the country is known.[7]

Examples:

- The food item in the NHS is *broadly described*, for example *rice*. In this case, the color (brown or white) of the rice is not specified. Therefore, a weighted average of the nutritional values of different types of rice is needed. If the food item description in the survey is *rice* and in the list of food items in the survey there is no mention of rice flour, then not only rice grain food commodities but also rice flour has to be included in the calculation of the average nutritional values.
- *Different types* of the same food product or different food products are listed together in the NHS as if they were one food item (for example, *white rice, grain or flour, wheat or corn flour*, and *eggplant, cauliflower, broccoli*). If the proportions of consumption are not known, a simple average of the nutritional values is done.
- *Fresh and dry* food items are listed together (for example, *fresh or powdered milk, whole milk* and *fresh or dried salmon*). If the proportions

of consumption are not known, a weighted average of the nutritional values is done assigning a maximum weight factor of 10 percent to the dry product.[8]

For instance, in tables 4.9 and 4.10, the protein value of the food item collected in the survey is obtained averaging the protein values of similar food items from the FCT. In tables 4.9 and 4.10 the total number of food items from the FCT is five. In table 4.9, equal weights[9] are applied so the weight factor for each food item is 0.2. Table 4.10 shows an example when the applied weights are different (e.g., they could be obtained from previous analysis of food consumption from household survey data).

Once the matching between the food items in the NHS list and those in the FCT is done, insert the food item index matching in column F, *Food Item Index Matching*, of the Archival worksheet. The values indicate

Table 4.9: Content of Protein in Rice Applying Equal Weights

Name of the FCT	Item code in the FCT	Item description in the FCT	Item weight factor	Grams of protein from the FCT
USDA	20036	Rice, brown, long-grain, raw	0.2	7.94
USDA	20040	Rice, brown, medium-grain, raw	0.2	7.5
USDA	20444	Rice, white, long-grain, regular, raw, unenriched	0.2	7.13
USDA	20450	Rice, white, medium-grain, raw, unenriched	0.2	6.61
USDA	20052	Rice, white, short-grain, raw	0.2	6.5

Item code in the survey	Item description in the survey	Grams of protein
4002	Rice grain	0.2 * 7.94 + 0.2 * 7.5 + 0.2 * 7.13 + 0.2 * 6.61 + 0.2 * 6.5 = 7.136

Table 4.10: Content of Protein in Rice Applying Different Weights

Name of the FCT	Item code in the FCT	Item description in the FCT	Item weight factor	Grams of protein from the FCT
Bolivia FCT	A77	Wheat flour	0.759	8.03
Bolivia FCT	A80	Corn flour	0.241	8.5

Item code in the survey	Item description in the survey	Grams of protein
4005	Wheat or corn flour	0.759 * 8.03 + 0.241 * 8.5 = 8.143

the type of matching between the food item listed in the survey and the food item selected from the FCT. These are the codes:

- A = Single, perfect match, no modifications required (apart from edible portion, if indicated)
- A2 = Exact match with multiple selections requiring average computation
- B = Similar, single match
- B2 = Similar match with multiple selections requiring average computation
- C = Poor, single match
- C2 = Poor match with multiple selections requiring average computation
- D = Calories estimated by ADePT using unit calorie cost (applies only to food consumed away from home for which it is not possible to know its composition, such as lunch, dinner or meal, other foods, etc.)

Step 3 In the worksheet Archival, in column G, *Refuse factor (refuse)*, insert the food item's refuse factor.[10] In column H, *Item group (item_grp)*, insert the food item group to which the food item belongs.

Step 4 In the worksheet Archival, fill all the columns highlighted in gray with the information available in the FCT corresponding to each food item, including total carbohydrates for further data-checking purposes. If a nutrient of a food item is missing in the selected FCT, look for the respective value in another FCT. Insert a comment in the Excel cell of the missing nutrient mentioning the name of the FCT from which the value was obtained as well as the food item code and description in the FCT.

In the specific case of missing ash content, the value found in another FCT has to be adjusted by the total content of solids using the formula:

$$Ash(g) = \frac{[Ash(g)\ in\ other\ FCT * (100 - Water(g)\ in\ the\ FCT)]}{100 - Water(g) in\ other\ FCT}$$

As for the nutrient values of the food items consumed away from home for which it is not possible to know their composition (meal, lunch, etc.), blank cells are allowed, because their respective nutrient values will be estimated by the ADePT-FSS Module.

The cells of the following columns *should not be filled* in the archival sheet:

- P: *Available carbohydrates by difference (fd_car)*
- R: *Computed calories (kcal) (fd_kcal)*
- U: *Animal iron (milligrams) (fe_anim)*
- V: *Nonanimal iron (milligrams) (fe_nanim)*

Once all the required information is inserted in the Archival worksheet, copy it to the Reference worksheet.

Step 5   In the Reference worksheet, compute the grams of *available carbohydrates by difference* in column P, *Available carbohydrates by difference (grams) (fd_car)*, as:

fd_car (column P) = 100 – *Water* (column I) – *Ash* (column J) – *Protein* (column K) – *Fat* (column L) – *Fiber* (column M) – *Alcohol* (column N)

Suggested checks:

- The sum of the values in columns M, *fd_fib*, and P, *fd_car*, should be similar to the value in column O, *Carbohydrates including fiber (Total) (grams)*.
- The values in column *fd_car* should be positive or equal to 0. If one value is negative and there was no data entry error in any of the nutrients involved in the computation, assign a value of 0.
- Ensure that the values of *fd_car = 100* do not come from having missing data on all the nutrient values involved in the formula. Since food items have at least one macronutrient, it is impossible to have all missing values.[11]

Step 6   In the Reference worksheet, compute the dietary energy value in column R, *Computed calories (kcal) (fd_kcal)*, as:

fd_kcal (column R) = *Protein* (column K) * 4 + *Fat* (column L) * 9 + *Fiber* (column M) * 2 + *Alcohol* (column N) * 7 + *Available carbohydrates by difference* (column P) * 4

Verify that the computed dietary energy values in column R, *Computed calories (kcal) (fd_kcal)*, are similar to those compiled from the FCT in column Q, *Calories (kcal)*. There will always be differences between the values of these two columns, but if there are *big* differences, verify that the nutrient values used in the computation are correct.[12] Two of the most common errors are wrong data entry of the food item nutrient content and wrong estimation of available carbohydrates.

Step 7   If the food item in the NHS is of animal origin (as previously defined in this document), in the Reference worksheet, copy the values of column T, *Iron (milligrams) (iron)*, to column U, *Animal iron (milligrams) (fe_anim)*. Similarly, if the food item is not of animal origin, copy the values of column T to column V, *Nonanimal iron (milligrams) (fe_nanim)*.

Step 8   In the Reference worksheet, insert the percentage of digestible protein in the food item in column AP, *Protein digestibility (%) (pro_dig)*.

Step 9   When all the above steps are completed, copy all the information of the Reference worksheet and paste it to the Upload worksheet. To paste the information, select the function **paste special > values** from the menu.

Only the columns whose variable name is red in the Upload worksheet are needed in dataset 4 and should be uploaded.

An example of a completed COUNTRY_NCT template for a country is available at http://www.fao.org/fileadmin/templates/ess/documents /food_security_statistics/Adept.zip.

Exogenous Parameters

To Estimate Dietary Energy Requirements[13]

The minimum and average dietary energy requirements (MDER and ADER, respectively) are produced by ADePT-FSM. To estimate the energy requirements, the values for the under-five mortality rate and birthrate are needed. Therefore, ADePT-FSM requires the user to insert these two country-specific parameters. Both parameters are computed at the country level and should refer to the year in which the survey was conducted.

Under-Five Mortality Rate

UNICEF defines the under-five mortality rate as the probability of dying between birth and exactly five years of age expressed per 1,000 live births. Estimates of the under-five mortality rate are available at http://www .childinfo.org/mortality_ufmrcountrydata.php.

Birthrate

The crude birthrate is the number of births over a given period of time divided by the person–years lived by the population over that period (UN 2011). Estimates of crude birthrate, expressed as the number of births per 1,000 people, are available at http://esa.un.org/unpd/wpp/unpp/panel _indicators.htm. In the ADePT module, the value of the birthrate parameter should be expressed *per person*.

To Estimate the Prevalence of Undernourishment[14]

The prevalence of undernourishment (PoU) is computed using a parametric approach under the assumption of a skewed normal distribution of dietary energy consumption. Such a distribution is defined by three parameters:

- The *average* dietary energy habitually consumed by a *representative* individual over one year
- The *coefficient of variation* of dietary energy consumption within the population
- The *skewness*, which is an indicator of the *asymmetry* of the distribution

The average dietary energy habitually consumed by a representative individual over one year can be estimated either from food balance sheets, which provide information on food available in a given country for human consumption (dietary energy supply [DES]), or directly from food consumption data obtained from NHS (dietary energy consumption). The MDG 1.9 indicator uses the DES for human consumption after having subtracted the calories lost at the retail level.[15]

The cutoff point used in the calculation of the PoU is the MDER. The depth of food deficit is estimated using the ADER. While ADePT-FSM computes the MDER and ADER using the structure of the population obtained from the survey, the MDER used to obtain the MDG 1.9 indicator and the ADER used to estimate the depth of food deficit consider the structure of the population published by the UN.

From the above, to estimate the PoU and depth of hunger using not only data from the survey but also from other sources, the user has to select the following parameters that are included in the software ADePT-FSM:

- Dietary energy consumption (estimated as the average DES from food balance sheets minus the calories lost at the retail level)
- Minimum dietary energy requirement
- Average dietary energy requirements

The values of these parameters used to estimate the MDG 1.9 indicator published in *The State of Food Insecurity in the World*[16] can be accessed at the FAO Statistics Division's website.[17]

Finally, while it is possible to infer at the population level estimates of the average consumption of calories and nutrients, at the subnational level the PoU and depth of food deficit can be inferred only for those population groups for which the survey has representativeness. Usually, surveys are designed in such a way that the sample is representative at national, regional, and/or urban/rural levels.

Notes

1. The information can be extrapolated from the survey documentation.
2. It is recommended to use the median height of each sex and age group, instead of the mean.
3. The analysis is done by characteristics of the household head.
4. For example: a household consumed potatoes; they were partly purchased on the market and partly obtained from own production. This household will have two entries (i.e., two lines) for the food item *potatoes*: one with quantity and expenditure related to the purchase, and the other with quantity and monetary value related to own production.
5. For example, without considering inedible parts such as peels, bones, etc.

6. For the food matching, consult FAO/INFOODS *Guidelines for Food Matching* (2012) available at http://www.fao.org/infoods/infoods /standards-guidelines/en/.

7. For example, from the analysis of previous national consumption surveys in the country, the milk consumption pattern is whole, 90 percent; partially skimmed, 7 percent; skimmed, 3 percent.

8. The figure 10 percent, though arbitrary, is used to avoid overestimation of nutrient content, as nutrients are more concentrated in dry foods, leading to higher nutrient values per 100 grams edible portion (FAO forthcoming).

9. A weighted average performed by applying equal weight factors is equal to a simple average.

10. In the survey, households report food quantities as purchased/acquired. But many foods have edible and nonedible parts. FCT report nutrients on edible quantities. Therefore, a refuse factor is needed to calculate the edible quantities contained in the quantities reported as purchased/ acquired. Only if we do so, can we apply the nutrients from the households to the food item list.

11. For example, mineral water has 100 grams of water; salt has about 99.8 grams of ash, etc.

12. A hypothetical example is that the value of calories for *rice white raw* published in the FCT is 346 kcal, while the value of calories estimated with the formula is 260 kcal.

13. Further details can be found in chapter 2.

14. Further details can be found in chapter 2.

15. Food waste within households is not subtracted.

16. The website is available at http://www.fao.org/publications/sofi/en/.

17. The website is available at http://www.fao.org/economic/ess/ess-fs /fs-methods/adept-fsn/en/.

References

FAO (Food and Agriculture Organization). Forthcoming. *AGN Proposition for an Improved Methodology to Attribute Nutrition Values to Foods in the FAO Commodity List (FCL)*. Rome: FAO.

FAO, and INFOODS (International Network of Food Data Systems). 2012. *Guidelines for Food Matching Version 1.2.* Rome: FAO. http://www.fao .org/infoods/infoods/standards-guidelines/en/.

James, W. P. T., and E. C. Schofield. 1990. *Human Energy Requirements: A Manual for Planners and Nutritionists.* Oxford, UK, Oxford Medical Publications under arrangement with FAO.

Chapter 5

Guide to Using ADePT-FSM

Ana Moltedo, Michael Lokshin, Zurab Sajaia

Introduction

Once the required four input data files are created they are used to execute the ADePT-Food Security Module (FSM). This chapter provides comprehensive instructions for installing and using the ADePT-Food Security Module. The instructions cover system requirements, installation, registration, updates, steps to launch the software, and the main characteristics of the ADePT-FSM.

System Requirements

To execute ADePT-FSM some requirements are needed for the system and the datasets. These requirements are shown in table 5.1 below.

Table 5.1: System Requirements

PC running Microsoft Windows XP (SP1 or later), Windows Vista, Windows Server 2003 and later, or Windows 7. ADePT runs in 32- and 64-bit environments.
.NET 2.0 or later (included with recent Windows installations), and all updates and patches.
80MB disk space to install, plus space for temporary data set copies.
At least 512MB RAM.
At least 1024 x 768 screen resolution.
At least one printer driver must be installed (even if no computer is connected).
Microsoft® Excel® for Windows® (XP or later), Microsoft® Excel Viewer or a compatible spreadsheet program for viewing reports generated by ADePT.
A Web browser and Internet access are needed to download ADePT. Internet access is needed for program updates and to load Web-based datasets into ADePT. Otherwise, ADePT runs without needing Internet access.
ADePT can process data in Stata (.dta) and SPSS (.sav) formats.

Installing ADePT

There are six main steps to installing ADePT:

1. Download the ADePT installer by clicking **Download the software ADePT-FSM (.exe)** located at http://www.fao.org/economic/ess /ess-fs/fs-methods/adept-fsn/en/.
2. Click the **Run** button and launch the installer immediately, or click the **Save** button and launch the installer later.
3. After the installer is launched, read the **License Agreement** dialog, then click the **I Agree** button.

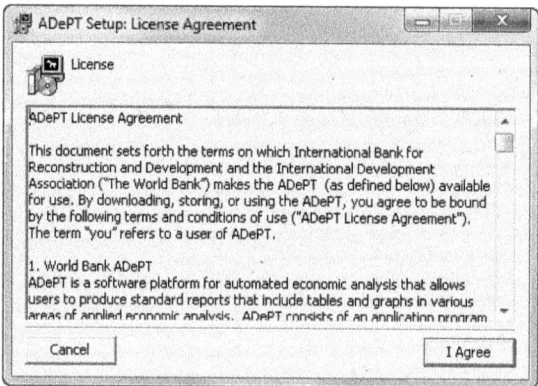

4. In the **Installation Folder** dialog:
   a. If desired, click the **Browse...** button to change the default installation folder.
   b. Click the **Install** button.

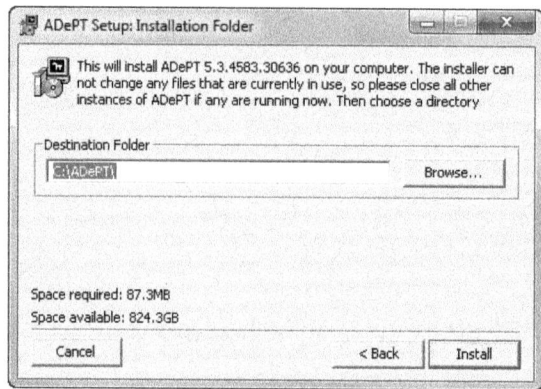

> **Note:** If a message mentioning that .NET is not installed cancel the ADePT installation, install the latest version of .NET (free download from the Microsoft® Website), then restart the ADePT installation.

5. Wait while ADePT is installed.
6. In the **Setup Completed** dialog, click the **Close** button.

ADePT is automatically launched after installation.

Registering ADePT

When installation is complete, the user is invited to register as an ADePT user in the **Welcome to ADePT!** dialog.

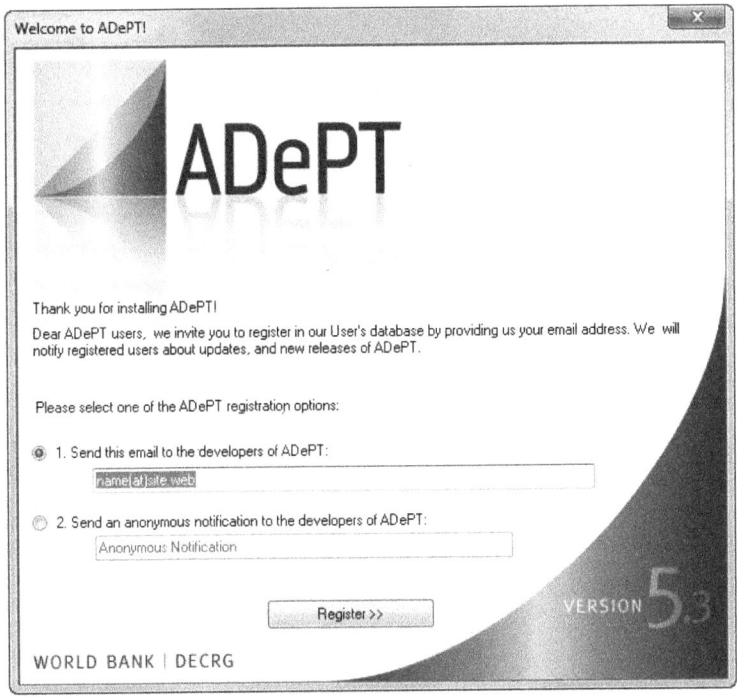

1. Select one of the registration options:

   To receive notifications about program updates and new releases:
   a. Click the **Send this email to the developers...** option.
   b. Enter the e-mail address.
   c. Click the **Register >>** button.

   To register anonymously:
   a. Click the **Send an anonymous...** option.
   b. Click the **Register >>** button.

To skip the registration process, click the **Close** button in the upper right corner.

Tip: The user can register for notifications later by using the **Help ▶ Register...** command to reopen the **Welcome to ADePT!** dialog.

---

2. In the **Select ADePT Module** dialog, double-click the name of the module to use.

Launching ADePT

After completing the installation and optional registration steps, the user is ready to launch the ADePT-FSM software. This can be done with the following two steps:

1. Click the ADePT icon in the Windows **Start** menu.
2. In the **Select ADePT Module** window, double-click Food Security (see arrow in the screenshot on the next page).

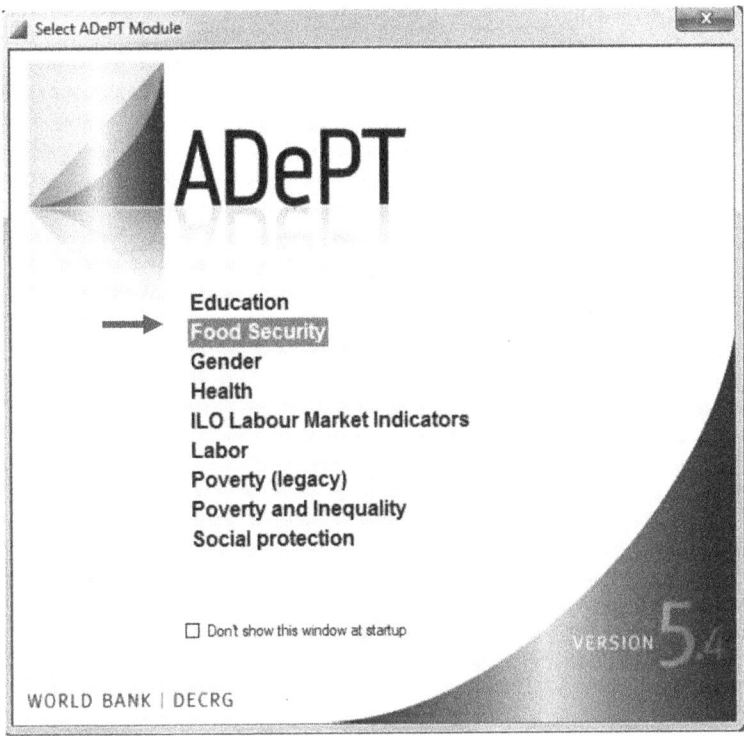

The **Select ADePT Module** dialog lists currently available modules. To work only with the **Food Security** module, suppress the **Select ADePT Module** dialog by activating the **Don't show this window at startup** option. ADePT will then automatically load the last-used module when it's launched.

3. Now the ADePT-FSM main window is shown.

Using the ADePT-FSM Main Window

In the screenshot below, the main window of the ADePT-FSM is divided into four areas; below the picture there is a description of each of these areas. The four areas correspond to the four general steps in the analysis process.

- **Area 1** contains the datasets and dataset variables where the user can load, remove, and examine datasets. The variable labels shown in the right column are read from the dataset.

Area 1

Area 3

Area 2

Area 4

- **Area 2** contains seven tab pages where the user maps the dataset variables and the exogenous parameters. The tab pages are classified according to **the information required on:** i) household characteristics, ii) household member characteristics, iii) food consumption, iv) macronutrient values, v) micronutrient values, vi) amino acid values and vii) exogenous parameters **needed to estimate the prevalence of undernourishment.**
- **Area 3** contains the list of tables the user can select to be generated.
- **Area 4** contains the description of the tables and the ADePT-FSM notifications created during the execution of the program.

Using ADePT-FSM

After completing the preliminary steps and becoming familiar with the user-friendly interactive window of the software, the user is ready to complete a comprehensive food security analysis. There are six main steps in performing an analysis:

1. Specify the four datasets needed to execute the software.
2. Map dataset variables.
3. Set parameters.
4. Select tables.
5. Generate the tables.
6. Analyze the notifications.

1. Specify Datasets

The first task in performing an analysis is to specify the four datasets. ADePT can process data in Stata (*.dta*) and SPSS (*.sav*) formats.

Operations in this section take place in the upper left corner of the ADePT main window where the

- First data file (**Household**) contains the household characteristics
- Second data file (**Individual**) contains household member characteristics
- Third data file (**Food**) contains the household food consumption
- Fourth data file (**Country**) contains nutrient values of the food

To add a dataset click the **Select** button. In the **Open dataset** dialog, locate and click the dataset to be analyzed, and then click the **Open** button.

Repeat the step to specify each additional dataset.

To remove a dataset: Click the dataset, and then click the Clear button.

Viewing a Dataset's Data and Variable Details

To view the content of a dataset: (1) in the **Datasets** tab click to the dataset to be examined, and (2) double-click in the text defining the dataset (e.g., **Household**).

This opens the **ADePT Data Browser**.

Data View Tab

- **The Data View** tab lists observations in rows and variables in columns.

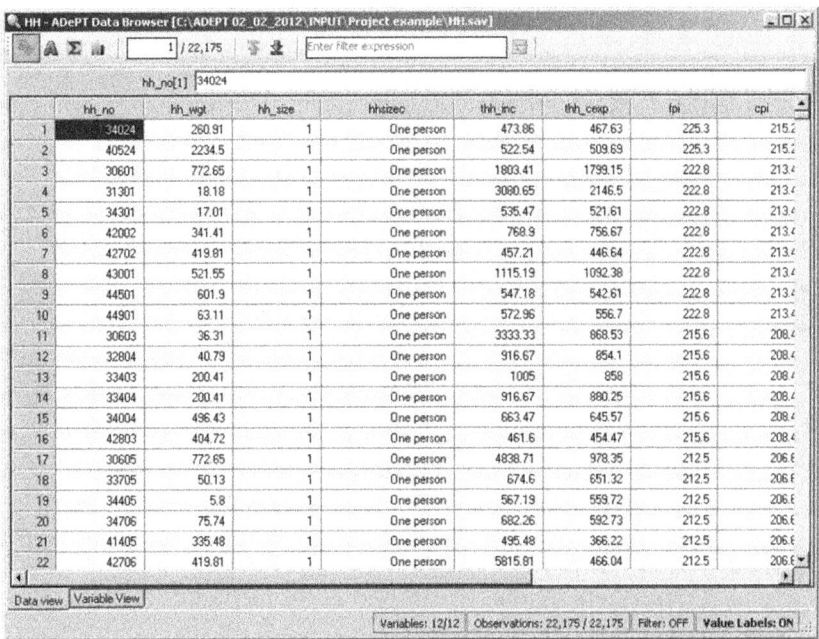

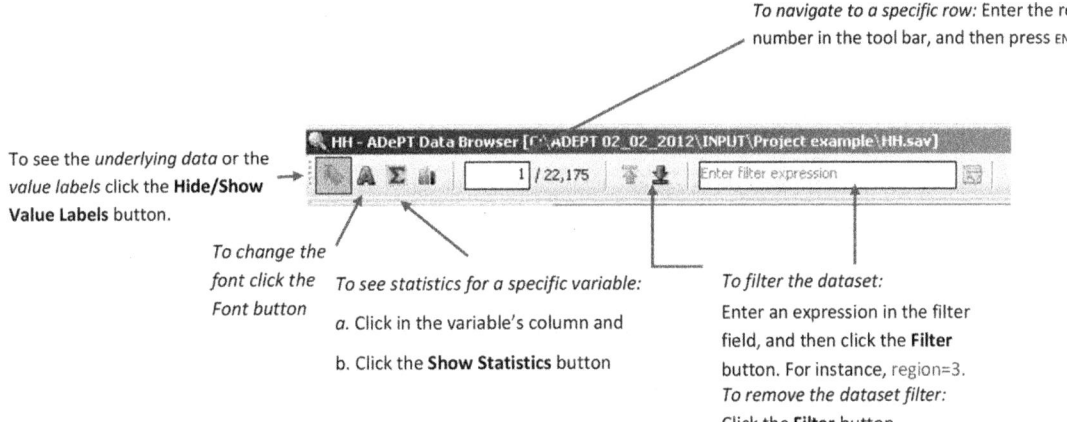

To navigate to a specific row: Enter the row number in the tool bar, and then press ENTER.

To see the *underlying data* or the *value labels* click the **Hide/Show Value Labels** button.

To change the font click the Font button

To see statistics for a specific variable:
a. Click in the variable's column and
b. Click the **Show Statistics** button

To filter the dataset:
Enter an expression in the filter field, and then click the **Filter** button. For instance, region=3. *To remove the dataset filter:* Click the **Filter** button.

> **Note:** Applying a filter in the **Data Browser** does not affect calculations. This filter only reduces the number of observations visible in the **Browser** according to the filter criteria in order to make it easier to examine the dataset.

> **Tip:** The status bar in the **Data Browser** windows indicates whether the filter and value labels are on or off.
>
>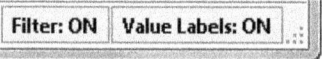

Right-click in the table to open this context menu:

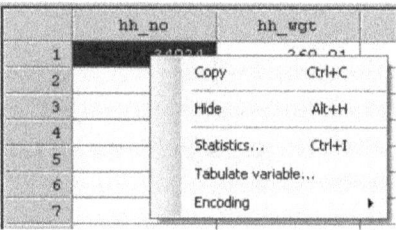

Table 5.2: Description of the Commands Displayed in the Menu

Command	Description
Copy	Copies the contents of the selected cell(s) to the clipboard.
Hide	Hides the column containing the selected variable. (Unhide columns in the **Data Browser's Variable View** tab.).
Statistics	Opens the **Statistics** window for the selected variable.
Tabulate variable	Opens the **Frequency tabulation** window for the selected variable.
Encoding	Opens a submenu listing character encoding for various languages. Click an encoding to properly display characters in the **Variables** tab.

Variable View Tab

The **Data Browser**'s **Variable View** tab lists detailed information about the dataset's variables. Maximize the window or scroll to see additional columns.

To hide or show variable columns in the *Data View* tab: In the **Variable View** tab, click the checkbox next to the variable name.

2. Map Dataset Variables

ADePT-FSM needs to know which variables in the datasets correspond to each type of information. In the second step of an ADePT-FSM analysis, the user manually maps the dataset variables to the corresponding field. The operations described in this section take place on the left-hand side of the ADePT-FSM main window.

At the bottom left of the main window, there are seven tab pages; in six of them the user has to map dataset variables, according to the type of analysis (table 5.3):

Table 5.3 Variables to Map According to the Type of Analysis

BASIC ANALYSIS
Map variables in the tab pages: **Household, Individual, Food**, and **Main factors**

BASIC AND MICRONUTRIENT ANALYSIS
Map variables in the tab pages: **Household, Individual, Food, Main factors**, and **Micronutrients**

BASIC AND AMINO ACIDS ANALYSIS
Map variables in the tab pages: **Household, Individual, Food, Main factors**, and **Amino acids**

COMPLETE ANALYSIS
Map variables in the tab pages: **Household, Individual, Food, Main factors, Micronutrients**, and **Amino acids**

Brief Description of the Tab Pages

- **Household:** maps dataset variables pertaining to household characteristics.
- **Individual:** maps dataset variables pertaining to household member characteristics.
- **Food:** maps dataset variables pertaining to household food consumption.
- **Main factors:** maps dataset variables pertaining to food commodity characteristics such as refuse factors and the contents of macronutrients for each food commodity listed in the survey.
- **Micronutrients:** maps dataset variables pertaining to the content of micronutrients for each food commodity listed in the survey.
- **Amino acids:** maps dataset variables pertaining to the content of amino acids for each food commodity listed in the survey.

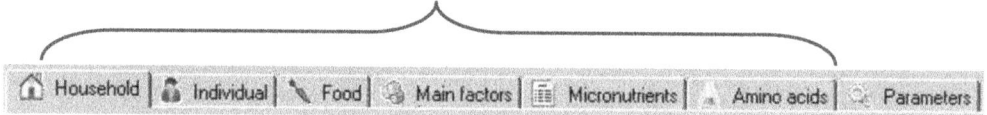

There are two methods for mapping variables:

Method 1

To illustrate the first method for mapping variables, an example is shown for the **Household** tab.

In the lower **Household** tab, open the variable's list, then click the corresponding dataset variable, as shown here for the **Household size** variable.

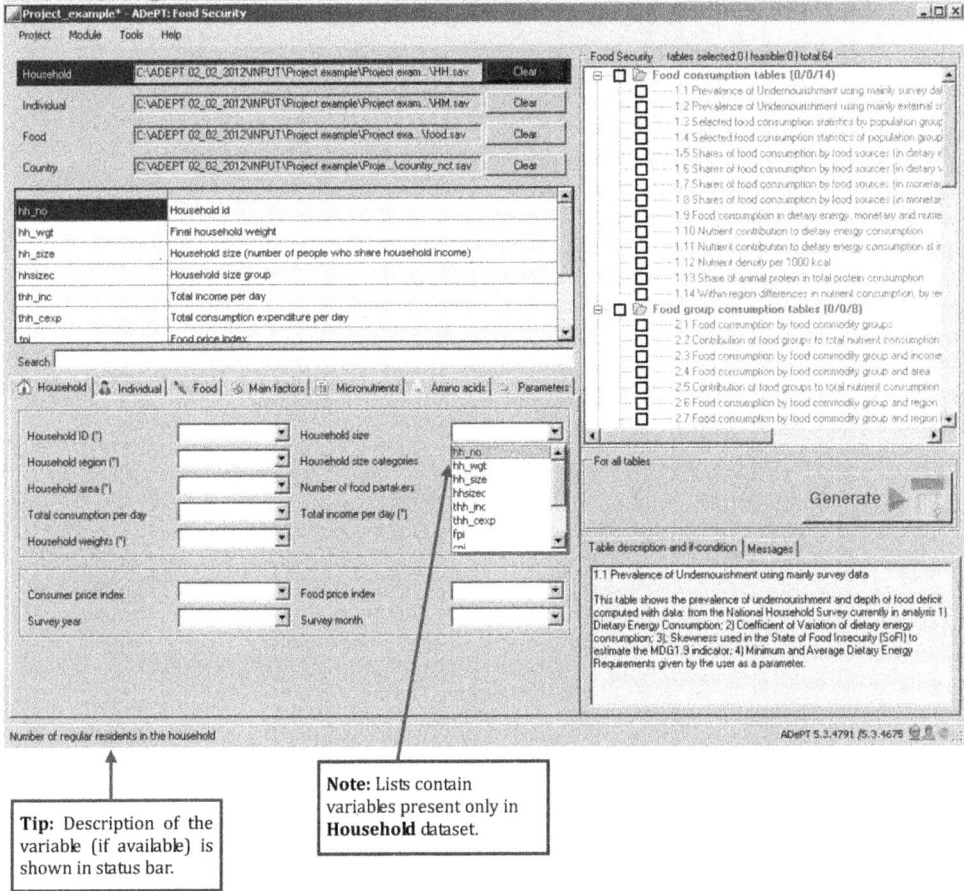

Tip: Description of the variable (if available) is shown in status bar.

Note: Lists contain variables present only in **Household** dataset.

To navigate a drop-down list quickly: Type a letter or two in the variable field, then open the drop-down list. The most closely matching variable name will be highlighted.

Method 2

One can also use a second method to map variables, and this method is illustrated here again using the **Household** tab as an example. In the middle left of the main window, the list of variables is shown and their description is included in the dataset selected above. Drag the variable name and drop it in the corresponding field in the lower **Household** tab.

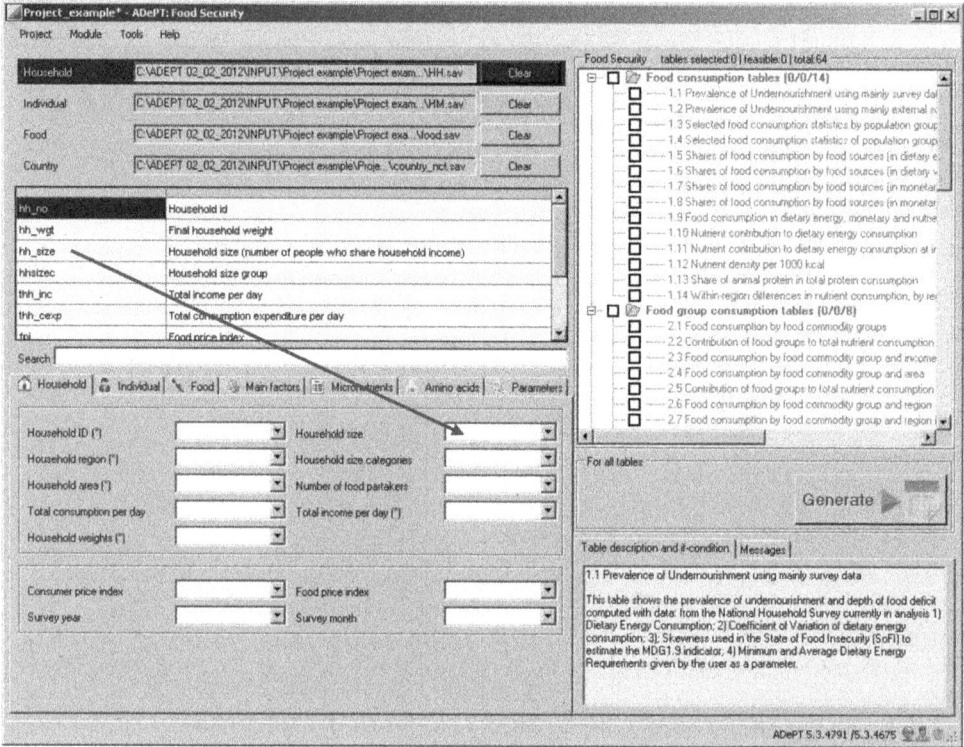

Tip: This method may be more efficient than method 1 when datasets have a large number of variables.

Note: Dataset variable names can be typed in the variable fields. The above methods are preferred since typing may introduce errors. A spelling error, syntax error, missing variable, or other problem is indicated by a red exclamation point next to the input variable field. However, pointing the cursor over the exclamation point allows one to see information about the error.

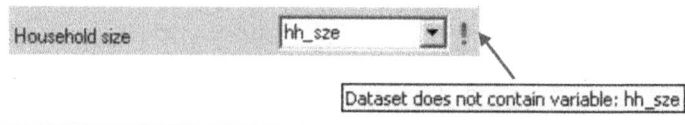

To remove a mapping: Select the variable name in the variable field, then press DELETE.

To locate a variable in the selected dataset: In the **Search** field, type a few characters in the variable name or variable label.

Custom Variables

In the tab page **Individual,** there is the possibility to customize variables to be analyzed. This means that the user can analyze country-specific groups of the population (e.g., ethnicity) or specific household characteristics (e.g., whether or not the household is receiving aid or the type of access the household has to drinkable water).

Write the label corresponding to the variable content.

Select the variable from the dataset.

Independently of the type of analysis (household or household member characteristics), the custom variable has to be in the dataset containing the household members' characteristics. Below, two different examples are shown for including an additional variable in the analysis. In the example on the left, the variable **hm_var1** is used to analyze differences between households. In the example on the right, the variable **hm_var1** is used to analyze characteristics of household members, and the variable can take on different values for different members of the same household.

225

Example where the variable **hm_var1** has a household characteristic:

	hh_no	hm_rel	hm_var1
1	100360011	1	2
2	100360011	3	2
3	100360081	1	1
4	100360081	2	1
5	100360081	3	1
6	100360081	3	1
7	100360081	3	1
8	100360161	1	3
9	100360161	2	3
10	100360231	1	2
11	100360231	2	2
12	100360231	3	2
13	100360311	1	3
14	100360311	2	3

Example where the variable **hm_var1** has household members characteristic:

	hh_no	hm_rel	hm_var1
1	100360011	1	2
2	100360011	3	1
3	100360081	1	1
4	100360081	2	5
5	100360081	3	3
6	100360081	3	4
7	100360081	3	4
8	100360161	1	1
9	100360161	2	3
10	100360231	1	1
11	100360231	2	2
12	100360231	3	3
13	100360311	1	3
14	100360311	2	4

As mentioned before, the ADePT-FSM has multiple variable tab pages; therefore, be sure to visit all tabs to map variables before starting the analysis.

Note: In the **Main factors** tab page, the user has the option of estimating the dietary energy consumption from the content of macronutrients in the food commodities or from calorie values of food commodities.

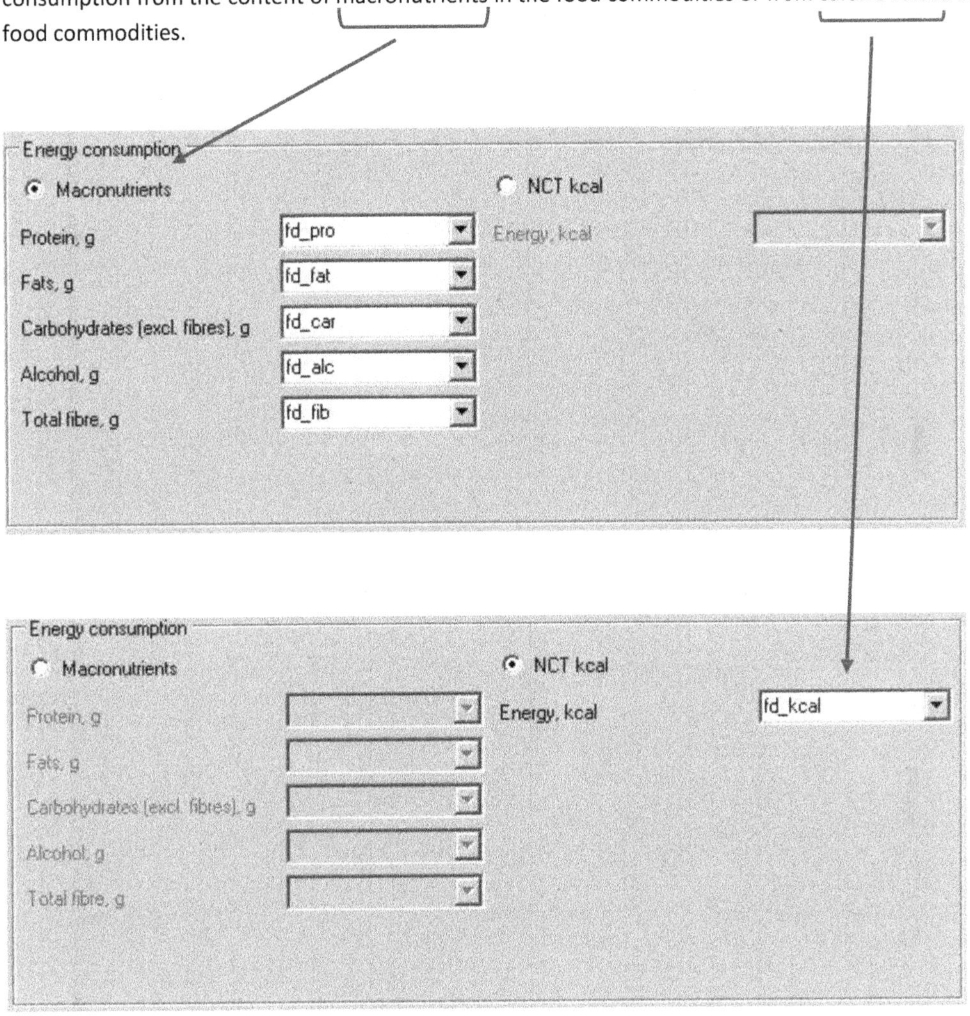

Energy consumption
- ⦿ Macronutrients   ○ NCT kcal

Protein, g	fd_pro
Fats, g	fd_fat
Carbohydrates (excl. fibres), g	fd_car
Alcohol, g	fd_alc
Total fibre, g	fd_fib

Energy, kcal

Energy consumption
- ○ Macronutrients   ⦿ NCT kcal

Protein, g	
Fats, g	
Carbohydrates (excl. fibres), g	
Alcohol, g	
Total fibre, g	

Energy, kcal   fd_kcal

3. Set Parameters

For the third step of a food security analysis using the ADePT-FSM, the values of exogenous parameters are assigned. In the **Parameters** tab, the data required are exogenous from the datasets.

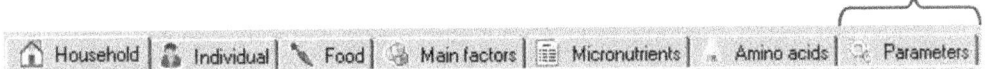

227

The tab page is split according to three types of information used to estimate (1) dietary energy requirements from household survey data, (2) the coefficient of variation due to sources different from income, and (3) the prevalence of undernourishment used to estimate the FAO MDG 1.9 indicator as in SOFI. The layout of the **Parameters** tab is shown and described below.

Place a check in the box **Under 5 mortality rate above 10 per 1000** if (at the year of the survey) the under-five mortality rate was above 10 per 1,000 live births for the country.

Add the birth rate in the country (at the year o the survey) either manually or by clicking on the magnifying glass.

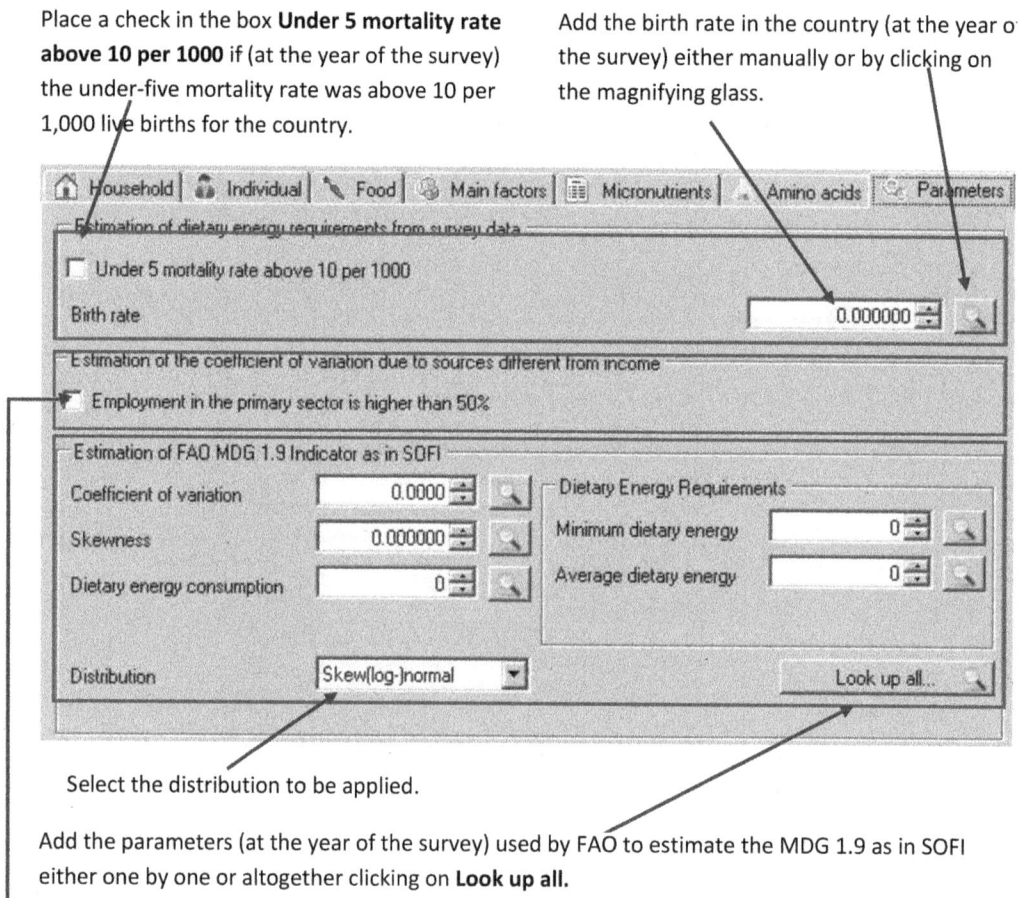

Select the distribution to be applied.

Add the parameters (at the year of the survey) used by FAO to estimate the MDG 1.9 as in SOFI either one by one or altogether clicking on **Look up all.**

Place a check in the box **Employment in the primary sector is higher than 50%** if (at the year of the survey) the proportion of people employed in the primary sector was higher than 50 percent for this country.

An example is shown for the selection of the **Coefficient of variation** for Australia in 2003, using the magnifying glass.

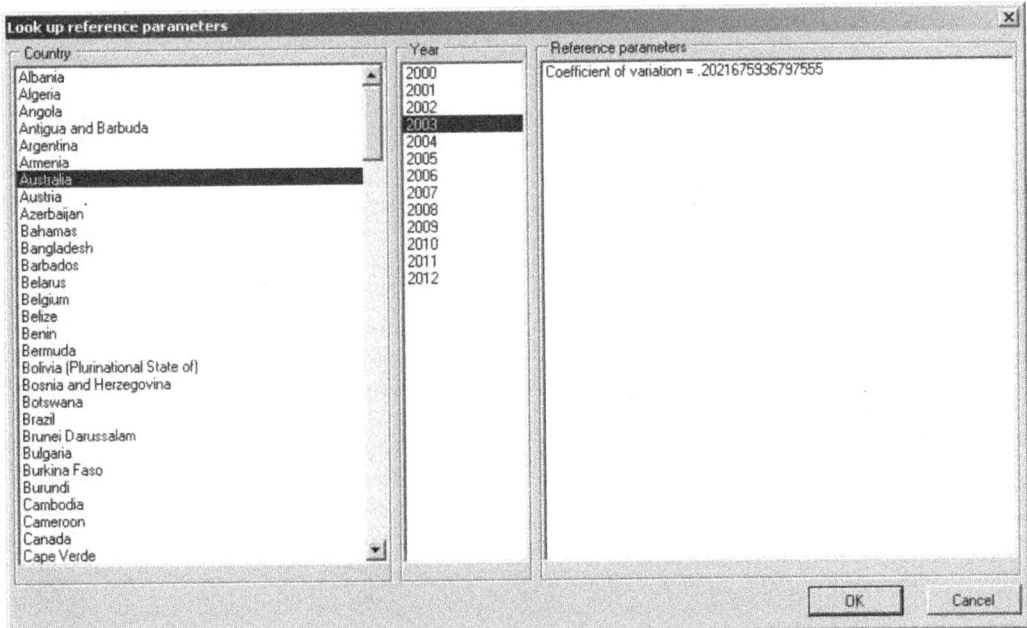

4. Select Tables

After mapping variables, the user is ready to complete step 4 of the food security analysis by selecting the tables to be generated by ADePT. The operations described in this section take place in the right side of the main window.

In the upper right (outputs) panel, place a check next to the tables to be generated.

Note: No variable was assigned to the **Household area** field, so some output tables are disabled.

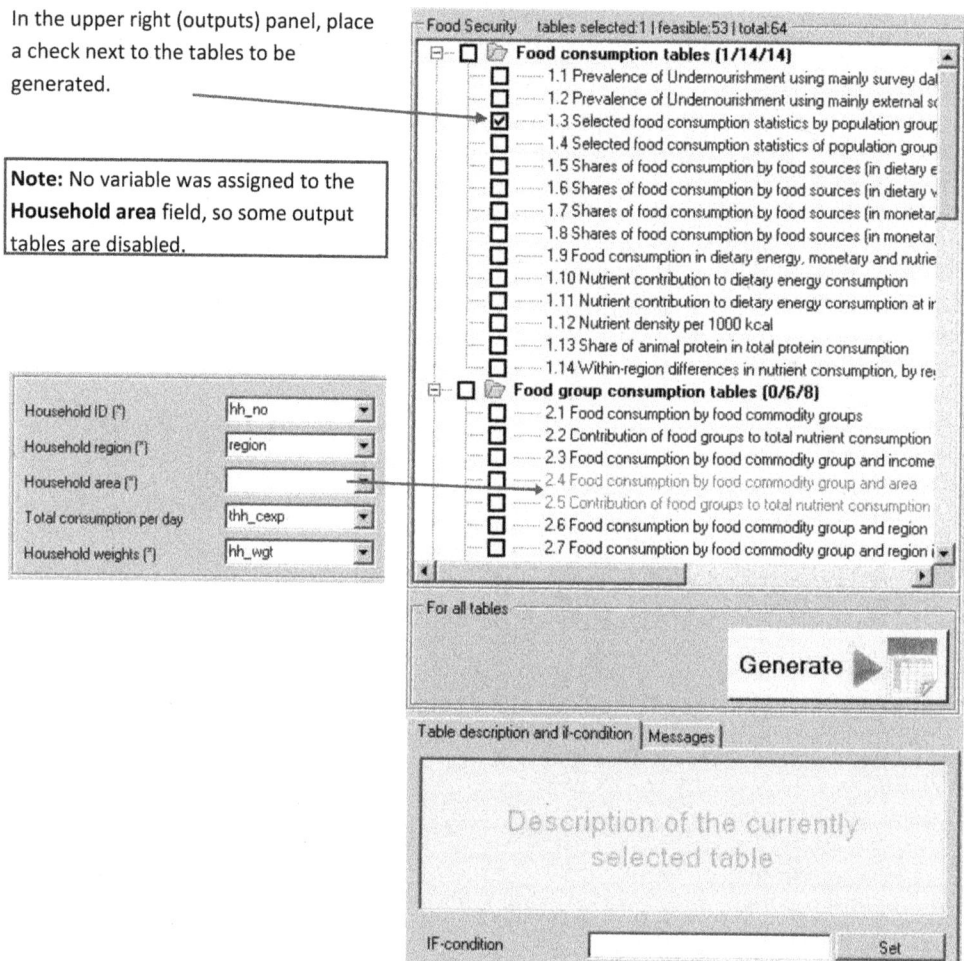

To see a description of a table: Click the name. Its description is displayed in the **Table description and if-condition** tab in the lower right corner of the main window.

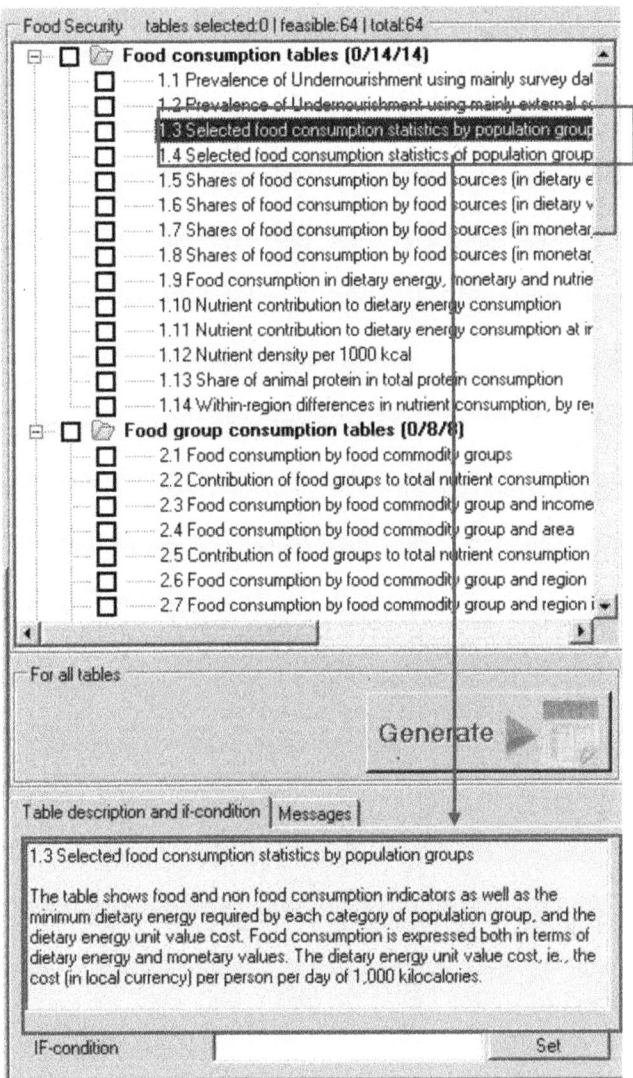

5. Generate the Tables

After completing the four initial steps described above, the user is ready to generate the tables selected previously.

Click the **Generate** button.

To stop calculations: Click the **Stop** button. (The selected tables are not generated if the user stops the calculations.)

6. Analyze the Notifications

It is possible that an error was committed in one of the steps above to generate the analysis, so it is important to analyze any notifications displayed after the generation of the output tables. Potential data problems can also be illuminated with these notifications.

1. Examine items in the **Messages** tab. ADePT-FSM lists potential problems in this tab.

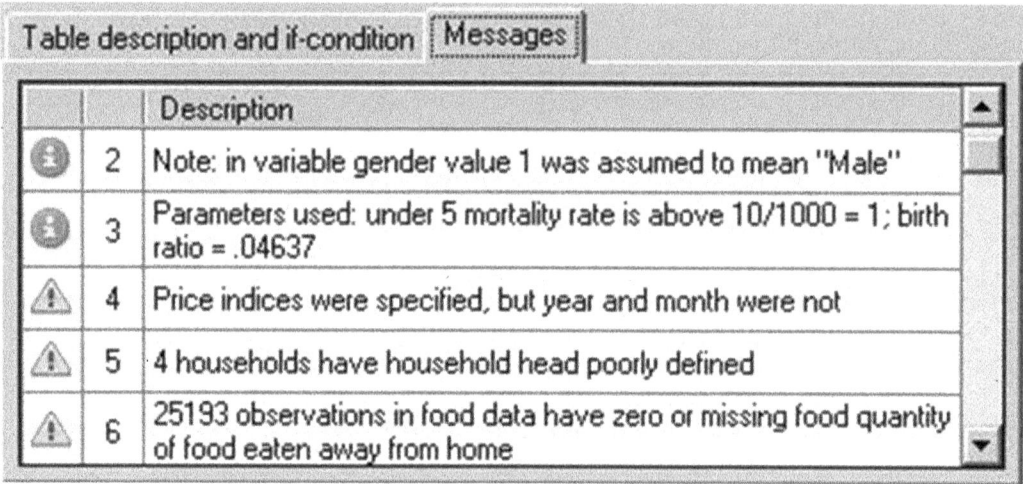

ADePT can identify three kinds of problems:

Notification provides information that may be of interest to the user. Notifications do not affect the content of reports generated by ADePT-FSM.

⚠ **Warning** indicates a suspicious situation in the data. Warnings are issued when ADePT-FSM cannot determine whether it is an impossible situation. Examples include presence of missing values or potential outliers in the datasets, inconsistent data, and inconsistent category definitions.

❌ **Error** prevents the use of a variable in the analysis. For example, a variable may not exist in a dataset (in this case, ADePT-FSM continues its calculations as if the variable wasn't specified). If ADePT can match the problem to a particular variable field, that field is highlighted in the input **Variables** tab.

2. As needed, correct problems, then generate the report again. If some problems were solved within a dataset, this dataset has to be uploaded again to refresh the information.

> **Note:** Notifications, warnings, and errors can negatively affect the results ADePT produces. Carefully review messages and correct critical problems before drawing conclusions from the tables.

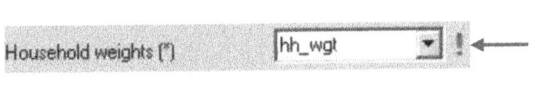

If a problem is found in a particular variable, an exclamation point is displayed next to the field in the input **Variables** tab in the lower left corner of the main window.

Examples of Notifications

When the **Generate** button is clicked ADePT checks the following:

Whether variables correspond to the requirements defined for each particular variable.

The values in **variable region** are numeric.

Table description and if-condition	Messages	
		Description
⊗	1	Variable region is of string type

The existence of invalid or missing data.

In variable **Food quantity per day** there are missing or 0 values of quantities associated to a food source different from consumed away from home.

Table description and if-condition	Messages	
		Description
⊗	6	8 observations in food data have zero or missing food quantity or food purchased, produced at home, or from other sources

There are missing values in variables **Total consumption per day** and **Total income per day.**

Table description and if-condition	Messages	
		Description
ⓘ	4	4 missing values of thh_inc found in HH data
ⓘ	5	3 missing values of thh_cexp found in HH data

The consistency of data between different datasets.

Some values in variable household size in the dataset **Household** are not equal to the number of records in the dataset **Individuals.**

Table description and if-condition	Messages	
		Description
⊗	16	Conflicting or missing household sizes in 2 household(s)

Note: Send any inquiry related to the notifications displayed in the **Messages** box to the FAO Statistics Division: **Food-Security-Statistics@ fao.org.**

Examining the Tables

When the analysis is complete, ADePT-FSM automatically opens the results as a spreadsheet in the spreadsheet program or viewer installed on the computer. This section will provide instructions on how to examine and interpret the output tables. The tables are organized in multiple worksheets, as follows:

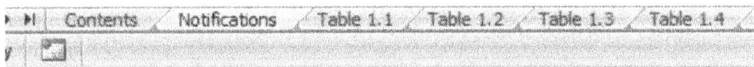

The **Contents** worksheet lists all the other worksheets, including titles for tables. Click a link to open a worksheet.

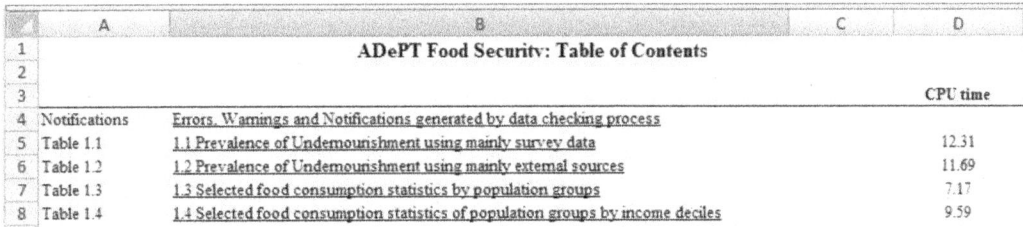

	A	B	C	D
1		ADePT Food Security: Table of Contents		
2				
3				CPU time
4	Notifications	Errors, Warnings and Notifications generated by data checking process		
5	Table 1.1	1.1 Prevalence of Undernourishment using mainly survey data		12.31
6	Table 1.2	1.2 Prevalence of Undernourishment using mainly external sources		11.69
7	Table 1.3	1.3 Selected food consumption statistics by population groups		7.17
8	Table 1.4	1.4 Selected food consumption statistics of population groups by income deciles		9.59

The **Notifications** worksheet lists errors, warnings, and notifications ADePT identified during its analysis. This worksheet may be more useful than the **Messages** tab in the main window because the problems are organized according to the relevant dataset.

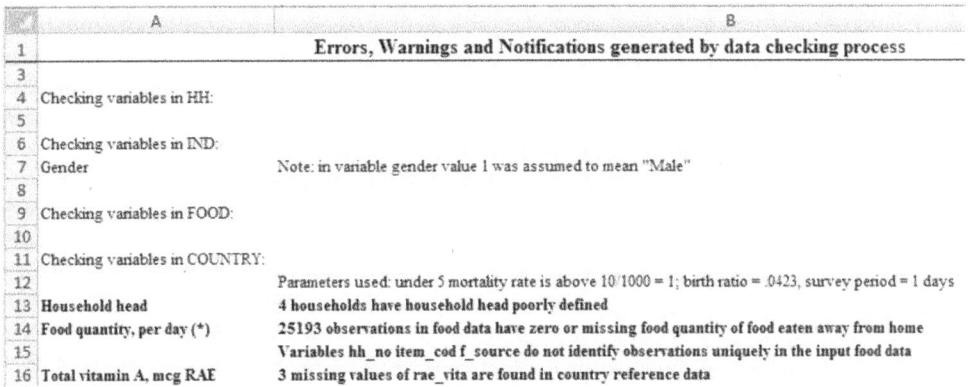

	A	B
1		Errors, Warnings and Notifications generated by data checking process
3		
4	Checking variables in HH:	
5		
6	Checking variables in IND:	
7	Gender	Note: in variable gender value 1 was assumed to mean "Male"
8		
9	Checking variables in FOOD:	
10		
11	Checking variables in COUNTRY:	
12		Parameters used: under 5 mortality rate is above 10/1000 = 1; birth ratio = .0423, survey period = 1 days
13	Household head	4 households have household head poorly defined
14	Food quantity, per day (*)	25193 observations in food data have zero or missing food quantity of food eaten away from home
15		Variables hh_no item_cod f_source do not identify observations uniquely in the input food data
16	Total vitamin A, mcg RAE	3 missing values of rae_vita are found in country reference data

The **Table** worksheets display tables generated by ADePT.

Tip: ADePT formats table data with a reasonable number of decimal places. Click in a cell to see the data with full resolution in the formula bar.

Viewing Basic Information about a Dataset's Variables

In addition to viewing the default output in the tables generated by the ADePT-FSM software, the user may wish to examine observations according to a specific set of criteria. Instructions on how to select specific variables, create new variables, and drop variables are given here; in addition, basic statistics and case frequencies will be generated for the variables selected or defined by the user.

1. Click the dataset to be examined. The list of variables within the dataset selected is displayed below. An example is shown for the input dataset **Household**.

hh_no	Household id
hh_wgt	Final household weight
hh_size	Household size (number of people who share household income)
hhsizec	Household size group
thh_inc	Total income per day
thh_cexp	Total consumption expenditure per day
fpi	Food price index

Search |

Note: Variable labels (in the right column) are read from the dataset file.

To search for a variable: In the **Search** field, type a few characters of the variable name or variable label.

2. Right-click in the variable's row and a pop-up menu appears.

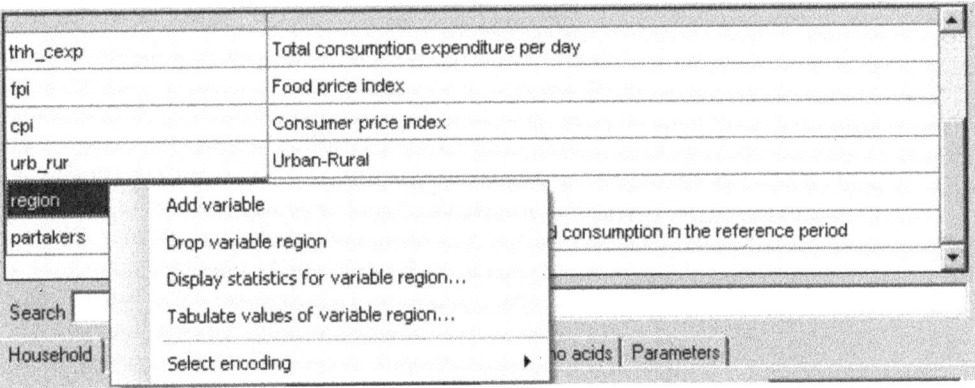

Table 5.4: Description of the Commands Displayed in the Pop-Up Menu

Command	Description
Add variable	Opens the **Generate/Replace Variable** dialog.
Drop variable [name]	Asks for confirmation that you want to remove the selected variable from the loaded dataset. Applies to generated variables and original variables, but does not remove original variables from the dataset.
Display statistics for variable [name]	Opens the **Statistics** window for the selected variable.
Tabulate values of variable [name]	Opens the **Frequency tabulation** window for the selected variable.
Select encoding	Opens a submenu listing character encoding for various languages. Click an encoding to properly display characters in the **Variables** tab.

Add a Variable

The user can create new numeric variables based on variables present in a dataset.

When in the pop-up menu the user selects **Add variable** the **Generate/ Replace Variable** dialog box is opened:

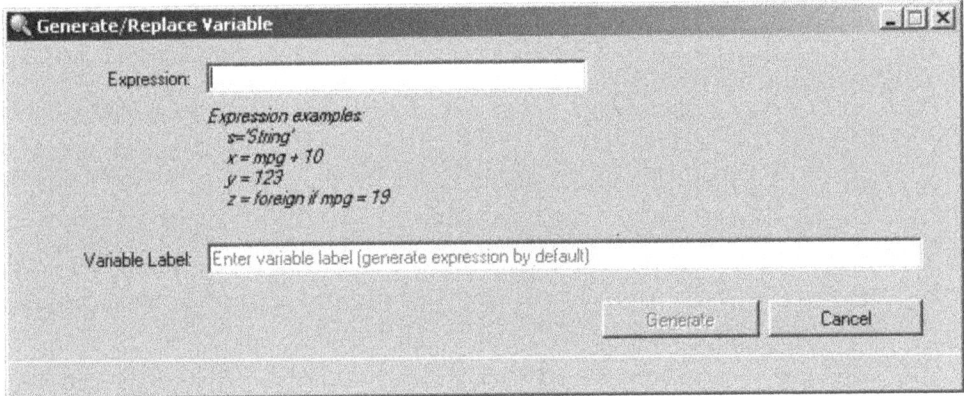

Table 5.5: Operators That Can Be Used in Expressions

Operator				Description
+	–	*	/	basic mathematical operators
abs	sign			
=	==			equality check operators
A	pow	sqrt		exponent (e.g., x^2 is x squared), power (e.g., pow(4,2) is $4^2 = 16$) and square root
round	truncate			shortenting operators
min	max			range operators
exp	log	log10		exponential and log operators
				indicates a missing value

Variable expressions can include constants, and strings can be used for variables that are of string type.

Table 5.6: Examples of Expressions

Expression	Effect
x = 1	sets all variable x observations to 1
x = y + z	sets variable x observations to y observation plus z observation
x = y = 1	sets variable x observations to 1 (true) if y is 1, otherwise sets to 0 (false)
x = 23 if z ==.	sets variable x observations to 23 if z is missing (.), otherwise sets to .
x = Log(y) if z = 1	sets variable x observations to log of y observation if z is 1, otherwise sets to.
s = "test"	sets all variable x observations to the string "test"

In the **Expression** field, define the new variable using the following syntax:

<new_variable_name> = <expression> [if <filter_expression>]

where

- **<new_variable_name>** is a unique name not already in the dataset(s)
- **<expression>** calculates new data for the variable
- **<filter_expression>** (optional) filters observations that take account in the calculation

Click the **Generate** button.

In the **Information** dialog, click the **OK** button.

The new variable will be listed in the **Variables** | [dataset label] tab, and in the **Data Browser**." You can change it with: The new variable will **be added to the list of variables shown in the main window and listed in the Data Browser.**

When the project is saved, the variable expressions are saved with the project. The variables are regenerated when that project is opened. Generating new variables does not change original datasets.

> **Note:** To replace a variable, specify an existing variable name instead of a new variable name. As with generated variables, these expressions are saved with a project and the variables are regenerated when the project is opened. Replacing variables does not change original datasets.

Drop a Variable

Variables can be removed from the working copy of a dataset that ADePT uses for its calculations. This operation does not change the original dataset. Native variables, as well as generated and replaced variables, can be deleted.

1. In the dataset **Variables** tab, right-click in the row containing the variable to be deleted, then click **Drop Variable [variable name]** in the pop-up menu.
2. In the **Confirmation** dialog, click the **Yes** button.

Display Statistics for a Variable

- When in the pop-up menu the user selects **Display statistics for variable [name]**, the window **Statistics** is opened and shows statistics for the selected variable.

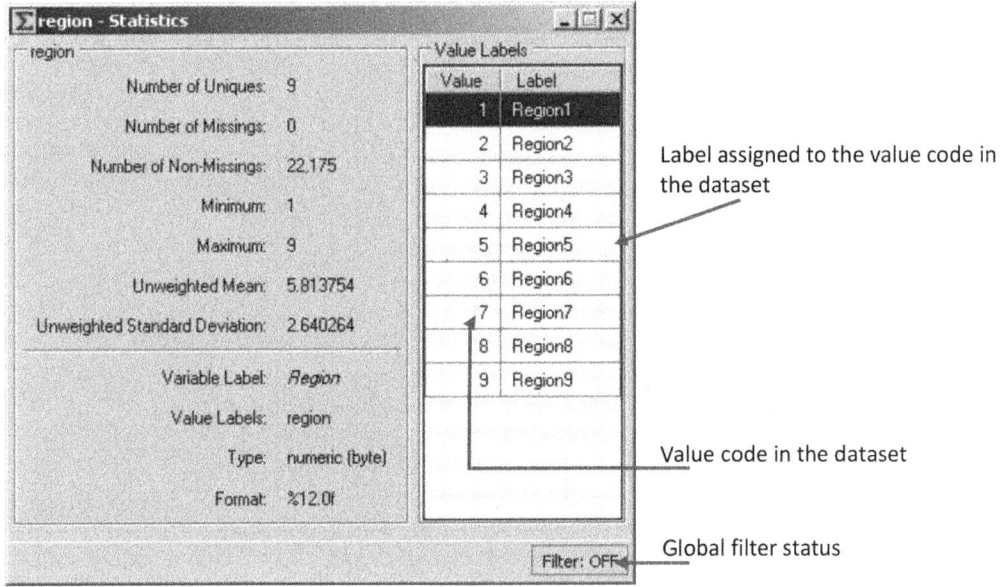

Tabulate Values of a Variable

When in the pop-up menu the user selects **Tabulates values of variable [name]** the window **Frequency tabulation** is opened and shows the frequency of values for the selected variable.

Value	Value label	Frequency	Percent
1	Region1	1,124	5.07 %
2	Region2	2,194	9.89 %
3	Region3	2,111	9.52 %
4	Region4	2,322	10.47 %
5	Region5	2,193	9.89 %
6	Region6	2,255	10.17 %
7	Region7	2,168	9.78 %
8	Region8	2,156	9.72 %
9	Region9	5,652	25.49 %
Total	Total	22,175	100.00 %

Value code in the dataset — Label assigned to the value code in the dataset — Frequency of the values in units — Frequency of the values in percentage

Working with Projects

A project is an ADePT configuration file that contains

- Paths for datasets and URLs for Web-based datasets
- Dataset transformations: generated, replaced, and dropped variables; variable mappings
- Global and dataset-specific filters
- Missing variable definitions
- Expressions used in the global filter

Projects *do not* retain table selections, corresponding if-conditions, and frequencies, because these are related to analysis outputs.

After specifying datasets and mapping variables the user can save the configuration for future use.

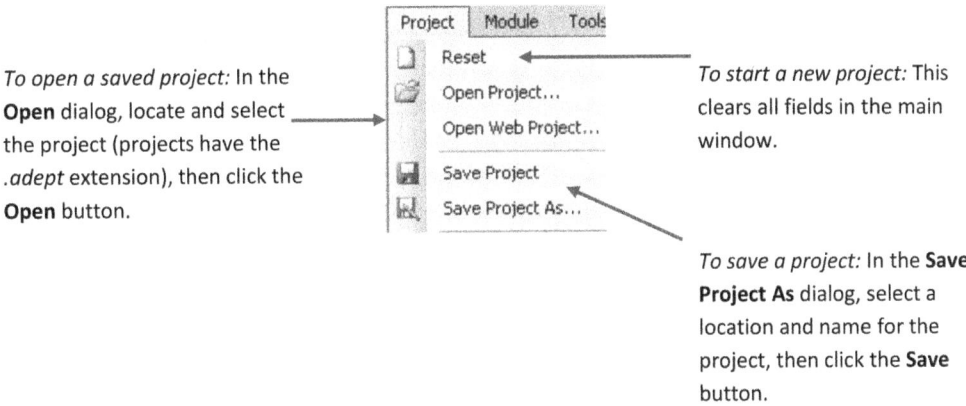

To open a saved project: In the **Open** dialog, locate and select the project (projects have the *.adept* extension), then click the **Open** button.

To start a new project: This clears all fields in the main window.

To save a project: In the **Save Project As** dialog, select a location and name for the project, then click the **Save** button.

Using a Project File on a Different Computer

The saved project files can be used on a different computer. ADePT projects contain absolute (not relative) paths to the data files. ADePT tries to load data files first from the locations stored in the project file; if this fails, it loads them from the directory where the project file is located. Thus, to use a project file in a situation where the locations of the data files are different from those saved in the project file, place the data files in the directory where the project file is located.

Replicating Results Obtained with ADePT

To reproduce the results obtained with ADePT, give the following to the person who will replicate the work:

- The link to download ADePT: http://www.fao.org/economic/ess /ess-fs/fs-methods/adept-fsn/en/. They will need to install ADePT.
- The project file with the input specifications used to generate the results.
- Datasets used to generate the results. (Datasets are not stored in project files. Only links to datasets are stored in project files.)

> **Note:** If the person who is using the files is unable or unwilling to re-create the same folder structure on their computer, instruct him or her to place the datasets in the same folder as the project files.

> **Tip:** The size of the transfer can be reduced by packaging the files in a single archive (e.g., a *.zip* file). The recipient will need to unzip the archive to access the files.

Exiting ADePT

The user cannot exit ADePT when it is performing computations. To close ADePT during its calculations, click the **Stop** button (which replaces the **Generate** button when computations are in progress).

When the user relaunches ADePT it will be in the same state as when it was closed, including the last-used module, settings, and contents of the input variable fields. However, the content of the input variable fields will be restored only if ADePT successfully generated output tables in the previous session.

Using ADePT in a Batch Mode

ADePT supports batch operations. This can be helpful when the user needs to produce several reports for many countries, or a set of reports with different parameters for the same country. Batch mode minimizes the effort by creating reports automatically based on settings that the user saved in a project file.

Here's how to set up and run a batch file:

For each analysis, prepare a project file in ADePT:

1. Load the dataset(s).
2. Map variables.
3. Set parameters.
4. Save the project (**Project ▸ Save Project**).

> **Note:** The user does not select tables when using batch mode. ADePT automatically determines which tables can be built based on the inputs. It always creates all feasible tables during batch processing.

5. Using a text editor (such as Windows Notepad), create a batch file (with extension *.bat*) containing one line for each analysis. Each line must have the following syntax:

<path>\ADePT.exe <path>\<project_file.adept> <path>\<report _name.xls>

where

<path>\ADePT.exe	is the full path to the ADePT program
<path>\<project_file. adept>	is the full path and name for the project file that the user created in step 1
<path>\<report_name. xls>	is the full path and name for the report file that ADePT will produce

Example:

C:\ADePT\ADePT.exe   C:\Projects\FirstProject.adept   C:\Reports\ FirstReport.xls

If a path or file name contains one or more spaces, enclose the entire path\name in DOUBLE QUOTES. For example:

"C:\Program Files\ADePT.exe" "C:\My Projects\First Project.adept" "C:\My Reports\First Report.xls"

6. Save the batch file. Be sure the file has the *.bat* extension.
7. Run the batch file by locating the batch file in Windows Explorer and double-clicking the batch file name. The user should see ADePT running.

If batch processing takes a long time, the user can use Windows® Task Scheduler to run the batch at night or some other time when the user is not using the computer. On a Windows® 7 computer, Task Scheduler can usually be found in the **Start ▶ All Programs ▶ Accessories ▶ System Tools** folder.

Batch Processing Tips

- Be sure to create the batch files using a text editor (i.e., not Microsoft® Word), and save them with the *.bat* extension so that the Windows® operating system can recognize them as batch files.

- To show the path where ADePT is installed, right-click its icon in the **Start** menu and then click **Properties** in the pop-up menu. In the **ADePT Properties** dialog, copy the text in the **Target** field, and then paste it in the batch file to specify the path to the ADePT program.
- Organize the files. Projects, reports, and data can be located in different folders, but it's a good idea to logically organize them. For example, store the prepared projects in one folder with data files in subfolders, and generate reports in a special output folder. Good file organization helps to find and back up the files more easily.
- Associate the project and its report with a common name. If the project file is *First.adept*, for example, then name the report *First.xls*.
- ADePT can be configured to run under another account in the background. Be sure to run it at least once interactively to correctly initialize all global parameters.

Debug Mode

ADePT is a complex computer program, and—as in any program—bugs and errors can occur. If the user experiences anything strange during the computations (in particular, if some tables are not generated or there are possible bugs), activate ADePT's debug mode. In debug mode, ADePT logs the commands issued during computations. This log can help identify problems with the algorithms on which ADePT is based.

Here's how to use debug mode: **Tools ▸ Debug mode**.

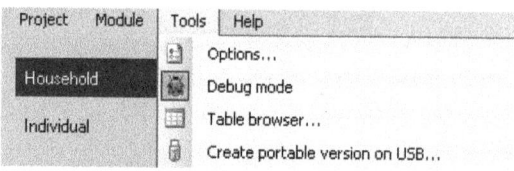

Once debug mode is activated, it will remain on until turned off. Check the ADePT title bar and status bar for debug mode status.

Generate a report following the normal procedure.

Click the **Generate** button.
After the report is displayed, a **Save As** dialog will appear. Save the log file (*ErrorReport.zip*). The file name and folder can be changed as needed.
Send the log file for analysis, as an e-mail attachment, to the ADePT Team at adept@worldbank.org.

The error report file includes the following items:

- Information entered in the ADePT main window
- Messages ADePT produced while checking the data and performing calculations
- Any reports (possibly incomplete) ADePT managed to generate before an error occurred
- Trace of the commands ADePT executed to transform the data and compute the indicators

The error report file does not include any unit-record data or user's datasets, which were used when the error occurred, for confidentiality reasons. However, this information would be useful for the developers in attempting to reproduce the problem. All the information can be checked in the error report before sending it to the ADePT Team—just open each file in the zip archive using a text editor.

Reference

World Bank. 2013. *ADePT Version 5 Technical User's Guide*. Washington, DC: World Bank.http://siteresources.worldbank.org/EXTADEPT /Resources/adept_ug.pdf or http://issuu.com/world.bank.publications /docs/adept_user_guide.

Index

Figures, notes, and tables are indicated by *f*, *n*, and *t* following the page number.